TAKING A CHANCE ON LOVE

AMERICAN POPULAR MUSIC SERIES
Advisory Board

Bob L. Blackburn, *Executive Director,
Oklahoma Historical Society*

Erika Brady, *Professor of Folk Studies,
Western Kentucky University*

Ronald D. Cohen, *Professor of History Emeritus,
Indiana University Northwest*

Charles L. Hughes, *Director of the Memphis Center,
Rhodes College*

Bill C. Malone, *Professor of History Emeritus,
Tulane University*

Andy Wilkinson, *Artist-in-Residence,
Crossroads Music Archive, Texas Tech University*

TAKING A CHANCE ON LOVE

THE LIFE AND MUSIC OF VERNON DUKE

GEORGE HARWOOD PHILLIPS

UNIVERSITY OF OKLAHOMA PRESS : NORMAN

LIBRARY OF CONGRESS CATALOGING-IN-PUBLICATION DATA

Names: Phillips, George Harwood, author.
Title: Taking a chance on love : the life and music of Vernon Duke / George Harwood Phillips.
Description: Norman : University of Oklahoma Press, [2019] | Series: American popular music series ; Volume 5 | Includes bibliographical references and index.
Identifiers: LCCN 2019007239 | ISBN 978-0-8061-6435-9 (pbk. : alk. paper)
Subjects: LCSH: Duke, Vernon, 1903-1969. | Composers—United States—Biography. | LCGFT: Biographies.
Classification: LCC ML410.D87 P55 2019 | DDC 780.92 [B] —dc23
LC record available at https://lccn.loc.gov/2019007239

Taking a Chance on Love: The Life and Music of Vernon Duke is Volume 5 in the American Popular Music Series.

The paper in this book meets the guidelines for permanence and durability of the Committee on Production Guidelines for Book Longevity of the Council on Library Resources, Inc. ∞

Copyright © 2019 by the University of Oklahoma Press, Norman, Publishing Division of the University. Manufactured in the U.S.A.

All rights reserved. No part of this publication may be reproduced, stored in a retrieval system, or transmitted, in any form or by any means, electronic, mechanical, photocopying, recording, or otherwise—except as permitted under Section 107 or 108 of the United States Copyright Act—without the prior written permission of the University of Oklahoma Press. To request permission to reproduce selections from this book, write to Permissions, University of Oklahoma Press, 2800 Venture Drive, Norman OK 73069, or email rights.oupress@ou.edu.

In its January 20, 2018, issue, *The Economist* paid tribute to a great musician:

> He was a composer not just of Broadway masterpieces..., but of ballet, opera, and chamber music, orchestral, instrumental, choral and vocal works, and even a film score. ... He was a fine concert pianist and pioneering broadcaster; ... an educator, ... lecturer, writer ... ; a husband, ... lover—a bona fide celebrity with the good looks [and] charisma ... of a film star. Such a multifaceted life was not without complexities, contradictions, and critics—but oh, what a life.

The tribute was to Leonard Bernstein. With a bit of editing, it could have been to Vernon Duke.

CONTENTS

List of Illustrations   IX

Acknowledgments   XI

Introduction: The Duke/Dukelsky Dichotomy   3

1. Dukelsky Emerges: Kiev and Odessa, 1903–1919   9
2. Duke Awakens: Constantinople and New York, 1919–1924   26
3. Dukelsky Triumphant: Paris, Monte Carlo, and London, 1924–1925   41
4. Duke Takes Charge: London, 1925–1929   59
5. Duke and Dukelsky Celebrated: New York, 1929–1935   77
6. Duke at His Very Best: New York, 1935–1940   97
7. Duke Serves His Country: New York and Palm Beach, 1940–1945   127
8. Dukelsky Reemerges: New York and Paris, 1945–1951   141
9. Duke and Dukelsky Become One: Los Angeles, 1951–1969   155

Conclusion: Duke and Dukelsky Rediscovered   193

Notes   211

Bibliography   235

Index   241

ILLUSTRATIONS

Anna Alexeevna Dukelsky, Kiev, 1917   20

Vladimir Dukelsky, 1921   36

Vladimir Dukelsky, 1924   51

Vittorio Rieti, Dukelsky, and Boris Kochno, 1925   61

Sheet music for "I Am Only Human After All"   83

Sheet music for "I Can't Get Started"   105

Record label for Victor recording of "I Can't Get Started"   109

Ira Gershwin and Vernon Duke, 1937   113

Hildegarde, Vernon Duke, and Leo Kahn, 1940   119

Advertisement for the Broadway production of *Cabin in the Sky*, 1940   122

Sheet music for "Taking a Chance on Love," 1940   123

Sheet music for songs in *Cabin in the Sky* by Vernon Duke and John Latouche, 1940   124

"Busy Month," item in *St. Louis Star and Times*, March 22, 1943   135

Vernon Duke, 1953   163

LP record label for *Vernon Duke Plays Vernon Duke*, 1953   165

Album cover for *Vernon Duke: The Serious Songs*, 1978   194

Program for Carnegie Hall performance of Dukelsky's Concerto in C Major, 1999   202

Poster announcing "Vernon Duke: A Centennial Celebration," concert at Bruno Walter Auditorium, New York City, 2003   203

ACKNOWLEDGMENTS

To members of the Library of Congress, I am forever indebted for your extended efforts in providing me with copies of the documents located in the George and Ira Gershwin Collection and in the Vernon Duke Collection. Several individuals were instrumental in getting the manuscript publishable and published. Peggy and Vincent Rossi searched the first and second drafts for misspellings and typographical errors. Acquisitions editor J. Kent Calder kept the faith when at times it looked as if the changes called for by the first readers could not be met. Copyeditor Elaine Durham Otto thoroughly edited the manuscript and improved it in innumerable ways. Beth Carmichael created the index and offered corrections. Biographer Philip Furia graciously read two drafts of the work and found the second one much improved.

Special thanks go to an Aaron and two Scotts—all outstanding musicians, Duke scholars, and interpreters of his music. Aaron Ziegel patiently went through two versions of the manuscript, correcting mistakes and offering very welcomed advice. Pianist Scott Holden provided me—a stranger—with the documents he had collected for his article and dissertation on Duke. He too examined my work in its manuscript form and made important suggestions for its improvement. Scott Dunn not only reviewed the manuscript but invited me to his home in Venice, California, to discuss its merits and shortcomings. He provided me with documents relevant to his impressive career as a collector, performer, recorder, and conductor of Duke's popular and classical compositions. It is bit scary for me to contemplate what this book would look like without the important assistance of these gentlemen.

TAKING A CHANCE ON LOVE

INTRODUCTION
THE DUKE/DUKELSKY DICHOTOMY

Brilliant, difficult, urbane, petty, charming, cantankerous, arrogant, loyal, impenetrable, sophisticated, argumentative, complex, foppish, gifted, dedicated, vain, opinionated, supportive, vindictive, witty, fastidious, cosmopolitan, and snobbish form a lexicon ascribed to Vernon Duke, also known as Vladimir Dukelsky. To his credit, Duke reveals these characteristics, often in self-deprecating ways, in his autobiography, *Passport to Paris*, published in 1955.

To prepare for his book, Duke read several autobiographies, concluding they could be divided into two types: those that stress facts and those that emphasize style. After considering "a tongue-in-the-cheek approach, the poker-face approach, the Dali or sensational-at-all-costs approach, the Freud or turn-over-a-new-fig-leaf approach," he decided to "stick to the facts and the hell with it. Just to record the facts is quite a job without indulging in the luxury of stylistic orgies."[1] Toward the end of the book, Duke paused again to reflect on his approach: "There is a righteous, hats-off-don't-you-know-who-I-am quality about composers' autobiographies (Stravinsky's, for one) that glosses over or skips ingenuously all that was not sublime, not godlike, in their lives. I have not hidden my frivolity, my ephemeral anecdotes—hardly germane to the lofty subject of my Musical Self—my preoccupation with *flânerie*, food, or clothes."[2]

The autobiography is about a man's life and about a man reflecting on his life. Perhaps this is the case with all autobiographies, but in this one it is particularly obvious. It begins with a complaint:

According to *Who's Who*, I have spent my "entire career" (come, come, I'm still spending it) writing two kinds of music: the serious or unrewarding kind as Vladimir Dukelsky and the unserious but lucrative variety as Vernon Duke. Almost every interview I've ever had has brought forth some tired references to "the Jekyll and Hyde of Music," "the Two-Headed Janus of Music," etc. There have been quite a few cases of composers who successfully managed to write in both the high- and low-brow genre, but I am entirely unique in one respect. Gershwin always remained Gershwin whether he wrote *Porgy* or "I Got Rhythm"; Weill was easily recognizable as Weill whether he tackled *Mahagonny* or *One Touch of Venus*; and even Lennie Bernstein is his ingratiating self whether he tears into *Jeremiah* or *On the Town*; but Dukelsky in no way resembles Duke.[3]

Duke's complaint is difficult to accept because throughout *Passport to Paris* he repeatedly references his dual musical life. He mentioned the time when his pregnant mother was frightened by a loud siren, causing her to grab and twist her left ear. Fears that her child would somehow be affected by the accident were "substantiated" at Vladimir's birth. His right lobe had a cleft. Tongue-in-cheek, Duke wrote: "Possibly my left ear has never heard what the right ear heareth, and there you have the whole mystery of Duke and Dukelsky in an earshell."[4] On another occasion, he was quoted as saying, "I always feel the duality in myself.... My light music is decidedly extrovert, my serious music is introvert. There's my Carnegie Hall self and my Lindy's [restaurant] self, my Russian heritage and my American influence. Can I help it if two people happen to be in my body?"[5] He even published an article in which Duke and Dukelsky engaged in a dialogue.[6] Initially Duke wanted to call his autobiography "The Two-Headed Monster," a title universally disliked by his friends.[7] His duality prompted friend and verbal sparring partner Oscar Levant to whimsically ask: "For a man who's destined for obscurity, why do you need two names?"[8]

Duke acknowledged that "my dichotomy, unnatural and irritating (because nonclassifiable) to my contemporaries, had now become an all-enveloping characteristic of my musical self-expression; in other words, it seemed impossible for me to stick to one kind of music without an occasional welcome excursion into the other field."⁹ Duke's contemporaries often commented on his ability to maintain separation. Elliott Carter noted that his popular songs have "no connection with his original and imaginative serious music in either style or content."¹⁰ Alec Wilder insisted that "Mr. Duke-Dukelsky kept his musical selves compartmentalized."¹¹

Depending on where and when Duke lived, the dichotomy manifested itself in different forms—the volatile Russian and the self-possessed American, the youthful Dukelsky and the elder Duke, the daring Dukelsky and the practical Duke, and the edgy New Yorker and the mellow Californian. But it was Duke, the wage earner, who allowed Dukelsky, the artiste, to compose. Before his thirtieth year, he had changed from being strictly a classical composer to one who could also write songs and entire scores for musicals. Although the Duke/Dukelsky dichotomy in no way implies a truly dual personality, there seems to be some stark differences in temperament between Duke and Dukelsky. Dancer Anton Dolin remarked: "Unless one knew him no one could believe that the two were the same person."¹² The dichotomy is most evident when Duke the tunesmith or Dukelsky the composer commented on musicians and those in the music business. The softer side of Duke is apparent in his discussions of contemporary producers, songwriters, and lyricists, whereas his meaner side emerges when writing about composers, conductors, and publishers.

Obviously, Duke was not the easiest person to get along with, even with his friends. Lyricist Ira Gershwin remembered him as "always arguing—with everyone. Everyone he worked with—me, Yip Harburg—he always had some supposed grievance." Duke thought he was a Grand Duke, recalled conductor Bernard Herrmann, "but there were times when he behaved like a Grand Duke's coachman. He could be very vulgar in many ways. But I always understood him, and I never took offense."¹³ Johnny Mercer once told record producer Ben Bagley, "The most interesting thing about you is that you managed to hang on to Vernon's friendship for almost ten years."¹⁴

Duke admitted he was "often overly fond of stinging letters, ill-timed righteous gestures, and experienced an exaggerated delight at putting a man in his place. These things do not make for popularity, and since quarrels are everyday fare in musical and theatrical circles, I have had more than my share of them. I have never hesitated about speaking my mind when it would have been far wiser to remain blandly noncommittal."¹⁵ And when he spoke his mind, some of his words may sound narrow-minded, sexist, and even occasionally bigoted today, but they also reveal the values and attitudes of a man of his time.

Duke once bragged to a friend that "NOBODY is as meticulous and prompt a correspondent as I am. A fat lot of good it does me! Most of my friends are simply hopeless in that respect and I am sick and tired of nudging them every week or so in vain hopes of getting them to write."¹⁶ Fortunately for the researcher, the carbon copies the correspondent made of many if not most of his letters provide an invaluable record of his life. And the scholarly and newspaper articles, book reviews, liner notes, and unpublished short stories he wrote often include information about himself. They and hundreds of other documents he preserved allowed him to jog his memory when writing his autobiography. Duke claimed not to remember what happened the previous year, but he also insisted that really important events were never lost. In his autobiography, the first two decades of his life are mainly based on a document written by his mother in 1930, but he never reveals when he is relying on the document or on his memory. Of course, the researcher must work with what is available, and without it much of Duke's early life would have been lost. The events of his later life are often corroborated by other sources. He is, however, sometimes inconsistent with chronology and loose with dates, and he gives some of his characters, even himself, dialogue. Contrary to what he said in his introduction, in many ways he was interested in style—but what a style it is.

In investigating the life of this man, I have searched the documents more for data about the person than about the persona, more about what he did than why he did it. Without some knowledge of his motivations, however, his behavior remains inexplicable. Therefore, when he reveals in his autobiography and in his letters and other documents how he dealt with his successes and failures, as a man and as a composer, I have quoted him extensively. As will become apparent, he took as many chances on love as on music.

His life, I contend, should be viewed less as a trajectory or arc than as a series of sharp turns, each directing him to a different place. His formative years in Kiev and Odessa prepared him for a life in music, but turning points came in places where he spent the least amount of time—Constantinople,

Monte Carlo, Paris, and London. Where he lived most of his adult life—New York and Los Angeles—he had some of his greatest successes and failures. The individuals he interacted with in each city contributed to his social and musical development. Substitute or eliminate any one of these places and his life would have been extremely different. Of course, eliminate the watersheds in any person's life and things would be different. But for Duke they would have been radically different.

Shortly before his death, he told a friend that more than three hundred of his works had been published in Europe and the United States, "and tracking them all down would be a gruesome job."[17] That task I will leave to others, but I have devoted more space than he did to discussing how well his classical compositions and popular songs were presented and received. Newspaper and journal articles written by musicians and critics provided much of the data on these issues. As a historical document, a music review can tell us how well an audience responded to a musical comedy or to a classical performance and what was musically conventional or daring at the time. For a brief moment in history, it identifies the musical values and norms of a least a segment of the population.

The importance of *Passport to Paris* as a historical source cannot be emphasized too much. I have read it more than once and parts of it several times, so I know its outline and much of the data in it. The problem with using it as a primary source is not what to include but what to exclude. For two chapters it was the main source, but I also used it as a reference book. If, for example, another work mentioned an incident involving Duke, I would check the autobiography to see what if anything he had to say about it. Because Duke tells us that he knew or was acquainted with nearly everyone in the fields of classical and popular music, this means everyone in these fields knew him. Many of them wrote autobiographies or had biographies and articles written about them, so I spent considerable time finding out what, if anything, they had to say about Duke. Because my book is designed not to replace the autobiography but to complement it, I have emphasized what I consider to be major events in Duke's musical and personal life and have left most of the specific details of that life behind in his fascinating book. Much of the autobiography is about the people Duke knew, whereas my biography is mainly about what he did. It is also shorter, much shorter.

In 1939, Vladimir Dukelsky became an American citizen and changed his name to Vernon Duke. He loved America, even Los Angeles, where he lived from 1951 to his death in 1969. Because *Passport to Paris* ends in 1954, this period has remained unexamined and therefore unappreciated. But Duke was remarkably active during these years, composing, performing, writing, lecturing, socializing, and appearing on radio and television shows. This period, moreover, saw the divide that had shaped his life become less pronounced, resulting in the tunesmith and the composer becoming figuratively, at least, one person.

DUKELSKY EMERGES
KIEV AND ODESSA, 1903–1919

The extraordinary life of Vladimir Dukelsky began in September or October 1903, when Anna Alexeevna Dukelsky unexpectedly went into labor at a railroad station at Parafianovo in the government of Minsk, then part of the Russian Empire. Mother and son continued on to their home in Kiev in Ukraine, where they were greeted by Alexander Vladimirovitch Dukelsky, Vladimir's father, whom he remembered as "a handsome man of medium height, with brilliant black hair and a resplendent mustache." A civil engineer, he specialized in railroad building and occasionally sang "gypsy songs in a pleasant baritone." Both mother, who played the piano, and father were "addicted to music in the customary manner of Russian dilettantes in comfortable circumstances."[1]

Because Alexander was often absent for months at a time with his work, Anna was Vladimir's primary caregiver:

> According to Mother's testimony, I was something of a sickeningly romantic child. Not only was my head adorned with curling brown locks, but my face perpetually wore a serious, not to say profound, expression, and of usual childish pranks I would have nothing. I cried only on the rarest occasions and then almost inaudibly, which perturbed the whole household, brought up in the belief that healthy children are also healthy vocalists. At the age of eleven months I apparently had quite a vocabulary of Russian and French and soon got used to being exhibited to the politely enthusiastic friends of the family.[2]

Between two and three he was reading, writing, and absorbing music. He often crawled under the piano while his mother played. And a "huge Gramophone with an imposing metal horn . . . was made to play an eclectic assortment of musical bits and pieces ranging from Italian operas sung by Battistini, Anselmi, Caruso, and the Russian gallery gods Sobinov and Smirnov (tenors both), to gypsy songs. A ritual was established of lulling me to sleep each night with florid Italian airs."[3] By stimulating his innate intelligence, this musical environment contributed greatly to the development of his prodigious musicality.

His brother, Alexis, arrived in April 1905, about the time the family moved from Kiev to Nikolaiev, where Alexander was employed as a railroad engineer. Situated on a peninsula forty miles from the Black Sea where the Bug and Inhul Rivers converge, the city was founded by Prince Grigory Potemkin after the Second Russo-Turkish War of 1787–92. Turkish prisoners were employed in laying out its broad, tree-lined avenues and its large park. Its first shipyards were built in 1788.[4]

During the nearly three years in Nikolaiev, Vladimir further demonstrated his precociousness. When taught typical children's games, he invented his own rules. He detested mechanical toys but loved stuffed animals, especially dogs and elephants. In the kingdom he and Alexis created, they assigned certain dogs to the roles of composers, novelists, painters, and sculptors. A tin frog governed the kingdom. Events in the kingdom were recorded in fat copybooks in hieroglyphics comprehensible only to Vladimir. This diversion did not concern his mother, but when at age four he began writing reams of meaningless poetry and reciting them to the cook and butler, she felt compelled to take him to a psychiatrist. Vladimir disarmed the doctor by nonchalantly answering his questions, but he was told to give up his pedantic pursuits for more physical ones.[5] In this stage of his development, Vladimir clearly demonstrated an egocentrism that would be revealed repeatedly in adulthood.

This characteristic was evident in his rivalry with his brother, a rivalry that would continue their entire lives. According to Vladimir, Alexis was an "insufferable brat in his early life" who inflicted physical harm "on whoever came within his reach." His attitude toward Vladimir was "one of awe mingled with contempt and ever-present jealously. Fully aware that I was a self-appointed genius, demanding and receiving rapturous attention at all times, he never failed to kick or bite me when least expected to do so."[6] Decades later, Alexis told an interviewer that Vladimir was a very spoiled child whose gifts were early recognized by their mother, who always defended his conduct.[7]

Alexis attempted to imitate all of Vladimir's creative attainments, such as writing in his diary as much as his brother did in his, even when he could barely write. The brothers joined in "punishing" a poodle named Caro for biting people. They fed him a concoction containing mustard and pepper that produced coughing and sneezing. Other than "Caro's banquets and the epic diaries," Vladimir's other recollection of his time in Nikolaiev was "an outing with Father to a country fair where he regaled himself with pickled watermelon, which I insisted on tasting and found so vile that I maliciously passed a piece of it to my brother, who swallowed it heroically, delighted at the thought of sharing his elders' pleasures."[8]

In 1910, the family moved to Kungur in the Ural Mountains. Founded in 1648 eleven miles above the mouth of the Iren River on the banks of the Kungurka River, Kungur, by the beginning of the eighteenth century, had developed its leather and footwear industries. During the next century, it became a transit trade center on the Siberia Road, and as the twentieth century progressed, it grew into an important industrial area, specializing in the manufacturing of leather footwear, gloves, and mittens.[9] There Alexander, who loved a nomadic life, worked on the construction of the Perm-Catherineberg Railroad. In his autobiography, Duke wrote:

> The magnificent Ural forests, the smells of fresh snow and crisp apples and the tart flavor of the birch juice from the young trees were a far cry from the semitropical, indolent atmosphere of Nikolaiev, but we all thrived on the change. According to Mother's notes, it was during the three years spent in Kungur that she grew from a simple young matron to a poised hostess and an avid student of letters and arts. She began entertaining her husband's business associates and soon presided over a group interested in philosophy and two-piano playing. Mother was very fond of teaching her sons a large repertoire of Russian nursery rhymes set to music, and while I had the better ear,

Alexis had the louder voice. However, since his r's, l's, and most of his sibilants were defective, he made a good deal of noise but very little sense, which gave me another opportunity to shine which I seldom failed to seize.[10]

While in the Urals, the brothers came under the guidance of a series of governesses—a Czech, a German, and a Swiss Italian. The boys developed a Franco-Russian-German patois comprehensible only to themselves. Of concern to his mother was a ballet Vladimir composed in which the notes looked like notes but were indecipherable to a musician. The ballet was in fourteen parts, one page to each act. He called it *Cassiopeia*. This exercise would prove to be prophetic.[11]

When Alexander was transferred to Crimea, the family sailed down the Volga to Nizhny-Novgorod, then by train to Sebastopol, and finally by steamer to Evpatoria. A brief interlude in Kiev allowed Vladimir to attend the theater for the first time. He saw Maeterlinck's *Blue Bird* and Massenet's opera *Cendrillon*.[12] Evidently it was while staying on his grandmother's estate that one of her employees, "a nineteen-year-old Polish amazon named Marylia took a great fancy to me, and I dimly recall certain liberties she took with me, to which I submitted rather sheepishly and for which I was rewarded by succulent sweets stolen from Grandmother's larder."[13]

With Alexander in the mountains working on the Crimean Railroad, Anna and the boys returned to Evpatoria and then moved to the nearby town of Alupka on the southeastern shore of the Black Sea. Known for its Neo-Moorish Vorontsov Palace constructed between 1824 and 1851, the town had been founded by Greeks, conquered by Byzantines, controlled by Tatars, and absorbed by the Russian Empire. By the beginning of the twentieth century, it had become a famous resort.[14] Dukelsky bragged that the Black Sea was bluer than the bluest Mediterranean, and the fish were tastier and more varied. But his most vivid recollection of Crimea was "the taste of the local grapes and the astonishing variety in their shape, size and flavor. I particularly remember three: the large yellow-green Chaoosh, the subtly perfumed Isabella, and the common but infinitely juicy Shashla. The everyday drink of the tourists and residents of Crimea was a fresh grape juice squeezed before your eyes from a pound of Shashla."[15]

After a summer and autumn in Alupka, the family moved to Yalta, but Alexander soon departed on an assignment and was absent for four mounts. During this time Anna began giving Vladimir piano lessons. His mother also hired a pretty young woman to tutor the brothers. Vladimir fell madly in love, prepared his lessons with great zeal, and was amply rewarded when she reported his progress glowingly to his mother. Alexis proceeded at a slower pace, but in 1911 he joined his brother in taking piano lessons and soon put Vladimir to shame.[16]

In March 1912, Alexander, at the age of thirty-nine, experienced a heart attack and was sent to Bad Nauheim, a German health resort, and then to Switzerland before returning to Kiev. Without Alexander, mother and sons vacationed at the resort of Mejigorye on the banks of the Dnieper. Run by the Mejigorye Convent for gentlewomen and their children, it allowed for nude bathing. There Vlaldimir's first sexual episode came back to him, and seeing so much feminine flesh made him cringe with remorse. He even considered suicide, but some of his companions "exhibited a premature interest in their surroundings." He recalled a boy called Petya being chased off the beach by an enraged naked sister with a huge black umbrella. Some of the local men were more successful. On an island in the river they gazed at their friends' wives through powerful binoculars.[17]

The vacation was cut short when the Dukelskys learned that Vladimir's maternal grandmother had died on September 28, 1912. By this time, Alexander's condition had deteriorated. He walked with considerable difficulty and in December was confined to his bed. On the twentieth-eight, he died of another heart attack. Vladimir recalled that the next few days

> brought all the paraphernalia of the Greek Orthodox conception of human frailty and untimely demise: swarms of hastily arriving relatives and yellow-faced nuns with ikonlike burning eyes, who mumbled inaudible but strangely terrifying prayers, their monotonous chants at the bier, the singing of the large choir brought back speedily after performing a similar chore for Grandmother, the frightening smell of incense mingled with that of unnaturally beautiful flowers and the damp leather of the servants' freshly varnished boots, the black crepe over the mirrors, and the hordes of the usual curious onlookers.[18]

The following year, Anna's younger brother, an officer in the celebrated Uhlan Regiment, put a bullet through his head. Declining to remain with her grandfather, where so much grief had recently visited, Anna found suitable accommodations in Kiev for her two boys and herself.[19] Thus from the age of nine, Vladimir faced life without a father and grew to adulthood in Kiev with little male supervision.

Founded early in the sixth century BP, Kiev was sequentially occupied by Slavs, Mongols, Lithuanians, Poles, Ukrainian Cossacks, and Muscovites. In 988 it adopted Orthodox Christianity and became a bulwark against the Catholic Church. Incorporated into the Russian Empire in 1686, a century later it had a population of 19,000. At the beginning of the twentieth century, Kiev was a metropolis of 250,000 inhabitants, the third most prominent city in the Russian Empire after Moscow and St. Petersburg. By specializing in sugar and grain, it became an important transportation center, and its wealth led to the founding of numerous education and cultural facilities.[20]

Vladimir Dukelsky fondly remembered the city where his musical life was to a large degree determined:

> Kiev was a world half-occidental and half-medieval Russian. The modern and luxurious thoroughfares of Kreschatik (Kiev's main street) and the exclusive Lipki residential section, named for its abundant young linden trees, seemed highly kinetic next to the peaceful golden domes of the city's many sixteenth-century churches; of these the Lavra of Petchersk was the Saint Mark's of Russian Christendom. The city's parks included the Gorka (Hill) of St. Vladimir, the splendid Czarski Sad (Gardens), and the Merchant's [sic] Gardens, the home of summer symphony concerts. Our street, the Bolshaya-Podvalnaya, was well paved, clean, and boasted a cinema where we saw the first super-colossal movie epic, *Cabiria*, the hilarious comedies of Max Linder, the monocled predecessor of Charlie Chaplin, the homemade sexy melodramas that starred the Russian favorites Vera Kholodnaya and Ivan Mozjoukin.[21]

Like other cities in the Empire, it benefited from the Revolution of 1905, resulting in Czar Nicholas II granting the historic October Manifesto, which promised civil liberties and order based on a lawful parliamentary government. But that year a terrible pogrom resulted in 47–100 Jews murdered, 300–400 injured, and 1,800 homes and business plundered, leaving 3,000 residents without a workplace.[22]

Immune to the violence that occasionally erupted in Kiev, Vladimir safely received an upper-middle-class education. His paternal uncle had enrolled him at birth at the St. Petersburg Naval Academy, and his mother sought to provide him with the necessary preparatory education for admission. Vladimir found the sea fascinating but was frightened by tales of the rigorous training at the academy, and he immediately began expanding his passion for music and writing longer and even more obscure poems. When Vladimir composed a long sonata, his mother concluded that a career in music would better suit his temperament than one in the navy.[23]

In the autumn of 1914, Anna took Vladimir and Alexis to a small resort on the Baltic Sea, where the boys made friends with the sons and daughters of Latvians and Germans vacationing there. In the evenings his mother accompanied on the piano a young Polish violinist, and Vladimir became enamored of Kreisler's "Liebestraum" and "Liebesfreud." The Dukelskys also visited Riga where Vladimir roamed the streets of this beautiful medieval town, heard violin music, and consumed quantities of smoked fish. Soon the family returned to Kiev.[24]

Enrolled in a private gymnasium (high school) run by a pedagogue named Naumenko, Vladimir and Alexis were forced to wear powder blue uniforms with golden buttons and caps with insignias. Those attending government schools considered the Dukelsky brothers sissies and were prepared to fight them at any opportunity. Clearly, athletics were not the strong suit of the "sissy," and when mistakenly assigned as goal keeper on the soccer team, he missed four goals. For his incompetence, he received a beating from the team and spent three days in bed. Nevertheless, he and Alexis got a good education, with Vladimir excelling in history, literature, languages, and geography but doing poorly in mathematics. He also learned to play the domra of the mandolin family, which was the lead instrument in the balalaika bands. Under the direction of Josephine Leskevitch, his piano studies progressed, but he neglected his homework, especially physics and math, flunking the latter. He focused instead on writing futuristic poems for the school magazine and playing his "revolutionary" piano pieces at children's parties.[25]

Because his mother had a box at the theater, the boys regularly attended operas and symphonies. In 1916, they heard the First Piano Concerto by a young Sergei Prokofiev, who would later play a major role in Vladimir's musical development. He remembered Prokofiev as "a tall young man of extraordinary appearance. He had white-blond hair, a small head with a large mouth and very thick lips . . . and very long, awkwardly dangling arms, terminating in a bruiser's powerful hands." More startling was his playing: "nothing but unrelenting energy and athletic joy of living. No wonder the first four notes of the concerto, oft-repeated, were later nicknamed '*pro cherepoo*' ('hit on the head'), which was Prokofiev's exact intention." But Vladimir remembered that the work contained not a single tune. His mother warned him not to write like that because melody should always come first.[26]

Reinhold Glière conducted the concert. Born in Kiev in 1875 of German-Polish ancestry (his original name being Reinhold Ernest Glier), Glière entered the Kiev school of music in 1891 and the Moscow Conservatory in 1894, graduating in 1900. He accepted a teaching post at the Moscow Gnessin School of Music, but also gave private lessons to eleven-year-old Prokofiev. From 1905 to 1908, he studied conducting in Berlin, one of his fellow students being Serge Koussevitzky, who would also play an important role in Vladimir's musical life. Between 1900 and 1911, Glière composed three symphonies, a symphonic poem, and two string quartets. In 1913, he became a member of the Kiev school of music and its director when it became the Kiev Conservatory of Music.[27]

Upon returning from a vacation in Moscow, Anna and Vladimir visited the Kiev Conservatory for an audition with Glière. Vladimir presented him with the sheet music of his sonata, asking him, if he cared, to follow the music while he played his work. The director had no choice but to accept the offering and listened intently for a time before asking the young man to stop. Vladimir had talent, he acknowledged, but suggested he take some advanced lessons with Marian Dombrovsky before entering the conservatory. As Vladimir recalled, "The interview was most satisfactory to Mother and me and we left Glière's office feeling that we had Euterpe by the tail."[28]

That confidence was reflected in Vladimir's next move. Determined to hasten his entrance into the conservatory, he deliberately made mistakes in his lessons at the gymnasium, and he passed out copies of his satirical journal, the *Ventilator*, which contained a drawing of his Russian language teacher in the embrace of one of his female students. The teacher showed the journal to the principal, and the next day Vladimir was expelled. As noted in his autobiography, "Mother was perturbed of course, but I set her right by claiming that my Pegasus was far more likely to be Glière than Naumenko, and that I would reach Olympus much faster in the Conservatory chariot."[29] It seems clear that Vladimir was demonstrating the traits of a rebellious personality: one that seeks independence, opposes being restrained, resists taking orders, thinks originally, and disrupts relationships. For the rest of his life, these traits would define the character of Vladimir Dukelsky.

At about the age of ten or eleven, he got his first taste of operettas and American music. His mother, after attending *The Chocolate Soldier*, *Sylvia*, and *The Merry Widow*, would return with the sheet music. And one of her admirers "presented Mother with some hot platters of American imported ragtime; the raging two-steps had such detestable titles as 'Automobile' and '*Très Moutarde*' (Very Mustard). Alexis and I watched aghast as the daring young man demonstrated, with Mother as his startled partner, the vigorous arm-pumping and jerky steps." At that stage in his musical life, Vladimir was not fond of dance music or the wailings of the early Russian crooners.[30] That would soon change.

Despite her ventures into popular music, Anna was determined that Vladimir receive a proper musical education, and she persuaded Glière to audition him as a private student. The harmony session did not go well, and Vladimir was dismissed, but he practiced diligently for his piano examination, which consisted of technical studies. At the performance, he inserted his own radical sonata and Glière stopped him. The admission committee nevertheless agreed that his general musicianship was excellent and his technique sufficient for lessons in an advanced piano class. Vladimir soon became a full-fledged conservatory student, and because the institution also ran a gymnasium, his general studies were not neglected. Unknown to his teachers, however, Vladimir wrote a piece purporting to be a string quartet and got it privately performed by some Ukrainians who were "gluttons for punishment." He also became friends with aspiring singers, violinists, and pianists, including Vladimir Horowitz and Nicolas Slonimsky, whom he remembered as "a Puckish young man of quick eye and ready tongue."[31] The life of Slonimsky would parallel Vladimir's in many ways, and for the remainder of their lives they would link up in several cities.

In the summer of 1915, Anna and the two boys visited Finland, St. Petersburg, and Moscow. Vladimir was awed by the phenomenon of the Nordic white night, and years later he would translate the experience musically into a cantata. Back in Kiev, Vladimir continued his piano studies, but practicing six hours a day proved to be odious to him. He tried not practicing at all for several days before the lesson and then spend the preceding day catching up. It worked, but for only a time. His instructor suggested he find a teacher "more interested in musical development than pianistic pyrotechnics."[32]

By this time, World War I, which had begun in 1914,

> made normal pursuits of learning more and more difficult. Mother and most of her female friends joined the Red Cross as volunteer nurses, and our apartment became the meeting place of young officers fresh from the front, quite a few of them wounded. Some of Glière's older pupils were mobilized, but on the other hand, there was an influx of aspiring composers from St. Petersburg and Moscow. Food was still plentiful in Kiev, and life was easy and carefree compared with the growing feeling of insecurity and unrest, as well as various economic restrictions, in the two Russian capitals.[33]

Nevertheless, martial law was declared in Kiev. Its industries were converted to the production of war materials, forcing the insular city government to ration firewood and to open a bakery and several bread shops to counter the rising cost of food. Efforts to persuade the imperial government to introduce a form of government that would best organize the city's resources were ignored.[34]

When the Russian Revolution broke out in St. Petersburg in 1917, Kiev initially supported the movement. Flower parades, military bands, and symphonic concerts were held to raise money for the war effort. There were occasional shootings and skirmishes with rapidly dwindling monarchists. Vladimir and Alexis, delighted at the never-ending recess from school, joined "little groups of happily shouting collegians whose chief fun was tearing the Imperial eagles from their caps and adorning their sleeves with flaming-red bands." With all of this going on, Vladimir got his first orchestral piece, a string intermezzo composed without Glière's knowledge, performed at one of the Merchants Garden Concerts. The work received a "respectable enough hand for me to come forward and take my first bow before a paying audience."[35] But he realized that the intermezzo was "the gloomiest piece of music imaginable, and that as a *Wunderkind*, I wasn't much of a *Wunder*."[36]

Because of the revolution, increasing numbers of students from St. Petersburg and Moscow were admitted to the conservatory, and soon the institution began to change. Vladimir, who had been accepted into Glière's composition class, witnessed

> old and respectable conservatory professors inexplicably vanish, their places taken by aggressive young men in military-style "frenchies" (as American and British officers' tunics were then called in Russia) and polished cavalry-issue boots. They talked music, but instead of using words like counterpoint, double fugue, recapitulation, main subject, etc., constantly referred to ideology, proletariat, class war, bourgeois tendencies, and social significance. Their talk sounded strange to us, but these early "commissars" were there to enforce the New Order, and we liked to consider ourselves "progressive" and to be part of it.[37]

During one summer, the Dukelskys ventured to the countryside, but getting there was no longer easy. Priorities on the trains were given to soldiers, revolutionary officials, and their staffs. In the eighteenth-century house of their hosts, Vladimir played an Erard piano at dusk. During the day he swam in the Psiol River and often observed the hostess floating naked on a bathing platform. The scene reminded Vladimir of the church-sanctioned nudity of the Mejigorye Convent, especially after witnessing "the numerous peasant wenches employed on the estate . . . swimming in the nude, singing, giggling, and splashing about like clumsy white seals." The village of Mirgorod, immortalized by Nikolai Gogol in *Mirgorod*, his collection of short stories, was nearby. Well stocked with food and yet to experience any real hardships, it was nevertheless experiencing insecurity and unrest.[38]

ANNA ALEXEEVNA DUKELSKY, KIEV, 1917. From Duke, *Passport to Paris*.
Reproduced with permission from Kay Duke Ingalls.

When the Dukelskys returned, Kiev had changed considerably. Men on street corners shouted threats and promises, large posters promised death to all enemies of the working class, lines lengthened at food shops, and clothing was rationed. Shots rang out periodically, and on certain evenings the populace was ordered to remain in their homes after sundown. Recognized by their dress, the bourgeois attending concerts and the opera were often forced to present their identification papers and were even held for interrogation. Vladimir and Alexis continued to attend the gymnasium, but they avoided crowded streets.[39]

Bolsheviks occupied the city on January 29, 1918. In Glière's composition class, a soviet official entered and informed the students that Comrade Trotsky demanded that to popularize the Communist Party they should write an opera in two weeks. Students worked on the libretto, the overture, and full orchestration, the ballet, and choral ensembles, and Vladimir was instructed to write three revolutionary arias. This he did in two days to the satisfaction of the young commissar, a conservatory-trained pianist in charge of the production. Vladimir admitted he was flattered, even though politically he was hardly a communist. The opera was completed on time, but Vladimir's health suffered from the ordeal, and he was confined to bed for three days. On the fourth he heard one of his revolutionary songs coming from the street. A soprano from the opera, accompanied by a pianist on a truck-borne piano, sang through a megaphone. When she heard the music, Anna, who strongly opposed Vladimir working on the Soviet propaganda, burst into tears. A short time later, however, she was cheered up when four Red Army soldiers appeared at her door. In appreciation of Vladimir's contribution to the opera, they presented her with much needed bags of flour.[40]

The residents of Kiev were now suffering from the revolution. Although better off than most, the Dukelskys were forced to drink carrot tea and coffee made from tree bark. Soup was cooked from the stock of bones of raw herring used over and over again, and horse meat was standard fare. The gums of the undernourished brothers bled, and they lost some teeth. Vladimir, the more vulnerable of the two, came down with a succession of diseases.[41]

This period saw the government of Kiev change nineteen times, with machine-gun battles in the streets and all-night bombardments accompanying each change. Vladimir recalled one dramatic episode:

> During these intense struggles, the house-committee leader ordered all tenants into the basement shelters, where we huddled together in fear and hunger. During one bombing which occurred in the middle of the day, I got acutely fed up with the whole thing—the evil-smelling fellow tenants, the prayer-mumbling old women, the ceaselessly whining children, and, I'm ashamed to say, my mother's exaggerated preoccupation with my welfare. I ran out of the shelter and up five flights to our apartment, where I stole to the piano. This sounds like an affected theatrical tour de force, but I truly began composing, oblivious of the crashing bombs outside. As I was picking out a Frenchified reverie, a bomb hit the top of our building and caved in the seventh floor, with the sixth floor above the only barrier between me and certain death. A heavy chandelier plunged to the floor, missing my head

by inches, and I tore back to the shelter, panic-stricken. I entered to a concerted wail led by Mother; her relief was as great as my delicious feeling of enveloping safety.⁴²

Despite the danger, in the spring of 1918 Vladimir composed a four-movement string sextet. It and his other works made up half of a concert presented by Glière, including some "rather flowery songs and a set of piano pieces. The soprano Znamenska acquitted herself well in the songs, the sextet made a favorable impression, and by the time I appeared in one of Mother's better sartorial creations, the audience gave me a warm reception. After the concert there were even some cheers, and pretty girls came back to the artists' room to shake my hand, which quite turned my head."⁴³

For the next year, the political and military situation in Kiev deteriorated so badly that in December 1919 the Dukelskys and Col. Alexis Fedorovitch Lvov, who had been rooming with them, boarded a railroad car designed for forty men and eight horses for what became a fifteen-day ordeal instead of the usual twenty hours. Their journey to Odessa began the first leg of what would become permanent exile.⁴⁴ Anna took her diamonds, and Vladimir took a bundle containing his collected poems, a prized green toothbrush, and music manuscripts. He saved "Five Novelles," "Trois Morceaux," which included a prelude in E-flat major, a nocturne in F-sharp major, and an étude in F minor, plus Sonata in G Minor, an eighteen-page piano work in one movement.⁴⁵ Thus began the first of several sharp turns in the life of Vladimir Dukelsky.

A port city on the Crimean coast, an area long occupied by Cimmerians, Scythians, and Greeks, Odessa was officially founded in 1794, making it the youngest of all contemporary European cities. It also experienced the most rapid growth rate of any European city during the nineteenth century. Its healthy climate drew to it wealthy individuals and business investors from all over western Europe. The British consul noted in 1908 that German was "spoken in every business house and in nearly all the principal shops in Odessa. French is known (more or less) by the upper quarter of the population. English is spoken by many of the upper classes and also (more or less) by seafarers and by many businessmen; but undoubtedly Russian is incomparably the most used language, and German stands in the second place." As described by a visitor in 1912, "The spirit of European capitalism reigned in the town center. There were black glass signs with impressive gold lettering in every European language at the entrance to banks and company offices. There were highly priced luxury goods in the windows of the English and French shops."[46]

It was, nevertheless, a port with a typical waterfront. As described by another visitor:

> Here, too, were the many beershops, taverns, eating-houses and inns, with flamboyant sign-boards in every known language, and not a few disorderly houses, at once obvious and secret, from the steps of which hideously painted women would call to the sailors in hoarse voices. There were Greek coffee-shops, where one used to play dominoes and cards, and Turkish coffee-shops, where one could smoke narghiles and get a night's shelter for five kopecks."[47]

Although the Dukelskys arrived at a commercially thriving and culturally vibrant city within the Russian Empire, it was, noted Vladimir, far less Russian than Kiev or Moscow with "an almost Mediterranean indolence and subtropical languor." Mother and sons were welcomed into the house occupied by Vladimir's paternal uncle, Col. Ilya Vladimirovitch Dukelsky, who held the title of head of evacuation of the City of Odessa.[48] The home was located in the neighborhood of Moldavanka, best known for its military barracks but also for its elegant country houses occupied by the city's wealthy. Close to the waterfront, Moldavanka was near old limestone quarries with catacombs that had long been the center of contraband activity.[49] It was probably this area that Vladimir remembered exploring with his brother: "My passion for *flânerie* (a sort of inspired strolling dear to the literary Frenchman), already begun in Tzarskoe Sielo, St. Petersburg, and Moscow, was now being indulged hourly, and since my sturdy brother was equally fond of walking, we soon explored the town very thoroughly indeed."[50]

When not strolling, Vladimir studied with Vitold Malishevsky, "a good-looking youngish Pole" who wrote "samovar and red boots music" but whose "fastidious taste led him . . . to tinker with a little Debussy."[51] Malishevsky was also a composer, pianist, conductor, musicologist, and former student of Nicolai Rimsky-Korsakov, and he became the first rector of the Odessa Conservatory. Founded in 1913, it attracted teachers and musicians from Italy, Poland, Czechia, Germany, and Austria, as well as from St. Petersburg and Moscow.[52]

Vladimir presented Malishevsky with some "highly spiced songs which he professed to like. One of them . . . is perhaps the first really decent piece I wrote, and Malishevsky praised it unreservedly; another ('Like the White Swans' was the title) intrigued him chiefly because of its inhuman range." During the day, Vladimir studied counterpoint problems Malishevsky sent him, but at night Colonel Ilya sometimes pressed him into playing polkas, tangos, and the increasingly popular American two-step. Thus Vladimir became increasingly familiar with American popular music.[53]

With the Red Army advancing on Odessa, Vladimir had little time to further develop his knowledge of popular or classical music. One day the city "awoke to the sounds of heavy bombing," he remembered, "and on rushing into the street, we beheld posters on which were printed a *prikaz* (order) calling for a general and immediate evacuation." The Dukelskys had prepared for this. Russian-born American soldiers were then assisting the Red Cross, and when they called for some English-speaking Russians to help guard the organization's warehouses, Vladimir volunteered, although his English was extremely limited. For his guard work he and his family were promised space on a transport named the *Navaho* bound for Constantinople. He was given an Enfield rifle, which he had no idea how to handle, an American khaki uniform way too big for his lean frame, and a Red Cross armband. On one occasion, he and his fellow "soldiers" were ordered to pick up a middle-aged general who was dead drunk and furious when he learned what was in store for him. But he followed his captors, as did a fat colonel who had to be forcibly separated from his blowzy mistress in bed with him. On another occasion, they "arrested" Col. Ilya Vladimirovitch Dukelsky.[54]

Vladimir vividly described the place where the prisoners and others were deposited:

> The port presented a spectacle worthy of Hogarth or Doré at their cruelest; literally thousands of citizens pushed and kicked madly, all

codes of decency abandoned, with men fighting women, lost children howling in a maze of luggage, bundles, and even furniture, with no one to organize the unwieldy mob and hold it in check. Two large transports were loaded to the point of danger, and the rest of the raging humanity apparently was to be squeezed into the rat-eaten entrails of the decrepit *Navaho*....

Suddenly furious shooting started nearby, and we learned that the Soviet cavalry was entering the Port of Odessa. Ours would be the last ship to leave, and the crowd knew that the ship was their only hope of avoiding mass slaughter. The scene that ensued was unforgettable. The danger-obsessed crowd crushed itself on board the creaking ship; we boys followed and were ordered to remain on deck ready to shoot if necessary.[55]

When the captain ordered full speed ahead, the second sharp turn in the life of Vladimir Dukelsky began, a turn that would result in him expanding his musical horizons in ways that would determine to a large degree the direction his adult life would take. A nascent Vernon Duke would emerge first in Constantinople and later in New York, where he would meet people who would be of great assistance in developing his dual musical careers. Getting there, however, was hardly guaranteed: "The rusty engines gave one tortured screech—and then stopped. The ice in the bay had us marooned. ... Luckily, the ship next to us, the *St. Andrew*, an old Imperial Navy icebreaker, pushed ahead, cracking the ice, with the *Navaho* following like a sacred Eliza out of range of the Soviet's hounds."[56]

DUKE AWAKENS
CONSTANTINOPLE AND NEW YORK, 1919–1924

The Dukelsky family fled Odessa as the Russian Empire was collapsing and arrived in Constantinople just after the Ottoman Empire had dissolved. It had sided with Germany in World War I, and its defeat by Allied forces led to its breakup in 1918. Constantinople was not at first officially occupied, but Allied warships cluttered the harbor and Allied diplomats and soldiers roamed about at will. The Allies divided the city into spheres of influence and took over most of its administration. They imposed their own courts and managed the local police. The Allies also enjoyed the cultural richness of the city and all its baser enticements. Life was "gay, and wicked and delightful," recounted an Englishman. "The cafes were full of drinking and dancing." But for Armenians seeking safety from Turkish retribution and Turks abandoning lands freed from Ottoman control, life in the city was hardly "gay." At least 100,000 slept on the city streets, often with little food.[1]

The *Navaho* dropped anchor in the middle of the Bosphorus. Two doctors, an immigration official, and an interpreter boarded the ship and inspected the crew and passengers. Because two of the passengers were infected with typhus, all were quarantined for three days until taken to the island of Proti. There Vladimir, his mother, brother, Uncle Ilya Vladimirovitch Dukelsky, and Col. Alexis Fedorovitch Lvov began their new lives. Vladimir and Alexis spent most of their time sick in bed. "Life on the wretched island was bleak enough," Vladimir recalled, "but viewed from a hospital cot, it was so desolate that I was inspired to write long pessimistic poems in the genre known to the French as *larmoyant*. One began with the fatalistic line: 'I want to die as simply as possible,' which was a poetic exaggeration as I had no intention of dying but was merely sick of being sick."[2]

Fortunately for the Dukelskys, the director of the Constantinople YMCA sought Anna's help in running the Russky Mayak (Russian Lighthouse), a club for refugees in Pera in the European quarter of Constantinople. The club was well appointed with a gym, a library, and a Steinway. Mother and sons found accommodations on the rue Agha-Hamam, Uncle Ilya in a more up-scale area, and Colonel Lvov at the Mayak. Anna spent her day in the kindergarten, where she was put in charge of the nursery teachers. Alexis joined a Russian Boy Scout organization, and Vladimir got three meals a day but no salary at the Mayak as music supervisor, concert manager, and accompanist at the Saturday concerts.[3]

Busy as he was, Vladimir found the time to explore Constantinople. More than its famous landmarks,

> it was the mysterious zigzagging sidestreets which intrigued me, peopled with masked matriarchs stolidly sitting on the curbs, vendors hawking pungent foods and liquids in fiercely polytonal counterpoint while whipping their donkeys along, bearded philosophers in white-tiled cafés tugging at their waterpipes or sipping the vile *duziko*, the baby lambs being roasted on a spit right in the street and being eaten without benefit of cutlery, the terrifying fat whores in Galata, their faces immobile and grotesquely painted, their bodies like gallons of inferior vanilla ice cream, squatting in cages to be gaped at by pencil-slim American sailors.[4]

Vladimir often missed dinner, which naturally disappointed his mother. He recalled one evening when her "troubled and infinitely loving glance scanning my face" irritated him greatly: "Mother knew I had plenty of free time to gad about, and she disapproved of most of my new friends. She was right, as mothers generally are, and I resented her rightness in the equally general fashion of recalcitrant sons." One of those friends was the son of a famed Russian baritone who took Vladimir to a feast presented by the chef of the sultan. Vladimir smoked hashish and got dead drunk. Three of his "fellow gay blades" deposited him in his mother's arms at 7:30 A.M.[5]

Vladimir also met respectable and influential people—artists, ballet dancers, and opera singers. Because the city was also "crawling with poets, young and old," he persuaded some Americans to subsidize a poet almanac in Russian. Boris Kochno, a young poet whose impeccable dress greatly impressed the young Russian who was becoming sartorially conscious, submitted some "prettyish" poems and was invited to join the group. As Vladimir recalled, "Kochno was of good height and figure, wore a well-tailored sack suit with a great air, sported a Doucet bowtie and even smoked an English cigarette in a long jade holder. His face, felinely soft, was quite beautiful, and his voice, although undeniably affected, had an ingratiating ring to it." Later Vladimir gave a Kochno poem to a composer who set it to music. It was sung at one of the Mayak's concerts, with Kochno in attendance. He soon departed for Paris, where a few years later he and Vladimir would collaborate on a ballet.[6]

Another meeting—this one with musicologist and magazine publisher Pierre Souvtchinsky—also proved to be rewarding. He was impressed with some of Vladimir's songs, especially "The Wooden Church," and later would support his compositional efforts in Paris. Vladimir also met pianist Nicholas Stember, who was playing Nikolai Medtner's piano sonatas all over town. He approved of Vladimir's G Minor Piano Sonata, perhaps his best work so far, begun in November 1920 and completed in April 1921.[7]

Regardless of the contacts being made and the experiences gained, Vladimir had to go to work, not to advance his intellectual pursuits but to make money to support his family. Events over which he had no control forced him to apply his considerable musical talents in a much different way. The practical side of him awakened rather rapidly, and he began to increasingly take musical chances. By adapting to the popular music then circulating in America and Europe, he developed the skills necessary to make a very good living for the rest of his life.

With a violinist and cellist, Vladimir formed a trio and performed in one of Pera's better restaurants, playing "O Sole Mio," Toselli's "Serenade," "Otchi Tchornya," and other favorites he soon grew to dislike. The job lasted about two weeks for which he was paid three liras per evening. He then played the piano at silent films. And at an English barracks, he accompanied drunken soldiers demanding songs like "K-K-K-Katy," "It's a Long Way to Tipperary," and "For Me and My Gal," which he knew, and English ballads he had never heard before. Somehow he got the Tommies to follow him, although one told him he was not much of a piano player. He also performed at the British embassy with a Russian baritone and received ten liras for his efforts.[8]

Although claiming to dislike popular songs, he admitted that during the first winter out of Russia he began "to function (unofficially and unprofitably) as Dukelsky and Duke." Because "the Rose of Jazz, healthy and blooming, was by now firmly planted on the European shore of the Bosphorus," the patrons at the Mayak began to request "Hindustan," "Tell Me," and "Till We Meet Again." He "promptly purchased all three, also Irving Berlin's early successes and a thing mysteriously entitled 'Swanee' by a man improbably styled Geo. Gershwin. The Berlins were good in their way, but the Gershwin sent me into ecstasies. The bold sweep of the tune, its rhythmic freshness and, especially, its syncopated gait hit me hard and I became an 'early-jazz' fiend." It was not really jazz that inspired him, however, but the jazz orientations and rhythmic inventiveness of Gershwin, Berlin, and others. He spent considerable time at the piano writing tunes in the American idiom, and even though his songs may have sounded American, he admitted that harmonically they were not. He signed his first songs as "Ivan Ivin" and later as the more American-sounding "Alan Lane."[9]

Vladimir's "agreeable wanderings" on the Asian side of the city resulted in "three Turkish songs, which I harmonized, and which my Turkish friends succeeded in having published by Pera's Maison André. One was called 'Telgirafin Tellerine,' which is about the beginnings of the telegraph in Turkey."[10] He also got his Kiev-composed string sextet performed, but it was poorly received. He and painter Pavlik Tchelitchev collaborated on a ballet that was produced in a music hall.[11] They would meet again in Paris. Nicolas Slonimsky, whom Dukelsky had met in Kiev, also played piano with a violinist and cellist at a cafe and had "Swanee" in his repertoire. American foxtrots, in particular "Dardanella," were especially popular in the city. Fascinated by its syncopated melody and rapid running base, Slonimsky decided to compose his own foxtrot. He remembered it had "a swinging syncopated melody, and it was set in the customary song form." He called it

"Yok, yok, effendi" (No, no, milord).[12] Vladimir thought the melody not bad but jerky like his own songs.[13]

While in Constantinople, Vladimir took a few chances on love. In *Passport to Paris*, he wrote:

> Things seemed to be humming on all fronts, except the lowly, but important, carnal domain. My adolescent technique of reciting verse to the belle of the moment and then progressing to sentimental kisses was a signal flop, because girls who liked poetry usually stopped right there and those who had designs on me (a distinct minority) didn't see any point in poetry prior to going to bed. Alas, it was the going to bed that I dreaded, because having adopted the pose of a jaded rake, I was ashamed of my anatomical status, which was certain to betray me. One uninhibited female, daughter of a naval officer, cut me short in the middle of a fancy ode, and proceeded to take off her clothes, complying realistically with the urgent entreaties of my verses. After a perfunctory caress or two, I invented some cockeyed excuse and fled, cursing my ode, the cause of my predicament.[14]

That relationship was about as brief as possible, but most of his friendships were also short-lived. For his acquaintances and late-arriving relatives, Constantinople was merely a layover station on their way to northern Europe and the United States. Anna, however, loved the city and her job as a teacher. Although she lacked teacher training, she had read many books on children's education in preparing her offspring for adulthood. She excelled at her work and was given the best room in the building with a view of the Golden Horn. As her classes became bigger and bigger, she was provided with more rooms.

> For two years I had great happiness. I loved it, but for my children I was uneasy. I was always busy, and they were at the age they needed me most. For myself, I should have liked to remain, but for my boys I could not. There was always about us the nervous tension as of a volcano about to go off, and I saw our family atmosphere needed quiet and strength. Dimir [Vladimir] should be progressing; there he could not. He played much, but he should have a higher education, impossible if we remained.[15]

Thus in the autumn of 1921, when an official in the YMCA secured for Alexis a scholarship to the Cushing Academy in Ashburnham, Massachusetts, mother, sons, and Colonel Lvov sailed for America.[16]

When the Dukelskys arrived in New York, a decade in American urban history called the Jazz Age had begun. In the 1920s morals declined, skirts shortened, stocks rose, crime increased, unemployment dropped, jobs expanded, and a new music called jazz either liberated or corrupted depending on one's point of view. Probably unaware of the social and musical changes sweeping through the city, the Dukelskys, like so many immigrants who came before them, were overjoyed at spotting the Statue of Liberty and the New Jersey Shore. The immigration authorities treated them well. Anna received immigration papers that included the boys, as they were too young for their own.[17]

Vladimir found New York dirtier than Constantinople, and the Manhattan skyline of 1921 was not as impressive as it was to become, "but there was electricity and feverish promise in the air. The town was new, ungainly and cocky, awkwardly young, rather like a wolfhound pup with legs too long for the rest of his body—not only the town's legs, but also the girls' were interminable, straight and perfect, like so many miniature skyscrapers." Vladimir's admiration of the young women of New York was matched by his fascination with Broadway. The great monuments of various cities—the Eiffel Tower, the Tower of London, and the skyscrapers of New York—often lost their appeal after a few days, but "Broadway at night was an awesome sight, nowhere equaled on earth."[18]

As he and his brother explored Broadway, they probably marveled at the marquees announcing *The Ziegfeld Follies, George White's Scandals,* and *Shuffle Along,* to name but a few. Vladimir had little time for sightseeing, however. As he recalled many years later, he was seventeen, no longer spoiled, "but unaccustomed to the dubious ways of the world, and quite unknown. Making music to pay for one's keep is no cinch, even now that I have a name—or rather, two names. How to be a composer without being a conductor or a virtuoso instrumentalist is a tough proposition—either get yourself a rich wife or write music for music consumers, *not* music lovers."[19]

A rich wife being out of the question, he chose the latter. In New York, he wrote songs for a magician, who gave him two hundred dollars for "a lullaby for a trick rabbit, a tango for vanishing handkerchiefs and suddenly appearing bouquets of roses, a languorous waltz for card tricks and a diabolic *galop* to denote the time-honored feat of sawing a woman in half." He also played piano for a small-time adagio team and for "ersatz gypsies" in a Second Avenue restaurant.[20]

Playing the piano and then conducting a pit band in a burlesque called *Jazz Babies* became routine, but the "spectacle of all that unsavory flesh pounding the runway over my head, twenty bare legs strutting lasciviously in a heady cloud of cheap talcum powder and sweat, proved too unnerving." He missed his cues, and the dance director resented that a member of the chorus—a "banana-haired bombshell"—took a liking to him. He either resigned or was fired at the end of the first week (he could not remember which).[21] Although Vladimir wrote about these experiences in a rather offhanded way, they proved to be valuable. It was his introduction to the hoi polloi of the entertainment industry, a class of people with whom he would frequently deal.

He became acquainted with people from the classical world as well. He picked up work accompanying aspiring opera singers being coached by retired opera singers. He met mezzo-soprano Isolde von Bernhardt through pianist Nicholas Stember, who was the accompanist of soprano Nina Koshetz, who entertained at her apartment on Riverside Drive. Like Dukelsky, Koshetz was a Russian Ukrainian who first lived in Kiev before moving to Moscow, where her musical training began and her considerable international fame was launched. At her apartment, Vladimir met composer Lazare Saminsky and critic Aaron Baron, who introduced him to more people, including composer Karol Szymanowski, who introduced him to violinist Paul Kochanski and his wife, Zosia.[22] He also met Sergei Prokofiev, who remembered him as "a rather detestable young man, and I purposely paid him no attention.[23]

Although many of these contacts would prove useful in the future, Vladimir was contributing little to the household. Anna sold the last of her diamonds and found work in a match factory, while Alexis studied various sciences in preparation for entering the Cushing Academy. Later Anna got a job designing children's clothes at a Fourth Avenue firm and moved to Washington Heights on West 172nd Street. Determined to make music pay for his share of the upkeep, every morning Vladimir would take the subway at 168th Street, alight at 50th Street, and wander around Tin Pan Alley, the conglomeration of music publishing firms where the collective pounding of pianists sounded like wives pounding on tin plates. With the assistance of tunesmith Lee David, he managed to get a hearing now and then, but his songs, not being in the idiom of the street, were rejected. He admitted that his melodies were not very good, and relying on a Russian–English dictionary, his lyrics were even worse. In a song called "Spooning on a Crowded Bus," he came up with "Underneath the bridge our paradise we *cross*, spooning on a crowded *bus*." Not surprisingly, the song was rejected, as was "Don't Waste Your Time Wasting Your Time on Me."[24] Leo Edwards, who was producing a nightclub revue on West 42nd Street for Murray's Roman Gardens, however, hired Vladimir as a pianist: "This was *Jazz Babies* on a higher and more refined level; the girls were slimmer and cleaner." They worked "in comparative harmony" until the show's quick demise.[25]

Working with showgirls did not prevent Vladimir from following his true Muse. He presented ten songs on avant-garde Russian poems to Nina Koshetz, but she could not decipher them and wondered why young men who are born old would rather die than write melodies. Vladimir agreed: "Poor melody became (unwittingly) a tawdry 32-bar refrain by Alan Lane or Ivan Ivin (Vernon Duke was yet to make his initial appearance), whereas Dukelsky, thus robbed—by himself—was in danger of sinking in a harmonic marsh." He realized he had been "leading a duel musical existence which became my trade-mark of the thirties. Out of an odd sort of self-defense, I began to torture and complicate the musical dialectics in my 'serious' output; thus, the simpler and more down-to-earth my tunes, the more cerebral and *voulu* my 'good' music became, until it was practically indistinguishable from that of the twelve-tone boys."[26]

Vladimir, however, offered his songs to soprano Éva Gauthier, who sang two of them at a concert presented by the International Composers' Guild. Vladimir noted in his autobiography that Gauthier mastered the songs, but the reception was cool, the critics silent.[27] Apparently he missed the review in the *New York Tribune*, which mentioned that the two songs by Vladimir

Dukelsky, an unknown Russian composer, "were quite melodious, while Stravinskyesque."[28]

George Gershwin, whose song "Swanee" had so impressed him in Constantinople, was in the audience and later told him he was surprised that someone so young could write such dry intellectual stuff. Although Gershwin was greatly impressed with Vladimir's musical background, he wondered what he was going to do with it. Vladimir responded by playing an extremely cerebral piano sonata, probably the one in G minor he had composed in Constantinople. There was no money or heart in that kind of stuff, said George. Don't be scared of going lowbrow. Write some popular tunes. They will open you up. In his autobiography, Vladimir wrote: "That rather startling remark of George's—'they will open you up'—stayed with me through all the years that we were friends."[29]

Following the Guild concert, an executive of the Wolfsohn Musical Bureau suggested that Vladimir write an orchestral piece, and he immediately went to work on an overture to a Russian poet's post-romantic tale of Iceland. He completed *Gondla* in a week and gave it to Dirk Foch, who had just formed the New York City Symphony. It was performed in Carnegie Hall with Vladimir in a box seat. The work received a meager applause, which allowed Vladimir to quickly bow from his box.[30] He later quipped that the overture "was less frozen than the audience and the critics."[31] A New York critic called it "a farrago of atrocious noises."[32] A female reporter said "it was barbaric in its harmonies, Icelandic in its frozen remoteness, and decidedly hunchback in its form."[33]

From this experience, Vladimir came to understand "the contemporary composer's plight; he gets a performance—then perhaps, another performance—then a seemingly interminable lull." Pondering his fate, Vladimir concluded that there was not much to ponder. A little pudgy man does not appear out of the blue and offer a composer $10,000 to write music. Of course this never happened in the past, "unless his name was Ludwig of Bavaria and yours Wagner." So Vladimir returned to playing with "synthetic gypsies," this time "at a pseudo-Russian midtown night spot."[34]

It was there that the "first clash between the embryo Duke, the wage earner, and Dukelsky, would-be composer," occurred. One night when a half-dozen composers entered the club, Vladimir was mortified because they were all practicing their craft while he was prostituting himself: "I closed my eyes, raced through the hateful 'Otchi' [Tchornya] at breakneck speed, causing the gypsy diva intense discomfort and annoyance." Vladimir apologized to Lazare Saminsky. The composer told him not to worry, that everyone had to eat. But the truth hurt so much that he decided, after a long talk with his mother, to renounce "the métier of an eatery piano player."[35]

When George Gershwin agreed to listen to some fresh tunes he had written, Vlaldimir was elated. His respect and affection for Gershwin are reflected in his recollection of that day: "He was a born *improvisatore* yet never changed tempo, nor played rubato, the relentless 4/4 beat carried him along—it was physically difficult for him to stop. This is just what he was doing when I walked in and sat down to listen." After Gershwin's sister sang a chorus and departed, George "began intoning Ira's lyrics," and no performer of his songs ever "invested them with such an arresting fervor." Ira joined George for the third chorus, but when he messed up a passage, the music stopped. A heated argument ensued, but Vladimir broke it up by sliding onto the piano stool. George shrugged off the first two songs he played, but the third so impressed him that he decided to take the young tunesmith to meet Max Dreyfus, the publisher of Harms, Inc. In the waiting room were notable musicians, composers, and lyricists, including Joe Meyer, Phil Charig, Harry Ruby, Vincent Youmans, and Oscar Levant. "The place was like a political hell," recalled Duke, "with Boss Dreyfus dispensing patronage to the Faithful and selling producers on commissioning entire musical-comedy scores to the older and better-established 'boys,' or interpolated numbers to promising beginners. Most of these privileged characters were drawing small weekly advances against future royalties on a yearly basis—and that's what I was after." To George's surprise, Dreyfus did not like the song.[36]

Obviously disappointed and full of self-doubts, Vladimir was again saved, this time by Nina Koshetz, who needed someone to assist her in preparing for an upcoming concert with conductor Leopold Stokowski. Given a room in her rented house in Monmouth Hills, New Jersey, Vladimir orchestrated two pieces for Nina to sing. Although his knowledge of orchestration was limited, with the proper manuals he finished the task to his satisfaction.

VLADIMIR DUKELSKY, MONMOUTH HILLS, NEW JERSEY, 1921.
From Duke, *Passport to Paris*. Reproduced with permission from Kay Duke Ingalls.

His romantic interest in a blonde of nineteen, however, proved to be unsatisfactory. Most of the young people who flowed in and out of the house spent their days swimming, playing tennis, and "some typically Fitzgeraldian petting in Stutz rumble seats." "Vladimir did not play tennis or drive a car, and he was too proud to borrow money from Princeton and Yale men. Instead, he composed and orchestrated."[37]

Then it was back to New York to search for work and to reflect on his future. The young men in their Wanamaker or Brooks Brothers suits, returning home from vacation, seemed "to have a purpose in life and a well-planned future, as did their 'dates,' pert, slim-limbed city sirens, complete with the new boyish bob, oriental earrings and a long cigarette holder, bent on marriage or a 'career'; they all had fresh memories of energetic necking at Princeton house parties or on the less recherché sands of Coney Island. I again felt suspended in thin air as I returned to my daily pursuits of Euterpe and greenbacks."[38]

Through his expanding network of contacts, Vladimir met actress-producer Edna James, who hired him to write the incidental music for a double-bill production of *Song of Songs* in pantomime and a one-act play by the Russian poet Alexander Blok. Vladimir's score was for seven instruments, including the piano part for himself. His music flowed continuously from the overture to the curtain without a break. Booked for three weeks at the Lyric Theatre on 42nd Street, it lasted two weeks, but one critic mentioned the music and its composer.[39]

During this time, Vladimir got caught up in a social swirl he called "The Bad Old Days" in his autobiography, in which "I wanna be Bad" was the "sophomoric motto of my New York companions, and how they loved achieving badness, not the involved post-Freudian aberrations, just drink and lechery in very large doses." Vernon decided to go bad in a big way, but "this proved simpler than chasing the Muse and the Moola at the same time. I was under twenty, not unattractive and wore my secondhand or borrowed clothes with an air, though without a cent." He "frequented musical Fifth Avenue—and dined at Hoytie Wiborg's, or Dorothy Monroe Robinson's, or Mrs. Otto Kahn's, three somewhat 'intellectual' hostesses who entertained splendidly"[40]

At Bob Chanler's home, a continuous party hosted by Louise Hellstrom ran from sundown to sunrise, with the most important guests occupying the third floor where "revelry reigned." The second and respectable floor was the domain of Chanler's debutante daughters, "who'd occasionally appear on the staircase, white-gloved and disdainful, to greet a white-tie eligible creature and make sure he didn't make a mistake and wind up on the wrong floor." At one such party, Vladimir found himself on the "correct" floor "dancing rapturously with a tall dark divinity, her Coty-scented arms locked around my neck." When asked what fraternity he belonged to, Vladimir said something that led to his immediate exit. Escorted to the third floor, Vladimir admitted he was not good at drinking or lechery and that the "sex business" still filled him with "uncomprehending terror."[41]

Yet he admitted having "a soft spot for the strange and lovable 'bad' couple, whose badness artfully disguised that very rare commodity—a big heart." And he did not complain about meeting at their parties Somerset Maugham, Jack Buchanan, Bea Lillie, Gertrude Lawrence, Arnold Bennett, Jane Cowl, Dorothy Parker, Judith Anderson, Augustus John, Alexander Woollcott, Arthur Bliss, Noel Coward, Marguerite d'Alvarez, Sam Hoffenstein, H. L. Mencken, Burton Rascoe, Arthur Guiterman, John Dos Passos, Blyth Daly, Tallulah Bankhead, and John Murray Anderson. Anderson was one of the most important directors and producers on Broadway and was then rehearsing a new show called *Jack and Jill*. Two chorus girls smuggled Vladimir into rehearsals, but Murray refused to listen to any of his songs. Vladimir did not blame him, because they were not very good. Neither was the show, which folded shortly after it opened.[42] In a few years, Anderson and Dukelsky would collaborate on a very successful Broadway show.

Pianist Arthur Rubinstein proved to be another important contact. When he heard Vladimir play some of his piano pieces at a party, he recommended that he compose a one-movement piano concerto. Completed in late 1923, Vladimir considered it his "first well-knit and technically adroit piece." He played it for Nicholas Stember, who promised to learn it, and at parties, but only after George Gershwin had stunned the guests with "Do it Again" and "Stairway to Paradise." He took the composition to Rubinstein, who received him "dressed in a brocaded silk dressing gown, with a large pearl stick-pin in his tie, affable and courtly as is his wont. The one thing I dreaded was a polite brush off: I had learned the concerto painstakingly, but, having given up practicing long ago, was barely equal to my task. I gave a fairly good account of my work, nevertheless, and Artur, bless him, was quite transported." Rubinstein praised the work because of its melodic content, which was often lacking in the works of new composers. He encouraged Vladimir to go to Paris, then the mecca of young composers. In looking back on his meeting with Rubinstein, Vladimir considered it a "turning point of major proportions." Without it he probably would have returned to playing "Otchi Tchornya."[43]

Vladimir needed money and turned to Gershwin for help:

It transpired that George, overburdened with work, needed a "ghost" writer for a black-and-white ballet—a simple bit of ragtime for a high-kicking precision routine—for the Tiller girls, who were to appear in the 1924 edition of George White's *Scandals*. I turned out the thing in a few hours and was paid $100 by George. Deeming the job satisfactory, George then desired to have me try my hand at "piano copies," publishable voice and piano versions of songs to be used in the revue. I arranged six of these and was paid twenty dollars apiece by Harms, Inc. The songs I "arranged" were the ever-popular "Somebody Loves Me," "In Araby," "Kongo Kate," "Tune In on Station J-O-Y," "Year after Year," and a rhythm song, the name of which escapes me. I was quite proud of the "fill-ins" I provided for "Somebody Loves Me" and was amused to find that they were also used in the stock orchestration—obviously, the arranger thought them eminently Gershwinesque, which indeed they were. That was another $120.[44]

Nothing could be more Gershwinesque than *Rhapsody in Blue*, which George performed with the Paul Whiteman Palais Royale Orchestra in Aeolian Hall on February 12, 1924. Gershwin had composed the work for two pianos with some indications as to how it should be scored. Ferde Grofé orchestrated the piece. To its premiere Whiteman invited some of the elites of the musical world, including Walter Damrosch, Victor Herbert, Jascha Heifetz, Sergei Rachmaninoff, Ernest Bloch, Willem Mengelberg, Leopold Stokowski, and Fritz Kreisler.[45]

Max Dreyfus hired Vladimir to write a solo piano arrangement of *Rhapsody in Blue*. In late May 1924, he wrote to George that he was "working on it, but the inability to indulge in all the intricacies that the two-piano arrangement would provide, drives me mad."[46] Apparently he finished the project, and with an additional $500 he got for playing at the house of a prominent Bostonian, he had accumulated $800, more than enough for a six-month sojourn in Paris. He got letters of introduction from his social mentors—Princesse Edmond de Polignac, Baron Adolph de Meyer, Misia Sert, and Karol Szymanovski. And he boldly asked Max Dreyfus for a letter to Francis Salabert, the top Paris publisher of light music. Dreyfus, "complete with the thin, long cigar, a thinner smile and few, very few words," ordered his secretary to type up the usual letter. With "a curt nod, a vague circular gesture with the cigar, indicating, I hoped, *bon voyage* and good luck," he dismissed Vladimir.[47]

Thus began another sharp turn in his life, but this one, unlike the others, he initiated himself. "It wasn't altogether clear to anyone, including myself, just what Paris would do for me," admitted Vladimir, "but supremely confident, I was determined to do something for Paris." Therefore, with a Greek Orthodox icon, a little theosophical pamphlet, and a thick wool sweater from his mother, Vladimir sailed on the *Rochambeau*, "a small, rickety vessel, but the passengers—wide-eyed students, for the most part—were young in search of happiness, the food excellent."[48]

DUKELSKY TRIUMPHANT
PARIS, MONTE CARLO, AND LONDON, 1924–1925

With a falling franc and a low cost of living after World War I, France beckoned those from the United States who, fed up with its rigid morality, sought the liquor, narcotics, and sexual freedom the country had to offer. By 1923 the expatriate community in Paris, which included Europeans, had expanded to thirty-two thousand. They found affordable, if barely livable, accommodations, cheap food, and other "necessities" in the run-down quarter known as the Montparnasse. The number of tourists who came for a day or night of hedonism gradually increased throughout the decade.[1]

Many American writers, artists, and performers, famous or soon to be, explored France for varying lengths of stay: Cole Porter, Ezra Pound, Gertrude Stein and Alice B. Toklas, Josephine Baker, Sherwood Anderson, John Dos Passos, Archibald MacLeish, F. Scott Fitzgerald and his wife, Zelda, and Ernest Hemingway. Sections of Hemingway's *The Sun Also Rises* and Fitzgerald's *Tender Is the Night* are set in 1920s Paris. The expatriate Americans, individuals from other countries, such as James Joyce, and some of the French formed what became known as the "Lost Generation," a term exemplifying the despondency and dissolution created by World War I. The French called the decade *les Années folles*.[2]

Like most first- and probably last-time visitors to Paris, twenty-year-old Vladimir Dukelsky was smitten, noting in his autobiography that he would "love her to my dying day." But the French themselves were another matter. He observed that

> French girls often had mustaches under their noses as well as under their arms; that their chunky bodies and voluminous busts were supported by bony toothpicklike legs, usually short; that the men were smallish and exceedingly badly dressed—even the dandies had an oddly overdressed "wrong" look; that the "flics" (cops) were corpulent, untidy and bewhiskered and spent most of their time arguing with even untidier taxi drivers, when the latter weren't too busy insulting one another; that the lady concierges were addicted to beards and glared at you until you give them *un petit franc*, at which point they displayed the most exquisite manners; that the *urinoirs* on street corners were none too safe as they were the habitual haunts of pederasts on the prowl; that the wine was incomparable and the beer deplorable; . . . that some people eat to live, others live to eat, but the French *eat to eat*; . . . that Paris children are the best-looking in the world, which argues well for the city's future; . . . that taxis were cheap and unsafe and telephones bewildering and unreliable; that snobs read Proust and Claudel, not the *Almanach de Gotha* or the social register and went to concerts, not just dinners, weddings and horse races; that everyone gave and took, and no one *gave a damn*—in short, that Paris was Paradise.[3]

Vladimir met people who would be, or who he thought would be, of enormous help in advancing his career. He immediately presented the letter of introduction that Max Dreyfus had written for him to the Paris publisher Francis Salabert. The letter, however, made no mention of the quantity or quality of Vladimir's music: "The bearer of this letter is Mr. Dukelsky, a young man who composes music. Any courtesies shown Mr. Dukelsky will be greatly appreciated." When the Frenchman icily asked if Dreyfus had heard any of his music, Vladimir said yes. He was then shown the door. He returned to his hotel room, tore up the other letters of introduction, and determined that his music alone would make or unmake him.[4]

When he ventured into Montparnasse, he received a much better reception at the apartment of painter Pavlik Tchelitchev, whom he had met in

Constantinople, and pianist Alan Tanner, both of whom took a liking to him. On one occasion, Tchelitchev coaxed Vladimir into playing the concerto he had come to conquer Paris with. Tanner was impressed and offered to introduce him to those preparing ballets for the coming season. Vladimir moved into a small hotel near his two friends, and through them he met composer Nicolas Nabokov. He did not like Nabokov's music, but he found him "an engaging young man with an open Russian face and the disarming clumsiness of adolescence." He also met Valitchka Nouvel, who, after listening to Vladimir's concerto, promised to mention him to Serge Pavlovitch Diaghilev.[5]

Born into an upper-middle-class family in Russia in 1872, Diaghilev studied at the St. Petersburg Conservatory of Music but gave up any thoughts of composing when told by Nikolai Rimsky-Korsakov that he had no talent for music. His love of art, however, led him to found a journal called the *World of Art* and later to produce plays, concerts, and operas. In 1909 he founded the Ballets Russes and throughout the years employed some of Russia's best young dancers. He commissioned ballet music from Nikolai Tcherepnin, Claude Debussy, Maurice Ravel, Erik Satie, Manuel de Falla, Richard Strauss, Sergei Prokofiev, Ottorino Respighi, and Francis Poulenc. Michel Fokine adapted much of the music for the ballets, and Léonide Massine did much of the choreography. Diaghilev also hired Igor Stravinsky to arrange some works by Chopin for the Ballets Russes, and he commissioned his *Firebird*, *Petrushka*, *The Rite of Spring*, *Pulcinella*, and *Les Noces*. Like Dukelsky, the Russian Revolution had forced Stravinsky into exile, in his case to Paris.[6]

A few days after their meeting, Nouvel informed Vladimir that he was invited to Diaghilev's box for a performance of Stravinsky's *Les Noces*. As Vladimir recalled,

> Sergei Pavlovitch Diaghilev was a big man—slightly over six feet tall—broad and big-limbed, but not corpulent; his head was enormous, and the face—a world in itself; you hardly noticed the rest of his body. The still-abundant graying hair was parted meticulously on the side and displayed the oft-described silver-white patch in the middle—no crafty coiffeur's trick but, from all accounts, something

of a birthmark. . . . The eyes had a piercing, mocking intensity about them, softened by unusually heavy eyelids, and he was fond of closing them slowly, as if persuaded by some unseen Morpheus, but only for a moment; they were soon peering at you again, not missing a thing. The mouth was cruel and soft at the same time, . . . the smile irresistible and oddly feminine. . . . He was well, although not conspicuously well, dressed. . . . His voice seemed monstrously affected at first—the Imperial Page's voice of aristocratic St. Petersburg—but you soon knew that he must have, too, been born with it.[7]

At the post-concert dinner party honoring Stravinsky, Vladimir told him how moved he was by *Les Noces*, "which effusion was graciously received." Many of the Paris elite were present, including Coco Chanel, "looking like a jockey in drag." Initially she showed some interest in the young man, suspecting he was a new dancer, but lost interest when Vladimir mentioned he was a composer. Also in attendance was Jean Cocteau "of the fallen angel-face, sleeve-cuffs unbuttoned to permit the bourgeoisie to feast their eyes on the fireman-red lining (a sartorial must with him) and the fanciful, if not always intelligible, line of gab. These people, including Stravinsky, talked of Stravinsky and I drank in every eloquent word."[8]

Two days after the concert, Nouvel told Vladimir that Diaghilev wanted to hear his piano concerto. He was to appear at the house of Baron Adolph de Meyer and his wife that afternoon. Vladimir described the ordeal. After much gossip he was too nervous to absorb and three martinis, he gave "a creditable account," but when he "hit the last crashing C-major chord, there was a moment of dreadful, complete silence—I didn't turn around but knew that the two de Meyers and Boris [Kochno] were looking at Diaghilev, awaiting his verdict. To my astonishment, the great man began clapping his hands thunderously and with such determination that the others soon joined the applause." He was further shocked when Diaghilev playfully wondered what Vladimir was going to call *his* ballet; that is, the composition he was to write for Ballets Russes.[9]

"The news of a new Diaghilev protégé emerging from out of nowhere—Russia via the United States was an unheard-of beginning—spread rapidly through the Paris salons," wrote Vladimir. "Diaghilev nicknamed me

Karsavina, as he claimed that I bore a striking resemblance to that dancer, and this led to obvious speculations as to the nature of our relationship; idle ones, I must add, because, quite outside my own 'normal' leanings, I just wasn't Sergei Pavlovich's 'type.'"[10] Diaghilev was gay. Dukelsky was still a virgin. Apparently their respective sexual orientations had little to do with their relationship, which evolved into true friendship.

Initially Vladimir's relationship with Stravinsky was more as an acquaintance than as a friend. Much later it would deteriorate. He recalled his meeting with the maestro, who agreed to listen to his concerto:

> The master, surrounded by multi-colored inks, erasers, pens, pencils, and music paper of every conceivable variety, all in meticulous order, sat in an ultra-modern chair behind an even more aggressively modern writing desk. As he got up to greet me with the rather fussy politeness so typical of him, I became conscious of the enormous goggles he wore, propped up *above* his eyes, the chin, in its turn, propped up by an elegantly tied ascot emerging from a monogrammed sport shirt. Stravinsky's body was small, taut, and compact, but in common with small men, he was fashion crazy.

Stravinsky liked the composition, praised Vladimir's technical proficiency, and predicted that he would write a good ballet for Diaghilev.[11]

Dukelsky was far more interested in meeting Sergei Prokofiev, whose Third Piano Concerto was the model for his First. Prokofiev had a reputation of being rude, blunt, and boorish, and Dukelsky was anxious about the meeting. He admitted being luckier than most, "because Serge the Second (I often think the twenties the Era of the Three Serges—Diaghilev, Prokofiev, and Koussevitzky) received me most cordially." On June 18, 1924, Prokofiev listened to his concerto, a date of significance to him, because "a great and durable friendship began on that day."[12] Prokofiev detected some of his own influences in the concerto and found it not bad.[13] He would become a champion of Dukelsky's serious works but a stern critic of his popular efforts.

Like Dukelsky, Prokofiev was born in Ukraine, although well before him on April 27, 1891. Like Dukelsky he was influenced by his mother's piano playing. Like Dukelsky he composed classical pieces at a very early age. Like Dukelsky he studied with Reinhold Glière, although as a private student in

Sontsovka rather than in Kiev. Prokofiev quickly achieved considerable fame as one who composed in numerous musical genres, including the ballet. After seeing the Ballets Russes in Paris and London in 1913 and 1914 and meeting Diaghilev in London, Prokofiev began collaborating with Diaghilev in 1921 on the never produced *Ala and Lolly* and the much postponed *Buffoon*.[14]

Presently, however, Diaghilev was sponsoring a new composer and instructed Vladimir and Boris Kochno, who had met in Constantinople, to create a ballet based on the legend of Zephyr and Flora. In an apartment above a bistro in the Chevreuse Valley, they went to work. As Vladimir recalled, "The honest bourgeois who patronized her establishment must have been bewildered by the distinctly un-French sounds emanating from upstairs, but no one seemed to mind. The bourgeois drank, I composed, and Boris went about the countryside faternizing [sic] with the villagers, a favorite pastime of his in those days." Diaghilev never paid them a visit, but Nouvel did and offered Vladimir a contract and a salary of 1,000 francs a month paid through the French Performing Rights Society. While in the valley, Vladimir finished almost half of the ballet.[15]

On August 4, 1924, Vladimir wrote to George Gershwin, then in London, about his good fortune, noting that his ballet was to be produced for the eighteenth season of the Ballets Russes. Although the score was to be very long from a difficult book, "you understand that nothing better could have happened to me, and, although speed is not required in this particular case, I'm writing and writing. In two weeks I'm going to Monte Carlo to join Diaghilev, finish the score and start rehearsals." He also told George that he had spoken to Diaghilev about him "and played nearly all your tunes to his secretary, who finds them amazing. . . . Do come to Paris before I leave."[16] At mid-month he sent Gershwin a postcard from Monte Carlo: "My ballet is progressing steadily. I already wrote the overture and three numbers. Diaghileff is quite satisfied."[17]

Diaghilev wrote to dancer Serge Lifar on August 13, 1924, noting that "Dukelsky came yesterday and played me the music for *Flore et Zéphyre* which I like enormously. I made such comments as I thought fit, and he very nicely said he would take note of it all, and go on working on it in Monte Carlo, under my eye: all of which pleases me greatly. For his twenty years he's extremely gifted and developed."[18]

The Monte Carlo Vladimir moved to had been created on the eastern edge of the Principality of Monaco in 1863, and a decade later its casino-resort was a famous gambling playground. It economically survived World War I, but postwar austerity measures, travel restrictions, and an influenza pandemic harmed the tourist industry. Business picked up in 1922, when hotels began to remain open during the summer months. In the prewar years, Monte Carlo, like other Riviera playgrounds, had few visitors between May and September—few people found much sense in sunbathing and swimming. That began to change in the summer of 1923 when Coco Chanel was observed sunbathing on the prow of the Duke of Westminster's yacht, becoming darker than some of the deckhands. Whether she invented sunbathing as some have suggested, the trend began about the time of her visit.[19]

Also a boon to the area and to Monte Carlo in particular was the relocation of the Ballets Russes to the city in 1922 on a somewhat permanent basis. The company was allowed to rehearse and perform at Theater de Monte Carlo for six months of the year. For the performers, the relocation was greatly welcomed. As recalled by Lydia Sokolova, "Dancers who had been obliged to leave their possessions scattered in hotels throughout Europe—many since 1913—were at last able to settle down in flats or lodgings which were semi-permanent."[20]

When Diaghilev, Kochno, and Dukelsky arrived at Monte Carlo, the two seniors checked in at Hotel de Paris. Vladimir found accommodations at a nearby hotel. The view was great, the room cheap and clean, the food limited and bad. He would often eat at the hotel and then join Diaghilev and Kochno in Monte Carlo for a second dinner. Vladimir's impressions of town were mixed. He could not "see why such astonishing natural beauty should be ruined by dingy and pretentious villas and, above all, the ever-present dirty-orange of the Riviera rooftops." His opinion of the casino was even worse. In its washed-out pink, it was "one of the saddest sights in the world." Losing money at roulette obviously shaped his view of the casino, where, ironically, Diaghilev got him a practice room with a piano.[21]

Prokofiev arrived during the last week in March 1925, and Dukelsky, who described the ballet as "classical with a whiff of Russian," played the score for him. Prokofiev later recalled that the first number,

> which was lively and not all that bad, answered to the description. But I already liked the theme of the second number, and the rest of the piece, especially the superb theme and variations (even though the theme itself was in some ways derivative and stylised). The penultimate number I liked less. All in all, though, this was an evening that happens all too rarely: having before one a genuinely important composer. I do not think I am mistaken. I congratulated Dukelsky most sincerely and returned home with the ballet ringing in my ears. Dukelsky was visibly delighted with my praise.[22]

On the evening of March 25, Prokofiev, his wife, Lina (better known as Ptashka), Diaghilev, and Dukelsky attended a performance of some of Diaghilev's earlier works and then had dinner in the Café de Paris. Seeing Vladimir dancing with Ptashka prompted Diaghilev to tease Prokofiev about the young man being better-looking than he. Diaghilev also mentioned that he now had three sons—Stravinsky, Prokofiev, and Dukelsky—but that Prokofiev was just his second son.[23]

Diaghilev wanted to stage a ballet similar to those once danced by private companies that Russian nobles had maintained during the reign of Alexander I. The subject had been performed in 1795, and the goal was to re-create the atmosphere of that period in the new production.[24] In the legend of Zephyr and Flora, the two characters are happily married, but Boreas, Zephyr's brother, is in love with Flora and invents a game of Blind Man's Bluff to separate the couple. Flora falls into the arms of Zephyr, and the jealous Boreas shoots the blindfolded Zephyr with an arrow. The Muses enter, dance with Flora, and depart. Boreas pursues Flora, who repulses him but falls into a swoon. The wounded Zephyr is carried out, and Boreas flees. Flora and the Muses lament the passing of Zephyr, but then he recovers. The Muses bind Zephyr and Flora together so they may never again be separated. They depart, and the Muses punish Boreas. The ballet was arranged in seven episodes. Georges Braque designed the scenery and costumes, Oliver Messel created the masks and symbols, and

Léonide Massine fashioned the choreography. Alice Nikitina was chosen to play Flora. Anton Dolin got the role of Zephyr and Serge Lifar that of Boreas.[25]

The dancer S. L. Grigoriev recalled, "Two novelties were on our list this year in the shape of two scores, one by George Auric (his second), and the other by a young Russian named Vladimir Dukelsky, the latter being a discovery of some of Diaghilev's friends. We all considered Dukelsky a most attractive person; and some of our young ladies even detected in him a likeness to Pushkin."[26]

Vladimir moved from his hotel to the nearby Villa des Genets. He would arise in the morning, breakfast with his two landladies, stroll to the casino to compose for two or three hours, hop on a bus to Larvotto Beach to swim and sunbathe, return to the casino to compose until six, and then dine with some of his new friends. Although Jean Cocteau was one of those friends, Vladimir failed to fall under his "spell, which, I fear, annoyed him not a little. . . . In spite of the marked and flattering interest Cocteau displayed in me, in spite of an enjoyable cruise in his famous boat *Ange Heurtebise* and the fact that he nicknamed me 'Le Duc Exquis,' (Dukelsky), I didn't very much care for these Villefranche outings."[27]

Cocteau was one of the rich and famous who took the Blue Train (the common name for the Calais-Méditerranée Express) to the Riviera. On one occasion, the *Menton and Monte Carlo News* announced, "The great and beautiful Blue Train arrived, fully conscious of its superiority." The passengers came to drink, dance, and swim. Permanent relationships were shunned. They can be linked to the "Lost Generation" but only superficially, as they preferred the frivolous to the serious.[28]

Disembarking one day was Karen, nicknamed Khaki, a nineteen-year-old English girl who was engaged to Biddy, a Cardiff football player, who was absent at the time. Vladimir fell in love, and deciding to become a man (he was still a virgin) and a husband at the same time, he proposed to Khaki. She told him to wait a few days. When informed of the proposal, Diaghilev was furious, having once told him to stay away from women. The dispute might have led to a rupture in their friendship and perhaps a disruption of the ballet had it not been for the arrival of Biddy. Khaki chose him, leaving Vladimir no choice but to find another outlet for his passion.[29]

While he was residing at Villa des Genets, a young English blonde named Sally led him to manhood, stole his watch, and infected him with a minor venereal disease. If that were not enough, a short time later in the room next to his, Vladimir overheard Sally and another man drinking and engaging in "heavy-handed horseplay" until the man noticed a splotch on her skin. Detecting a venereal disease, he dressed quickly, gave Sally some money, and fled. Dukelsky rushed to his doctor, fearful he had contracted another type of the disease, but the tests proved negative. Monaco authorities later deported Sally.[30]

None of this prevented Vladimir from flirting with Tamara Geva, whom he remembered as a "standard Nordic beauty—pale and fair-haired, with cool blue eyes and a perfectly proportioned body." One of the nine Muses, she was married to Georgi Melitonovich Balanchivadze. Born in 1904 in St. Petersburg to a Georgian father and a Russian mother, Georgi entered the Imperial Ballet School at the age of thirteen. Graduating in 1921, he enrolled in the Petrograd Conservatory where he studied the piano, counterpoint, harmony, and composition. He graduated in 1923 but remained with the conservatory as a dancer. While on a visit to Germany with a Soviet dance troupe, he, his wife, and other dancers fled to Paris. There Diaghilev invited him to join the Ballets Russes as a choreographer.[31] Vladimir, however, was not impressed by Georgi, whom he remembered as a short, slender man with a slight facial twitch. Unaware of his "prodigious gifts as choreographer I thought he was merely an inevitable nuisance in his lucky role as Tamara's husband."[32] A decade later, Duke and George Balanchine (as Georgi became known) would collaborate on several ballets.

To publicize his most recent ballet, Diaghilev wined and dined French and English critics and got Dukelsky to play the entire score of *Zephyr and Flora* for the composer Francis Poulenc. In an article in a Paris musical review, Poulenc wrote that Dukelsky earned a living playing "jazz" but was

> too intelligent not to realize the danger of assimilating such music into his.... Isn't it the most beautiful lesson to those who believe that jazz is destined to renovate music? . . . Dukelsky, without archness or affectations, touches the heart by the freshness of his melody. The harmony, always direct, and the boldness of the development give his

VLADIMIR DUKELSKY, MONTE CARLO, 1924. From Duke, *Passport to Paris*.
Reproduced with permission from Kay Duke Ingalls.

charm the framework indispensable in living music.... His art, rather remote from the great Stravinsky, is perhaps closer to that of Prokofiev, but if there exists a spiritual relationship, the realization differs profoundly in one and the other. Truly, Dukelsky is already himself.[33]

During this period, Duke occasionally appeared. As recalled by Anton Dolin,

> He used to sit for hours playing all the latest Gershwin song hits of the day. There were times when this annoyed Diaghileff. He would arrive after dinner to attend a rehearsal and on entering the room the strains of "Lady Be Good" or some equally popular song of the

moment would greet him, and there, clustered round the piano listening to Dukelsky, he would discover Lifar, Kochno, and me. If the great man was in a good humour, well and good; but if he were not, the rehearsal that evening would be accompanied by more than the usual shouts and lectures.[34]

The orchestral rehearsals revealed many mistakes that had to be weeded out, and with the orchestra continually stopping, it was difficult for Dukelsky to tell if the orchestration was good, adequate, or poor. He admitted that it was "no more than adequate for the most part. At times, what seemed like a lofty musical conception became muddled and distorted almost beyond recognition; the harmony seemed too thick, the basses that boomed so splendidly on the piano were hardly discernible, and the inner voices stuck out for no good reason. . . . The music managed to overcome this self-imposed handicap to some extent."[35] Although Dukelsky's "music proved very refreshing," recalled Serge Lifar, "its rhythmic design was somewhat difficult, and but little helped by the manner of its scoring."[36]

Nevertheless, the ballet opened in Monte Carlo on April 28, 1925.[37] Serge Leonidovich Grigoriev was there:

The performance in fact went smoothly, but the ballet failed to produce any great impression. As far as I could judge there were several reasons for this ineffectiveness. In the first place, the scenery and costumes by Bracque were attractive but quite unsuited to the subject; indeed I wondered how Diaghilev could have passed the designs, and could only suppose he had been mesmerized by the artist's celebrity. Then Dukelsky's music suffered from similar defects: it too was interesting but ill-suited to the plot. Finally there was Massine's choreography; though he made good use in it of the young dancers, it seemed deficient in both style and inspiration and devoid of any fresh ideas. As for the dancing, Lifar's technique has enormously improved during the previous two years, but he was still somewhat raw and uncertain. The only performers who were entirely satisfactory were Dolin, with his sure, well-shapen movements, and the executants of a charming *variation* for four Muses, namely Tchernicheva, Danilova,

Doubrovska, and Sokolova. Diaghilev was, of course, fully conscious of the shortcomings of *Zéphire et Flore*, which very clearly disappointed him, and when he left Monte Carlo he was still considering how it might be improved before being shown in Paris.[38]

Dukelsky's recollection of the opening differed:

> The *première*, before a bejeweled and befurred audience, went off without a hitch. The ballet obtained a sizable success, all three principals—the ethereal Alice Nikitina, bouncy Dolin, and fervent Lifar—were applauded and cheered to a faretheewell.... At the final curtain, following the bows of the three principals, Bracque, Massine, and myself appeared on the stage and I was presented with a laurel wreath of such gigantic proportions that, on accepting it, I almost fell under its tremendous weight.[39]

After the performance, Dukelsky went to Paris to prepare for the ballet's opening there. At a gathering with the Prokofievs, Vladimir "turned on the charm and chattered away nineteen to the dozen, mildly irritating Ptashka by his tendency to boast which, however, he restrained in front of me." He asked her "if she could fix him up with an introduction to an attractive woman, preferably single. My guess is that he was deliberately drawing attention to his desires because of rumours about the nature of Diaghilev's interest in him."[40] A few days later, Vladimir visited Prokofiev at his home where an attractive American divorcée flirted with him, and he sought to impress her by playing some foxtrots. Prokofiev found them nauseatingly banal. Vladimir then played his concerto, which Sergei thought began well before deteriorating. But he was most impressed with the first number and the theme and variations from *Zephyr and Flora*.[41]

Prokofiev was further dismayed when Dukelsky dragged him and Pierre Souvtchinsky to a nightclub where in a separate room naked girls began washing themselves in preparation for a "live Cinema." He dashed out of the room, "pursued by a furious Dukelsky disconcerted by my 'abandonment midstream,' followed by a chortling Suvchinsky, who said that the most enjoyable part of the evening had been watching Dukelsky." They repaired to a respectable restaurant where Dukelsky informed them about losing his virginity the previous year and about other intimate details of his life. Prokofiev considered his shamelessness bordering on the naive.[42]

On June 15, 1925, Diaghilev's season opened with the premiere of *Zephyr and Flora*. Having only heard Dukelsky's piano rendition, Prokofiev was disappointed. The orchestration sounded clumsy, Braque's setting seemed flabby, and Kohno's libretto lacked a point of view: "Only in the finale, when the nymphs fan out lying on their backs around Boreas and invite him to give himself to them, did the audience get much in the way of pleasure. The success was lukewarm. Dukelsky came out once to take a bow, anxiety written endearingly on his brow. To sum up it was rather a disappointment." The ballet, however, could be reorchestrated and the settings redesigned, "because purely as music it is one of the most significant events of the season."[43]

The following day, George Auric and Dukelsky met with Prokofiev, and Vladimir defended his orchestration. He wanted a "chamber-music" orchestration, not "Rimsky-Korsakovian fireworks." Prokofiev retorted that chamber music was one thing, bad orchestration another. He and Auric teased Vladimir about his inability to orchestrate his own ballet, which, according to Sergei, "drove him completely out of his mind."[44]

A critic, however, asserted that Dukelsky discovered "in one fell swoop a liberated style for which we, in our country, are searching in vain. The score of 'Zephire' offers a richness and an abundance of rhythms and a savor of sounds that make it a perpetual treat for the ear." Another critic thought that the score was "a copious work, filled, I would almost say *stuffed* with music, which reveals qualities of the first order." Even though the composer did not yet know how to curb his language, "Can you think of a more praiseworthy defect? So many composers have nothing to choose from, since they have nothing to say!" The debut contained "more than merely promises and Mr. Dukelsky can be proud of a most merited success." The *Herald Tribune* of Paris enthused: "This score, so new and so alive, seems to me, next to the gigantic production of Stravinsky's, one of the most significant works of modern music, and Russian music in particular."[45]

In *Nouvelle Revue Française*, Boris de Schloezer wrote: "One expected jazz band effects; fortunately, the author avoided them, and one finds in *Zéphire* no trace of the Negroid Americanism that has become the very mark of musical modernism, as the whole tone scale was yesterday."[46]

Prokofiev told a friend, "The most interesting item among the new music I heard during the Paris spring *grande saison* turned out to be *Zéphire et Flore* by Dukelsky, a young composer (age 21), a former student of Glière. . . . The ballet is very well done, with a mass of very beautiful material. At the center is a theme with variations."[47]

André Cœuroy was more critical of the critics than of Dukelsky: "The musician's friends committed the great imprudence to announce the arrival of a new Messiah. . . . No uncertainty in the disposition of this quasi-classical suite in separate numbers, not a blemish of taste in the orchestral sensibility, no shocking surprises in the rhythmic monotony. . . . Here's an occasion to reflect, yawning a little, on the dangers of and merits of abstract art." Dukelsky and Diaghilev, however, were delighted with the reviews, and Vladimir was certainly happy with the six thousand francs he received for his work on the ballet. He was further rewarded with a check of five thousand francs from the Heugel publishing firm for his piano concerto.[48]

On the evening of the second performance, while parading up and down in the foyer, "complete with tails, monocle and the usual outlandish flower in my button hole," Vladimir spotted "a fine-looking man in a fur-lined overcoat." Serge Koussevitzky was the conductor of the Boston Symphony and founder and editor of Editions Russes de Musique, which had published the works of Prokofiev and others. Nicolas Slonimsky introduced Vladimir to the conductor, who had just missed the ballet. Unexpectedly, Koussevitzky announced that he wanted to sign him to a life contract, to print everything he wrote, and to commission a symphony. Reflecting on this turn of events, Vladimir concluded that he had three people to thank: "Prokofiev, Slonimsky—and Diaghilev, who issued my passport to Paris, which was now miraculously turning into a passport to fame."[49]

Dukelsky remained in Paris, dining with the Prokofievs and others on July 1 and pursuing an American woman just in from the States. As Prokofiev noted in his diary, "She gave no sign of not welcoming the attention. Our little company was greatly amused by this, not the least by the figure Dukelsky cut in his exaggeratedly wide-trousered grey suit, which he assured us was the very latest fashion and had been custom-made for him by a superb London tailor."[50] These were the Oxford Bags, which were soon all the rage in England.

Two days later, Prokofiev became extremely irritated when Vladimir barged into his study. As Ptashka escorted him out, "a chagrined Dukelsky babbled, 'I only came because I am so very fond of Sergey Sergeyevich. I appreciate that he is working but I don't see why it is necessary to be so peremptory about it. . . .' In short, he took offense, and then went to London and temporarily disappeared over the horizon."[51]

In October 1925, a drawing of Dukelsky appeared on the "We Nominate for the Hall of Fame" page in the London *Vogue*. Part of the caption reads: "Diaghilev, with his flair for new talent, suggested his writing the music for 'Zephyr and Flora,' which we hope to see in London."[52] They were not disappointed. Dukelsky, Kochno, Nouvel, and Diaghilev soon arrived in England to prepare *Zephyr and Flora* for its opening. On October 22, 1925, the *Stage* announced that "the Diaghileff Ballet will begin another season at the London Coliseum. . . . Besides numerous familiar ballets the season's programme will embrace at least two important novelties: 'Zephyr and Flora,' music by Vladimir Dukelsky to be presented in the third week of the season, and at a later date 'Barabau' by Vittorio Rieti."[53]

Zephyr and Flora opened at the Coliseum on November 12.[54] The *Era* reported:

> Once more Massine has startled us with the novelty of his choreography. Though 'Zephyr and Flora,' his latest ballet, which has just been introduced into the repertoire of Serge Diaghileff's company at the Coliseum, is nothing more original in outline than the fable of Greek mythology, yet his method of arranging gesture, pose, and dance is a revelation. At first the movements seem awkward, bizarre, and even a trifle ludicrous; but very soon the general design becomes familiar without losing its strangeness.[55]

Another critic noted that the choreography "embraces angular movements that are not always pretty to watch. Dukelsky's music suggests a Handel influence in its opening passages, but later develops characteristics that no ordinary fellow can understand if his musical education has been restricted to accepted ideas of harmony and tunefulness. But the dancers interpret it with all their accustomed grace and skill which, after all, is the main thing."[56]

Cyril W. Beaumont described the dress and scenery:

The costumes were fanciful. Nikitina wore a hat trimmed at the peak with flowers, short tunic, and tights which were decorated from the knee to the toe with leaf design. [Constantin] Tcherkas wore a jockey's cap and a tunic sewn with large petals. Lifar's costume was composed of a helmet and gold trunks. The settings consisted of small blackcloths, framed in a false proscenium and painted simply to suggest a landscape by means of several undulating masses of contrasting colour. I recall one particularly pleasant composition in varied tones of gold.[57]

Dukelsky bragged:

If the Paris *premiére* had but a moderate success, there were no such reservations to be made of the London one. In the pet phrase of society columnists, it was rapturously received. No laurel wreath this time, but I wore a large chrysanthemum in my buttonhole to match the floral tributes bestowed on Alice Nikitina by Lord Rothermere. Except for the outrageous chrysanthemum, reported by the tabloids the next day, my clothes were those of a gentleman at long last, thanks to Messrs. Anderson & Sheppard, and, like Noel [Coward] in *Present Indicative*, I "savoured to the full the sensation of being well-dressed for the first time."[58]

More interested in his ballet than his clothes, a critic from the *London Sunday Times* wrote: "It is a pleasure to welcome a work which not only avoids mere silliness but shows that the young composer really has something to say." The music struck Francis Toye, the biographer of Rossini and Verdi, "as by far the most interesting of all the compositions associated with Mr. Diaghilev's most recent ballets.... Here is a young man who, despite the discordant idiom of the times, knows how to shape a musical phrase and conceive a musical idea." Another critic wrote: "It is a rich score—possibly even a little too rich, for there are things in it which scarcely come through—and does not need any of the indulgence that one accords to an early effort, for, apart from a certain youthful exuberance, its style is usually settled and consistent."[59]

Shortly after the opening, Dukelsky departed for the continent, and while on the Promenade des Anglais in Nice, he "came face to face" with

Nicolas Nabokov. Nabokov mentioned a piano sonata he had recently completed, and they hurried to Vernon's hotel to go over it. Vladimir found the music dry, but "one or two passages showed real and unexpected promise," and he promised to take it with him when he dined with Igor Stravinsky.[60]

Stravinsky greeted him cordially. They drank vodka, talked music, and with Stravinsky's wife and children, they consumed a copious dinner.[61] After playing some of his "own music and some bad jazz" and excerpts from Nabokov's work, which he played atrociously, Stravinsky concluded that the latter was "far from silly."[62] But Dukelsky was then forced to listen to a Stravinsky diatribe about Diaghilev. Worshipping the man and "realizing that before me sat a Diaghilev-made composer, who owed Diaghilev his entire career, I became intensely uncomfortable. . . . I restrained myself with difficulty from what would have been an unpleasant argument and kept silent."[63]

Despite the success of his ballet, Dukelsky was not sure he had a future in classical music. Contemplating another sharp turn in his life, he had written to his mother in May that shortly his music might sound significantly different than it did now: "I'm doing nothing at present, except trying to clarify my affairs; contacting publishers, authors' societies, etc.—anything to make a little money, of which I'm in dire need. . . . All my hopes are in jazz, which is well paid in London and in great demand everywhere." Already Duke was "stirring in Dukelsky's breast, ready to come to his rescue."[64] Later he reflected on his decision: "Instead of going on with my work, I decided to take things easily and (with the exception of three songs on words by N. Bogdanovitch) didn't write anything for a year. The call of saxophones was too strong to resist, and so back to London I went to write a musical comedy."[65]

4

DUKE TAKES CHARGE
LONDON, 1925–1929

When Vladimir Dukelsky visited London with Diaghilev, Kochno, and Nouvel, his impressions of the city were mixed. After a terrible dinner but a better breakfast in a shabby hotel in the Bloomsbury section, he ventured

> past squalid Greek and Italian grocery stores and supposedly French restaurants of Soho into the more animated but strangely shabby Shaftesbury Avenue. Things were getting livelier by the minute; big red buses, antique Daimler taxicabs, policemen twice the size of the French "flics," signs lauding Bovril, Guinness, and Player's cigarettes, unfamiliar products all, had a cozy, comfortable look about them—naive and outdated, perhaps, but oddly reassuring. If Paris smelled of lilacs and gasoline, the prevailing London odor was that of rotting apples.[1]

The scene changed dramatically when he reached Piccadilly: "Never have I encountered so many faultlessly turned out men, bowlers and Homburgs at just the right angle, suits beautifully yet unobtrusively cut, ties a model of sobriety, umbrellas, like trained black eels, dangling effortlessly from the left arm, in spite of the blazing sun." But he found London women frumpy and unkempt. Some of the girls were pretty, "in the fresh Anglo-Saxon way, with the well-advertised glowing skin and sturdy, substantial legs, but the clothes were for the most part deplorable." So was his own dress. Catching his reflection in a store window, Vladimir dashed into the nearest pub for a beer and then spent half of his money in the Burlington Arcade on a hat, shirts, ties, and the "most eel-like umbrella obtainable."[2]

When Vernon Duke moved to London in 1925, he found a city tailored to his tastes and needs. As recalled by Patrick Balfour, the city was in a state of flux, changing

> from quails in aspic to eggs and bacon, from champagne to lager, from coal fires to electricity, from mansions to mansion flats, and from balls to cocktail parties; an age in the course of which peers became Socialists and Socialists became peers, actors and actresses tried to be ladies and gentlemen and ladies and gentlemen behaved like actors and actresses, novelists were men-about-town, and men-about-town wrote novels, persons of rank became shopkeepers and shopkeepers drew persons of rank to their houses, the Speed King supplanted the Guards officer as the *beau ideal* of modern woman and modern woman herself grew each day slimmer and slimmer—and slimmer.
>
> It was in every sense an age of transition, and therein lies its virtue. For it had the best of both worlds: the remaining dignity of an aristocratic order combined with the luxuries of a cosmopolitan machine-civilization; the Spanish Embassy *and* the Embassy Club, Norfork House *and* the Blue Lantern, the Russian Ballet *and* the Prince of Wales in butter at Wembley. It was an age in which the traditions of the old dovetailed into the ideas of the new.[3]

"What parties they gave!" recalled Balfour. "Parties for the Blackbirds; an unforgettable Russian party in Gerald Road, with a negro band, where a whole house and studio had been specially redecorated for a single night; the swimming party in the St. George's Baths; David Tennant's Mozart party, where the eighteenth century was recaptured for a night; Tallulah parties; Guinness parties; impromptu wild parties, in fancy undress, in the Royal Hospital Road."[4] Vladimir bragged that he attended all of them: "Wasn't my portrait in *Vogue*, my ballet announced and extolled by Almighty God Diaghilev himself, weren't my clothes Anderson & Sheppard's best?"[5]

The well-dressed composer fell madly in love with a gifted young actress, Frances Doble. He remembered "Bunny" as

> rarely beautiful with her shining, almond-shaped eyes, voluptuous yet shy mouth, dark-brown hair, the natural sheen of which set off

VITTORIO RIETI, VLADIMIR DUKELSKY, AND BORIS KOCHNO, LONDON, 1925.
From *Sphere*, December 26, 1925.

the cool, even pallor of her skin, almost free of cosmetics. . . . Our first meeting was an exact duplicate of countless such meetings in countless third-rate films, where the hero and heroine, speechless and dumbfounded by each other's charms, utter unbearable banalities, while the audience's collective heart palpitates wildly and enviously."[6]

Later, when Vladimir came down with a bad bout of gastric fever, Bunny spent considerable time at his bedside, feeling responsible for insisting he attend one of her parties after he had become ill. "There was talk of marriage," remembered Vladimir, "of never leaving each other—Bunny in tears, I in bed with a high temperature, which according to the girl gave me a magnificent color. Bunny then left and, I fear, Love left us shortly afterwards."[7]

Fortunately, there was work to do. Charles B. Cochran, the most important music producer at the time, signed him to write a musical comedy and advanced him three hundred pounds, a very large sum for those days. Cochran's generosity reflected his love of stealing talent from Serge

Diaghilev as much as it identified Duke's potential.[8] In a letter to Cochran, Diaghilev expressed his outrage: "I very much regret . . . the way you exploit the Russian artists whom I have discovered and trained. Dukelsky writing bad foxtrots for musicals is not doing what he is destined to do."[9]

Cochran, however, canceled his musical with Duke but retained him as arranger and orchestrator. Vladimir made a few arrangements for Léonide Massine, who was then staging cabaret shows for Cochran, and one night while he was dining with Diaghilev at the Trocadero, a dancer performed one of his arrangements. After the dance, an employee of Cochran's congratulated Vladimir on his music, and "Diaghilev went blue with rage, said nothing, drummed on the table with his knuckles and demanded the bill. I was handed my coat, ebony walking stick and brand-new top hat by the hat-check girl; no sooner were we out in the street than Diaghilev knocked my top hat off my head with my own stick, trampled upon it savagely, reducing it to a messy pulp, and with a one-syllable parting shot, "Whore!" disappeared in the dark."[10]

For the "whore," there was no turning back. From now on, he would write not just in two genres but live in the vastly different worlds of the musical theater and the concert hall. Taking George Gershwin's advice, he adopted "Vernon Duke" for his "lowbrow" music.[11] Cutting "Dukelsky" in half to form "Duke" made sense, but there being no English cognate for "Vladimir," the best choice may have been "Vernon." Although the "Duke" side of him had appeared in Constantinople, with the new name he could present a more accessible persona to those in show business. For his "highbrow" music, he retained his original name.

Duke had already learned that there was an immediate return in writing theater songs. That is, he could hear and often see performed what he had recently written. He had spent months composing *Zephyr and Flora*. "Try a Little Kiss," his first published song as the tunesmith Vernon Duke, took a few hours, if that, to write. It and "Back to My Heart" were interpolated into *Katja, the Dancer*, an operetta that had opened on February 21, 1925, at London's Gaiety Theatre and would run for 505 performances.[12] In its second year, producer Jimmy White had contracted Vernon to "pep up" the show with some of "that bloody Yankee monkey music." To Vernon, it was "a mystery that White should have applied to me, a Parisian Russian, according to the London press, for Yankee monkey music, but he handed me a very welcome contract and I started a career of 'doctoring' ailing Viennese operettas and 'jazzing 'em up.'"[13]

Duke now had the financial security to shuttle between England and France, where he often paid unannounced visits to Sergei Prokofiev. The surprise visit on March 22, 1926, prompted Prokofiev to record the event:

> He is just in from London, where he has spent the winter composing operettas and revues and earning tidy sums of money. For some operetta or other he now earns a "pension" of £15 a week. New suits, ties and erotic adventures, which he recounts with me with naive brazenness. He also played me the beginning of his new 'serious' ballet. It was interesting. It defeats my understanding how he can combine composing foxtrots with real music, and good music at that.[14]

Back in London, Duke became good friends with George Balanchine, whom he had met in Paris. Vernon now considered him "probably the most lovable creature that ever lived." He was already his well-known unpredictable self, "mixing sheer lunacy with phlegmatic *laissez aller*, carried to unheard of lengths. Ever a diligent and inspired worker, he lived in a cozy little world of his own, disorganized and ill-assembled to the naked eye, but very dear to him. Untranslatable Armenian [Georgian?] jokes and good Russian food were enough to make him happy." Diaghilev promised him that he would choreograph his next ballet, the *Three Seasons*, the music to be composed by Dukelsky.[15] The ballet was to be based on *Tales of Belkin* by Alexander Pushkin.

It was Duke, however, who wrote most of the score for *Yvonne*, a revue that opened at Daly's Theatre in London on May 22 after a tryout in Manchester. While it was in rehearsal, a reporter for the *Daily Sketch* noted that "composers of ultra-modern ballets are not above picking up quite an honest penny or two by being a trifle lower in the brow for the nonce. Dukelsky, for instance, has written some songs, duly approved by Mr. James White, for 'Yvonne' at Daly's under the name of 'Vernon Dukes' [*sic*]." Although the lyricist found his American-style tunes rather difficult to lyricize, Vernon wrote several numbers he thought were "mildly pleasant, comfortably Kern-like in spots." He considered "Magic of the Moon" one of his better songs, "a fair mixture of Kern and corn." "Day Dreams" was "agreeably sung and danced by Ivy Tresmand." But Hal Sherman brought the house down with a Chaplinesque routine to "Don't Forget the Waiter." Duke was also fond of a sketch in which Tresmand sang "It's Rather Nicer to Be Naughty (than to be always quite good)." The play ran for 280 performances.[16]

Although Duke was gaining recognition, Dukelsky was far from forgotten. In June, Ballets Russes presented a program of three ballets, one of them Stravinsky's *Les Noces*, which Dukelsky had seen in Paris. The ballet was designed to express semipagan rites and old ceremonies associated with the marriage of peasants in provincial Russia. The score called for percussion, four solo singers, a chorus, and four pianos.[17] According to Vladimir, who was one of the pianists, the music was extremely difficult, and the opening was "a scandalous triumph, unique in London's theatrical annals. . . . The noise was deafening—boos, hisses and catcalls mingling with cheers and thunderous applause." The program was closed after seven performances.[18] H. G. Wells insisted that the ballet was "a rendering in sound and vision of the peasant soul."[19]

As soon as the Prokofievs arrived in Paris in June, Dukelsky appeared unannounced at their hotel:

> He sports dazzling new suits, expensive shirts and gorgeous ties but apparently very little in the way of new compositions—a few pages of a second ballet (this made me laugh: dedicated to Diaghilev and no more than two bars of music!), and three songs, part of which he had played to us some time before. Espying a young American woman in our hotel, Dukelsky immediately took out his monocle and subjected her to a detailed examination. We appealed to him not to ruin our reputation in the hotel.[20]

Sergei Prokofiev was highly critical of the performance of *Zephyr and Flora*. Dukelsky, attired in full evening dress with top hat, white gloves, and cane,

> sat with us and held his head in his hand on account of the dreadful performance. Of late it has been Diaghilev's practice not to allow much time to rehearse the music. This evening's performance was so

bad it was impossible to tell whether the changes Dukelsky made to the score were any good or not. But whatever the case I am inclined to think that even in a good performance Dukelsky's orchestration will sound like a poor man's Brahms.[21]

Vladimir's recollection of the performance differed. With two additional sets, it was "again almost unanimously approved."[22] To one critic, moreover, the ballet was a recurrent theme "of very great beauty, and there are passages in the prelude and in the first three scenes of real excellence; but in this work Dukelsky shows no staying powers and the music of the last scenes might have been written by Poulenc or Auric at their worst."[23] To another, the music was excellent and "greatly superior to that of either Poulenc or Auric, and it is to be hoped that he will be given further opportunities."[24]

In early August, Vladimir returned to Paris with a young Irish girl he had gotten pregnant. The several doctors he had contacted in London about performing an abortion declined his pleas, pointing out that such activities in England sent people to jail. After a successful operation in Paris, Vladimir gave the girl a tour of the city that she greatly enjoyed, but the entire adventure cost him 10,000 francs. Late at night on August 10, he imposed himself on the Prokofievs, now living in a country house on the Seine in Samoreau near Fontainebleau. His excuse for arriving so late was that Kochno had given him misleading directions. After explaining why he had come to France, the Prokofievs put him to bed in their parents' room. He returned to Paris the following day.[25]

The Prokofievs were expecting a return visit on August 21, but Dukelsky, well prepared to explain everything, arrived late. As recorded by Sergei, "At first I received him frigidly—what a louse he is, after all!—but this provoked a torrent of excuses and accounts of extraordinary occurrences. At lunch he had choked on a bone, which had to be removed in hospital with the aid of pincers and two mirrors." The following day he and Sergei got into a furor over classical and popular music:

> He defended his position with equal fervour, saying that operetta music existed on such a different plane that it could have no possible effect on his serious composition. I retorted that the influence most

certainly did make itself felt, moreover in a way of which he was not himself conscious. One fine day he would find real musicians beginning to distance themselves from his music and he himself descending to the status of a second-rate composer. At that point he would abandon serious music altogether and would confine himself to operettas. We were separated by Ptashka, who worried that the neighbours, hearing our raised voices, would say that "les monsieurs russes ont trop bu."[26]

Like previous dustups, this one did not harm the relationship between Dukelsky and Prokofiev, it being rather typical of Russians to explode in disagreement over an issue one moment only to have forgotten about it the next. For the remainder of his life, however, in the spoken and written word, Dukelsky would exhibit this trait, apparently unaware or unconcerned that it was often misunderstood by non-Russians. His egotistical, often arrogant, personality only compounded the matter.

When Dukelsky received a letter from Prokofiev, congratulating him on becoming a "full-fledged cocotte" for his popular music but inviting him nevertheless to Fontainebleau where he was vacationing, Dukelsky turned down the offer, needing the time to work on his ballet, the *Three Seasons*. In early September 1926, after a month of composing in Villennes, he and Balanchine departed for Florence where Diaghilev had established his headquarters.[27] Dukelsky and Diaghilev quarreled over the ballet's adagio, which Serge claimed was too frivolous and Italian in spirit.[28] But all was not lost. From a cafe in the Piazza Vittorio Emanuele, Dukelsky enthused about the city in a letter to his mother: "This is the most miraculous city of all cities.... One feels like remaining idle permanently here; it's impossible to do anything except look, think and absorb."[29]

By the beginning of October, Dukelsky was back in Paris. Prokofiev played for him his Fifth Sonata, but Vladimir found it dry and exceedingly complicated. Sergei told him he was a fool and ordered him to listen again. Before he could resume, three women, including his wife, slipped in. Prokofiev ordered them out and continued playing his sonata. Because Dukelsky liked it no better than before, he too was thrown out, "with a short speech in which 'lazy London tarts' and 'lousy chess players' figured frequently." Duke returned to London to learn that he was overlooked as the composer of a new musical and that Diaghilev was not going to include *Zephyr and Flora* in the next season. Only one of Duke's songs was added to the score of Franz Lehár's *Blue Mazurka*, which closed after 140 performances.[30]

His "Somebody's Sunday" with his own lyric, however, was added to *Two Little Girls in Blue*, which had opened in Portsmouth in April 1927. Most of the music was by Paul Lannin and Vincent Youmans, and most of the lyrics were by Ira Gershwin. Although they were hardly collaborators on the show, it was the first time Vernon and Ira were associated with one. It closed in its pre-London tryout.[31] In a letter to George Gershwin, he mentioned that he had sold ten songs to different managers, two of which were in *Two Little Girls in Blue*. He claimed to now write all his lyrics, which was "great fun." He congratulated George on his recent hit, "Someone to Watch over Me." London was dreary, the parties boring.[32]

On June 4, 1927, Dukelsky returned to Paris to perform Sonata for Piano and Orchestra, which he had recently and hastily composed, with Serge Koussevitzky and the Boston Symphony. His recollection of the event was told with great irony. He appeared on stage to "an audible gasp and some spotty applause" in a tight-fitting morning coat with balloon-shaped trousers cut by Anderson & Sheppard. The French, however, never "took to Oxford bags and I presented a strange spectacle." He got through the performance, but the applause was "even spottier than at my entrance." A French critic could not refrain from noting that "Mr. Dukelsky's music was barely visible behind his sumptuous trousers."[33]

While in the city, he attended the premiere of Prokofiev's ballet *Le Pas d'acier*, a pro-Soviet political epic. Prior to its opening, newspapers devoted much space to the ballet, and Diaghilev gave numerous interviews in which he avoided the political issues but defended the music and design.[34] Although the expected protests from Russian émigrés did not occur, there was, remembered Vladimir, "plenty of noise, deafening cheers, and piercing catcalls."[35]

The act following the performance could have come from some theater of the absurd. While Vladimir was discussing the ballet with Prokofiev, Jean Cocteau appeared, screamed an insult at Vladimir, slapped him in the face, and departed. When Vladimir finally found Cocteau, he deported himself well but challenged the Frenchman to a duel. Astonished, Cocteau refused, but to settle the dispute, he commanded Vladimir to slap him. Before the request could be accommodated, he was restrained. When Vladimir encountered Cocteau a short time later addressing a large crowd outside the theater, the Russian promised the Frenchman that the following day his seconds would appear at his house to make preparations for a duel. The seconds, however, could not get past Cocteau's servant, forcing Vladimir to appear alone. The servant, recognizing only a well-dressed gentleman in a morning coat with striped trousers, allowed Dukelsky to enter. In the encounter, Vladimir slapped Jean and again challenged him to a duel. But Cocteau embraced him, and Vladimir departed nonplussed. They never spoke to one another again.[36]

In a letter to Boris Kochno, Cocteau explained his actions:

> I very much regret having caused a disturbance on Serge's stage, but in view of Dima's ugly mug, his rose, his top hat, and Louis XV cane, his denunciation of Parisian frivolity was hard to take. . . . Do tell Serge how much I regret this incident. . . . My views were of aesthetic as well as of a moral order. I do reproach Massine for having turned something as great as the Russian Revolution into a cotillion-like spectacle within the intellectual grasp of ladies who pay six thousand francs for a box. I was not attacking the composer or the stage designer.[37]

After this incident, Dukelsky joined the Prokofievs and another couple on a long motor trip to the Haute-Savoie Mountains, but the Prokofievs' constant quarreling ruined it for him. Moreover, the weight Vladimir gained due to the unsurpassable cuisine began a process that would eventually cost him his boyish looks. On his return to Pairs, he wrote an article on Diaghilev for the magazine *Versty* that contained criticism of Stravinsky's neoclassical period. His article was the first in what would be numerous publications in magazines, journals, and newspapers.[38] Prokofiev noted in his diary that a friend was very impressed with the article "and professed astonishment that such a flirtatious popinjay should command such an acute intelligence."[39]

The "popinjay" returned to England to write the symphony he had promised Serge Koussevitzky. Sir David and Lady Baird provided him the time and space to undertake the work on their estate in Scotland. As he recalled,

"Lady Baird was maternally fond of me, but I, too, baffled her. I wasn't a bona fide White Russian as I had no title and wrote music for a living. I came from America without being American, and looked and talked not unlike her daughter's 'aesthetic' English friends, without being English." Although Lady Baird was troubled that Vladimir showed too much interest in some of her daughter's friends, she had no cause to worry, because "English and Scottish girls are just as good as any in spotting the 'right' man, and there was nothing 'right' about me, except my clothes." Despite the distraction, Dukelsky composed his First Symphony. Only sixteen minutes long, the first and third movements contained a lot of Prokofiev, he admitted.[40]

With his symphony completed but his debts accumulating, Dukelsky deferred to Duke, who joined Jimmy Dyrenforth in writing "For Goodness' Sake."[41] The song was added to *The Bow-Wows*, which ran for 124 performances at the Prince of Wales.[42] Vernon considered the song "his first respectable effort in the idiom," and its "unusual rhythmic pattern" attracted some attention.[43] So did Duke's first complete score for a musical. *Yellow Mask* premiered on November 15, 1927, at the Birmingham Theater Royal. The outstanding review it got in the *Era* included a reference to the music: "There is some really tuneful music by Vernon Duke and acceptable lyrics by Desmond Carter."[44] On February 8, 1928, it began a run at the Carlton Theatre in London and received a good notice from the *Daily Mail* and a congratulatory letter from Gershwin.[45] The *Stage* was far less enthusiastic. The vocal and orchestral music came from "the rather jazzish pen of a young composer now choosing to be known as 'Vernon Duke,' whose work, like that of Desmond Carter, in the writing of the lyrics, does not rise above the standard found in commonplace musical comedy."[46] The *Diss Express*, however, congratulated the composer "on writing such entrancing melodies." The two most notable were "Half a Kiss" and "Deep Sea."[47] Along with "Blowing the Blues Away," wrote another critic, "the haunting 'Half a Kiss,' 'Deep Sea,' and 'Mary' will be the popular favorites. Mr. Desmond Carter's lyrics are, as usual, fresh and snappy."[48]

By this time, the *Diss Express* had "exposed" the Duke-Dukelsky masquerade: "The successful Russian Ballet 'Zephyr and Flora,' composed by Vladimir Dukelsky, and the musical comedy 'The Yellow Mask,' composed by Vernon Duke, are, as a matter of fact, the work of one and the same musician. Mr. Duke, indeed, has in America been dubbed 'the Dr. Jekyll and Mr. Hyde of modern music.'"[49] Writing in the third person, "Jekyll/Hyde" bragged that the royalties from a show that "a certain Mr. 'Vernon Duke' wrote ... enabled Mr. Vladimir Dukelsky to go on with his operas and symphonies for nearly two years." And finally he could send some money to his mother.[50]

In early December 1927, Prokofiev and his wife arrived in London for a performance of his Second Piano Concerto. Speaking like an Englishman, Dukelsky took them to lunch and later played his First Symphony, which Sergei found interesting. If well orchestrated, it would be a good work.[51] Sergei mentioned in a letter to a friend that Dukelsky could not come to the first performance of his concerto "because that evening he was giving a bath to a maiden of questionable virtue. But he has written a symphony that isn't bad at all. . . . His symphony is well-crafted and not especially long (15–20 minutes). He is now orchestrating it and I promised as much as possible to give him my suggestions, for orchestration is not his strong suit."[52] Prokofiev offered a similar assessment to another correspondent: "I have seen the manuscript of Dukelsky's new symphony—it's a very cheerful and pleasant thing, with some good ideas and cleverly put together; but I'm not entirely confident that he'll be able to orchestrate it sufficiently well."[53]

Vladimir escorted the Prokofievs around London, pointing out the best places for value and style in men's clothing. Although the revue he took them to included one of his songs, they found it boring and bewailed Vladimir for "being at home in such an atmosphere."[54] Vladimir, however, had just been advanced two hundred pounds to write a new operetta.[55] Apparently it was during this visit that Vladimir recalled being happy "to get back to 'music talk' after English theatrical slang, which is a queer mixture of Cockney and Broadway." Dukelsky was curious about conditions in the Soviet Union, but since they never talked politics, he wisely avoided the subject. Prokofiev mentioned that some of Dukelsky's classical songs had been sung in Kiev and that he was attempting to get *Zephyr and Flora* performed in Moscow. On the Prokofievs' last day in England, they dined and drank a lot of lager with Dukelsky in a gaudy nightclub called the Silver Slipper. There, however, Dukelsky's past caught up with him. The "loudly dressed tart" who passed their table was the disease-spreading Sally from

Monte Carlo. She told him he was getting fat. Vernon said she had no right to address someone she had treated so shabbily. Dukelsky and the Prokofievs fled the club, with Vladimir remaining silent about the incident. One can only imagine what Prokofiev thought, but he invited Dukelsky to join him on another gastronomic tour of the South of France, which he gladly accepted.[56]

Back in Paris, on April 6, 1928, he visited George and Ira Gershwin, their sister, Frances, and Ira's wife, Leonore, at Hotel Majestic. George told Vladimir about a party hosted the previous night by the Polish French composer Alexandre Tansman. George sought his views on several composers including Tansman. Although Dukelsky considered him a second-rater, the Italian Vittorio Rieti was very good; E. Robert Schmitz was also very good; but Jacques Ibert was second-rate. When George mentioned a few more composers, Vladimir's response was curt: "You shouldn't have gone to that party. It will hurt you, people like that." Vladimir also got into an argument with George over parts of *American in Paris*, claiming he had allowed himself to become saccharine. When Vladimir left, the English composer Sir William Walton, a friend of both men, advised George to disregard Dukelsky's remarks because he was under the spell of Sergei Prokofiev and considered anyone who wrote in any other style old-fashioned.[57]

The following month Vladimir got into an argument with Prokofiev over composer Alexander Scriabin. When Vladimir "dismissed him with a shrug of the shoulders," Sergei was so annoyed that he told him "he was merely influenced by the opinions of others without having any himself. For the first time Dukelsky was seriously offended, and I said, 'There was a time when the only really good thing about you was your good character, but now even that has left you.' Dukelsky walked out."[58]

Nevertheless, Dukelsky took Prokofiev and Diaghilev to a concert at the Paris Opera in which Dimitri Tiomkin played Gershwin's Concerto in F. Tiomkin was no Gershwin, and the French musicians were allergic to jazz, insisted Vladimir. Prokofiev was intrigued by some of the pianistic inventions, and he asked Vernon to bring Gershwin to his apartment the following day. There George played song after song. Prokofiev liked the tunes and the flavorsome embellishments, but thought little of the concerto, repeated by Gershwin, which he later said consisted of thirty-two-bar choruses ineptly bridged together. But he thought highly of Gershwin's gifts, both as a composer and pianist.[59]

In Paris at Salle Pleyel on June 14, 1928, Dukelsky attended the premiere of his First Symphony, orchestrated with the help of Prokofiev and conducted by Koussevitzky of the Boston Symphony Orchestra. Also on the program were fragments of Prokofiev's opera *The Fiery Angel*. Vernon thought his work held up against the master's.[60] Prokofiev admitted that it went well and was warmly received, but so was his own work.[61] In a letter to a friend he wrote: "Dukelsky's symphony has turned out to be very interesting and sounds not bad at all in the orchestra."[62] Koussevitzky informed Anna, Vladimir's mother, that the symphony, a wonderful piece, was dedicated to her.[63]

While Vladimir was in Europe, Alexis graduated from the Massachusetts Institute of Technology, and with a Fontainebleau Scholarship was soon to enter the master's degree program.[64] But before undertaking his studies, he went to Paris. "I met his train at the Gare St. Lazare," recalled Vladimir, "and he had difficulty in recognizing me—that's how much I had changed in the four years since we had seen each other. He was surrounded by rah-rah boys and girls bent on raising a little traditional Franco-American hell. . . . My brother's enthusiasm for every thing French, especially food and scenery, was contagious, and I loved impersonating a true Parisian and showing him the sights."[65]

Dukelsky and a friend then departed for Berlin for the simple reason that he had never been there. He disliked the city largely because the Berliners wore ill-fitting clothes, smoked evil-smelling cigars, and had "porcine necks and triple chins." He saw two performances, one being *"Jonny Spielt Auf,* Krenek's tuneless and jazzless jazz opera; the other was *Evelyne*, an elephantine operetta by Bruno Granichstaedten, fully as unpalatable and Teutonic as the composer's name. The badly lipsticked and atrociously garbed chorus girls kicked sausagelike legs and shrilled, 'Yes,' 'Okay,' and 'Get hot,' at the top of their beer-greased lungs, to the accompaniment of three trombones, a tuba, and the inevitable celeste and xylophone, all played in unison, which to anyone familiar with German musical comedy is an orchestrator's 'must.'"[66]

Returning to London, he was dismayed to discover that *Zephyr and Flora* was long forgotten, that *The Yellow Mask* was not doing very well, and that his symphony was unknown.[67] Then it was back to Paris where in November,

Dukelsky played for Prokofiev some of the songs for his opera *Mistress into Maid*, based on a story by Alexander Pushkin that Sergei did not like. They dined at a Russian restaurant where "tipsy retired generals" sang with gypsy singers and wallowed "in memories of the past." Dinner over, Vladimir invited Sergei to accompany him to "a certain establishment," but Sergei declined.[68] The following day, Vladimir played nearly all of the first act of the opera, although only a quarter of it contained music. Prokofiev, however, found the dialogue entertaining.[69] Dining the next night with the Prokofievs, publisher Pierre Souvtchinsky, and Mr. and Mrs. Vsevolod Meyerhold, Vladimir took a fancy to Mrs. Meyerhold, suggesting that he could help her make her lips more shapely in applying her lipstick. He also told a number of risqué jokes, prompting Sergei to note in his diary, "How fashionable it has become among the émigré community to tell indecent stories; this is something that people coming from Russia never do."[70]

On January 8, 1929, Vladimir accompanied soprano Vera Vajevska in her recital, half of which was devoted to his music: the Pushkin songs, his songs based on the poems of Ippolit Fyodorovich Bogdanovitch, and an aria from *Mistress into Maid*. As remembered by Vladimir, "There weren't too many people in the hall but we had a good success and pleasant notices, although *Le Monde Musical* harped chiefly on my great talent as ... pianist."[71]

Once back in England, he concluded that "the London-dwelling Dukelsky was weakening by the minute. Other people's music was applauded at the ballet and discussed at dinner tables, Gershwin reigned supreme as Musical Comedy King, and many other writers with the U.S.A. stamp had their fling. There was no getting away from it—America ruled the musical theater and I was neither American, nor British, nor Russian for that matter, with my aptly named League of Nations passport." In a letter to his mother, he asked, "Why should I languish in London, up to my neck in debt, where they don't pay you half as much as they do on Broadway and resent your writing for the theater into the bargain?" He could not wait to get back to the States, "where people of worth are properly remunerated, not just lionized."[72]

Prior to his departure and thus unknown to him, the Boston *Evening Transcript* announced that Dukelsky's First Symphony would soon be performed. And in an newspaper article, his friend from Constantinople, Nicolas Slonimsky, briefly recounted Dukelsky's history to 1929. He compared him to Charlie Chaplin in "*The Circus*, rope-walking and gamboling in the air, not realizing that his support has gone. Dukelsky started gorgeously, and betrays so far no sign of weakness. Why not grant him that high order of distinction—originality?"[73] On March 15, 1929, the Boston Symphony performed his First Symphony, attended by his mother, Anna, whom Mrs. Koussevitzky had invited to the concert.[74]

An article in the *Boston Globe* briefly traces the life of Anna with her sons, and the three photographs—one of her at the piano and one each of Alexis and Vladimir—represent an early visual record. The article acknowledged that mothers were easily "lost in the crowds that acclaim their grown sons." Anna mentioned how good the boys were and "how happy she will be when Dimir comes home again," even though she might not recognize him. When asked about listening to the symphony, she said, "I felt such a contact with my son. I was very deeply happy."[75]

Philip Hale of the *Boston Herald* found the symphony

> an interesting work. Like all the compositions of young men who are at all worthy of attention, in their joy of invention, in their desire to strike out a new path, to be individual, the symphony's first movement was yeasty. . . . The second movement, with its broad, flowing chief theme, ingeniously ornamented, shows the Dukelsky of whose future one may entertain reasonable hopes; and the final with its exciting rhythms, and not too scholastic treatments shows fancy as well as originality.[76]

Before returning to the States, Dukelsky visited Paris for what would be the last time for several years. The city had changed. *Les Années folles* was winding down, its end often attributed to the Wall Street Crash of October 1929. But the demise had already begun. Bohemian Montparnasse had become "rich, prosperous, brightly lighted, . . . and they sold caviar at the Dome," complained Ernest Hemingway, who added: "The Era for what it was worth, and personally I don't think it was worth much, was over." Expatriates from the United States had become frugal and thus sought accommodations elsewhere or returned home.[77]

While in the city Dukelsky met the celebrated Russian critic and musicologist Igor Glebov, who professed to like his music and who was interested in his friendship with George Gershwin, a legendary figure even in the Soviet Union. Glebov asked Vladimir to translate some of the librettos and lyrics of *Lady Be Good* and *Funny Face*. And "no better anti-Soviet propaganda could be imagined than a big, healthy dose of Gershwin music." He succeeded in "Russianizing them quite expertly," and Glebov took them to Russia. Vladimir never heard from him again.[78]

Vladimir also socialized with the Prokofievs, informing them that the tour of his operetta in the English provinces had brought him enough money to journey to the United States to see his mother and to get a commission for another operetta. Prokofiev wrote in his diary that Dukelsky's "turn towards the world of operetta and his lack of success in serious music has made him less interesting. All the same we chatted until midnight and I went out with him to have supper, which made Ptashka cross."[79]

The following day, the chatter became strained. Prokofiev played the first movement of his Fourth Symphony, which pleased Dukelsky until Sergei told him that some of the music was left over from his ballet *Prodigal Son*. Vladimir insisted that combining ballet music with symphonic music was the height of ignorance. Sergei pointed out that Vladimir had approved of the work before he knew it was a "half-brother" of a ballet: "The point is that everything depends on the composer's skill in using his material, and it may be that it was in demonstrating this I particularly wished to shine."[80] Dukelsky would not see his mentor again for some time.

While in Paris, Dukelsky bumped, literally, into Diaghilev at a performance of *Blackbirds*, starring Florence Mills. When reproached by a large man in a beaver coat for knocking into him, Dukelsky was shocked at his haggard appearance. Diaghilev was delighted to see his subject and invited Dukelsky to visit him in Venice and perform his *Mistress into Maid*. He would never see him again.[81]

Returning to London, Duke sold some songs to a producer of a show called *Open Your Eyes* that included "Happily Ever After," "Jack and Jill," "Open Your Eyes," "Such a Funny Feeling," "You'd Do for Me—I'd Do for You," and "Too, Too Divine."[82] It opened in Edinburgh on August 26, with the *Era* noting that the "dramatist has been well seconded by Mr. Vernon Duke who has composed the musical score which contains a number of flowing melodies."[83] The billing credited Duke and Collie Knox for the songs, and a critic singled out "You'd Do for Me" as successfully presented but in a show that musically was a little above average.[84] Duke considered the song his best and the music "better and fresher than that of *The Yellow Mask*."[85]

These successes brought Duke to a crucial moment in his musical life. In *Passport to Paris* he wrote:

> Looking back at my London debut, which took place almost thirty years ago, it becomes clear to me that I missed my big chance and made the unpardonable mistake of dissipating the excellent first impression my music made, by not taking myself at all seriously. Had I but the stick-to-itiveness of, say, Prokofiev (I am not comparing his music with mine), I would have followed *Zephyr* with a yet better work, would have orchestrated the early concerto—a sure applause getter whatever its faults—and, first and foremost, gotten back to study, especially study of orchestration. I had Diaghilev and Koussevitzky where I wanted them, my meteoric rise gave me an entree to almost any conductor you could name, and Cochran, the greatest showman of his time, was commissioning a musical comedy from me—me, who had not a single printed song to his credit! Yet, with all these wondrous opportunities, I let all these birds in my hand fly away—and did little of consequence for the next three years—except, in the current colorful phrase, have myself a ball.[86]

Duke, the elder, seems to have forgotten that Dukelsky, the junior, was then only twenty-five and had spent most of his youth not having a ball but studying, composing, and working at odd jobs. Lady Luck, however, soon appeared in the shape of a pianist, Herman Wasserman, who thought highly of Duke's music. He told Duke what he already knew—that he was wasting his time in London—and persuaded him to return with him to the States, where he would find him the right producers. Duke settled a few debts, talked the American consul into granting him a visitor's visa, paid a fraction of the British taxes he owed, and on June 22, 1929, boarded the *Laconia* "with the firm intention of giving America a second chance to discover me."[87]

DUKE AND DUKELSKY CELEBRATED
NEW YORK, 1929–1935

When Vladimir Dukelsky arrived in the United States in 1921, the Jazz Age had begun. When Vernon Duke returned to America in 1929, the Great Depression (1929–1939) was about to begin. The Depression is seldom mentioned in his autobiography, but it greatly affected his chosen profession. Money once easily obtained for investment in musicals dried up. In 1930, twenty-eight new musicals opened. By 1933 the number had dropped to thirteen. During the decade only four musicals had more than four hundred performances. With some exceptions, such as *The Cradle Will Rock* and *Americana,* which included "Brother, Can You Spare a Dime?" the shows of the period avoided the political and economic turmoil that the nation was undergoing. Left-leaning dramatists, of whom there were many, however, set their plays squarely in the Depression and used them as vehicles to comment on how the crisis was affecting ordinary Americans. *Waiting for Lefty* by Clifford Odets is perhaps the quintessential dialectic play of the times.[1]

Oblivious to all of this when he arrived, Duke reminisced about his return to New York:

> I felt oddly at home in this overpopulated overadvertised city—inhumanly beautiful when viewed at a distance, inhumanly ugly and wretched at close quarters. Yet it was part of America, the country to which we Dukelskys owed everything—our exodus from enslaved

Russia, our subsistence in Constantinople, Alex's brilliant scholastic career, made possible by Americans who had faith in him. Outside of Diaghilev and a chance of my *Mistress into Maid* being produced by him, there was really nothing for me in Europe—not in England . . . and not in France, as Koussevitzky was abandoning his summer concerts and concentrating on the Boston job. . . . I felt I belonged here; I knew I wanted to be close to Mother and Alex and their adopted country, not the countries I had left behind.[2]

Duke fondly remembered the ten days he spent in Natick, Massachusetts, where his mother, Anna, was "rather perplexed" by his English accent and London clothes, but she "looked rested and well, but was, as always, inclined to minimize all the trials and privations she had undergone while I was riding high in Europe." New England reminded him of central Russia, which "made the home-coming feeling even stronger." The food was devoid of frills, and the girls were provocatively dowdy in their "no nonsense" clothes. He was reunited with Col. Alexis Fedorovitch Lvov, who bombarded him "with questions, arguing, giving advice and carrying on as if they had never left the good island of Proti—which, I dimly recalled, was just another Ellis Island, but with olive trees."[3]

Duke also had pleasant memories of the party he attended in January 1930, given by a millionaire in honor of the Gershwins' revival of *Strike Up the Band*. Sergei and Ptashka Prokofiev were in town, and Vladimir persuaded them to attend. All the stars of the operetta and musical worlds would be there, he claimed. It would be the most spectacular party of the season. Sergei recorded the event: "At midnight he came around for us so we dressed and went with him even though our real desire was to go to bed. It proved to be rather a strange evening. A cabaret diva sang in a bass voice, a beautiful woman who is said to earn $4,000 a week. Gershwin himself played." His father, "a semi-intelligent Jew who has forgotten nearly all his Russian, stood beside me (I was sitting in a chair) and delivered himself of various ludicrous malapropisms." At two o'clock, the Prokofievs, finding it hard to keep their eyes open, left, "chuckling over Dukelsky and his 'most spectacular party of the season.'"[4]

Four days later, Dukelsky played for Prokofiev excerpts from his recently composed double-bass concerto. Sergei was not impressed: "The music is feeble; nor does he understand the instrument. . . . Dukelsky seems to be withering on the vine. I had been afraid that flirting with operetta would damage him, and evidently he thought the same as he has gone in quite the opposite direction, towards aridness."[5]

The Prokofievs had arrived in the States on January 1 for a series of concerts in several cities. Late in the month, the Boston Symphony Orchestra performed Sergei's Second Piano Concerto and *Scythian Suite*, the sound of the latter overwhelming Dukelsky, who heard it for the first time. Nevertheless, he told his mentor that he was not on the right track when he composed it and that the material was no more than average. Apparently his views did not disrupt the relationships because Dukelsky accompanied the Prokofievs on their return trip from Boston to New York, making up verses about Stravinsky's inability to compose a tune of his own and embellishing them with drawings of the composer.[6]

Shortly after Duke arrived in New York, H. T. Parker commissioned him to write three articles, at fifteen dollars each, on Diaghilev, Prokofiev, and Nabokov for the *Boston Evening Transcript*. The newspaper published his tribute to Prokofiev in early 1930. Dukelsky considered Prokofiev "one of the greatest living composers" and denounced English critics for virtually ignoring him. He briefly outlined his accomplishments, noting, "With the Third Piano Concerto (1930) Prokofiev becomes the finest melodist of our time," but it remained "for him to give us that monumental piece of musical epos which is expected of every great man."[7] A year later Dukelsky would write another article for the Boston paper that briefly traced the musical life of Nicolas Nabokov. He admitted "that much as I admired Nabokov (only a year older than myself) as a person, I developed a positive distaste to his compositions. Those first efforts were, in reality, rather pointless and dry and extremely imitative." Later he heard Vera Vajeersla sing some of Nabokov's songs. They were "no longer merely promising; they contained a rich and real warmth, a satisfying fulness that left no doubts as to the talent of the composer."[8]

Because newspaper articles hardly brought in enough money to live on, Duke asked George Gershwin for a loan of $120, which he promised to repay within a month. George was not to mention his request to anyone and to send the money immediately, if he were so inclined.[9] Once the money arrived,

Vernon quickly responded: "You have already done so much for me that I only hope to be able to repay you one day for your true friendship, which I value more than anybody else's."[10] A short time later, he asked George to contact Max Dreyfus, who had hired him to write some songs, about his contract, which had not arrived. Until it came he could not afford to live in New York.[11] And still later, he requested another $150, promising to repay him "as promptly as the sum I borrowed last time." If George agreed, he was to make out the check to Vernon Duke.[12]

Apparently the money arrived, because after a brief vacation in Philadelphia, Duke moved in with his mother and brother, Alex, as he was now called, now employed at an architectural firm in Broad Street and the main provider, in an apartment in an uptown residential area of New York. There, the Dukelsky in him orchestrated his Second Symphony, and from there he ventured to the huge Russian gatherings held by his mother's friends, the Polevitzkys. He took a chance on someone named Irene but failed to sweep her off her feet "with adolescent horseplay, a 'must' in America, an enigma to Europeans. My vanity was hurt, my heart (luckily) unbroken."[13] If he needed a vanity boost, it came in October 1930 in an article in the *New York Times*. It mentioned that Duke was "a good friend of George Gershwin and that he credits Mr. Gershwin with having supplied the formula whereby even an excellent musician is enabled to write hit tunes." The article held that Duke showed much promise and predicted that his songs would be heard a lot this season.[14]

Until that day arrived, Duke needed to make some money, and thus he was obviously pleased when the Paramount Publix Corporation, which had studios in Astoria, Long Island, hired him at seventy-five dollars per week and paid him fifty dollars for each song accepted. He was "given a freshly scrubbed cubbyhole of an office, with my name in modest-size letters on the door, a tinny upright, a writing desk, a music cabinet, and a telephone and told to write whatever music Paramount needed. I enjoyed turning out a song with [E. Y.] Harburg for a two-reel short in the morning and a few pages of 'emotional' background music for a dramatic feature in the afternoon." Because the music cabinet contained hundreds of stock arrangements, all he had to do was open one of the drawers labeled "Anger," "Hysteria," "Seduction," "Passion," or "Religion" and select something that fit the particular scene he was assigned to.[15]

Director Edmund Goulding took a liking to Duke, and Duke was impressed with the "well-turned-out Englishman with a unique gift of unconventional gab," who was a "professional man about town, first-nighter, and lady killer." Duke assisted Goulding on *Night Angel*, a melodrama set in Prague starring Fredric March and Nancy Carroll. It was not a musical, but when Goulding wanted intervals of background music of caviar and champagne or enthusiastic whistling, it was "faithfully taken down by me and blown up to symphonic proportions." Duke admitted that the movie was a colossal fiasco.[16]

So did the *New York Times*: "It seems as though Edmund Goulding aspired to be an Eisenstein in his direction . . . and that the stellar player, Nancy Carroll, had hopes of being a Bernhardt or a Duse. Neither is successful and therefore this screen offering results merely in being an affected study in direction and acting."[17] Duke also worked on *Tarnished Lady*, directed by George Cukor and starring Tallulah Bankhead in her first movie. Duke considered it one of her worst pictures.[18] Bankhead "acquits herself with considerable distinction," reported the *Times*, "but the vehicle to which she lends her talent is no masterpiece."[19]

Called on to write a song for a musical short called *Devil Sea*, he and Harburg composed "Old Devil Sea" for Ethel Merman, then appearing on Broadway in *Girl Crazy*. In a highly expressionistic set of white-and-black tones depicting part of a wrecked ship, an officer played by Leslie Stowe tells Merman that the sea has taken her man. She then sings about her loss. Obviously written for one person in a unique setting, the song captures in a dark and moody way the feelings of despair. It begins in the thirty-two bar format of the popular song, but then it drifts away into the ether, as it were, which makes it seem like a new song has been introduced. This is an early example of Duke's creativity in the "popular" field. In "Glory, Glory," by Harburg and Johnny Green, the mood shifts when Merman learns that her man has been found.[20]

Duke, Harburg, and Green also wrote the music for *The Sap from Syracuse*, starring Jack Oakie and featuring Ginger Rogers.[21] Duke mentioned meeting Rogers, "an apple-cheeked, wholesome lass" of nineteen, whom he bought lunch at the commissary and learned that her strange Christian name came from her vaudeville days when she and her husband were billed as "Ginger and Pepper." Duke took her to a dinner or two and on a ride in a hansom through Central Park. Because Ginger was anxious to learn French, Duke "taught her all manner of amorous nonsense during the hansom ride—of verbal variety only, I hasten to add."[22] Rogers was also featured in *Honor among Lovers*, with March and Claudette Colbert. Duke and Green provided the music.[23]

Duke enjoyed working on *Laughter*, starring Nancy Carroll as a Ziegfeld Follies dancer who marries a millionaire but takes up with a composer played by Fredric March. The score of the movie reflects both Duke and Dukelsky. During one scene, March was "required to play a three-minute 'rhapsody' (composed by me) on the piano; I also performed this piece in the film, with March going manfully through the correct pianistics—in this I had to coach him." In another scene, March pretends to play a jazz piece also composed and performed by Duke. Soon Vernon was earning ninety dollars a week, and when not scoring for Paramount, he was lent to other companies, such as Warner Brothers, to "'musicalize' trailers, those idiotic few-minutes previews of a coming attraction."[24]

Duke also met important theater people. At a party hosted by the Gershwins, he played a song called "I Am Only Human After All."[25] Present was Theresa Helburn, one of the founders of New York's Theatre Guild. She encouraged him to audition the song and others for the Guild's production of the third (1930) edition of *Garrick Gaieties*. The first two editions had launched the careers of Richard Rodgers and Lorenz Hart. Although one of several tunesmiths who got their songs accepted, Duke managed to convince the producers that five of his were worthy of inclusion, including "I'm Grover."[26] Also accepted was "Too, Too, Divine," from *Open Your Eyes*, which became "Shavian Shivers" with a new lyric by Harburg, and "I Am Only Human After All," with the lyric by Harburg and Ira Gershwin. The latter was published by Harms Inc. and received a positive review in the *New Yorker*. The revue had a four-month run in New York, and for its out-of-town tour Duke and Harburg wrote five more songs, including the critics' favorites, "Unaccustomed as I Am" and "A Little Privacy."[27] In 1930 the Colonial Club Orchestra, the Arden and Ohman Orchestra, and Joe Venuti and his New Yorkers recorded "I Am Only Human After All."[28]

Sergei Prokofiev was not pleased with Duke's commercial successes. In November he wrote: "No matter how you might pretend and prevaricate, the fact is that you like your half-respectable bread. You can't hide the excitement you feel because your lousy record is number one in sales. But if I were

"I AM ONLY HUMAN AFTER ALL." HARMS, 1930. Author's Collection.

to ask you what you have accomplished in the last year in the field of *real* music, then aside from two rather dry piano pieces you couldn't show me a single thing." Nevertheless, he looked forward to Vladimir "rehabilitating" his name, "which is now half-forgotten in Europe" and promised to promote his Second Symphony.[29]

Duke wrote to Gershwin in April 1930 about the Boston Symphony's third rehearsal of his Second Symphony. The first movement was "very satisfactory," and although the coda was taken twice too fast, it would be corrected at the next and final rehearsal. He was dying for George's opinion of the work.[30] Duke admitted he was "apprehensive about the symphony's Boston fate, owing to my inability to make suggestions or last-minute alterations in the score. For once my fears were groundless; Koussevitzky straightened out the sore spots or glossed them over and the symphony scored an emphatic success."[31] It was performed in Boston on April 25.[32]

Apparently this success was not enough to satisfy Prokofiev, who told a friend the following year that he doubted the composer had a future in classical music: "Dukelsky, who now lives in New York, sent me his latest manuscripts, but his inspiration has somehow just completely dried up. It's a pity, for he had a lot of promise."[33] In a letter to Dukelsky, he noted that the defect of *Dushenka*, scored for two sopranos, chorus, and chamber orchestra, was its "patchwork quality," the music flowing "between indecision and decisiveness." On another occasion, he told Dukelsky that his Second Symphony had no direction.[34]

Duke, however, was doing well and becoming so well known that *Billboard*, in its September 5, 1930, issue, listed him and Arthur Schwartz as Broadway's most prolific composers, each with songs in four productions. *Three's a Crowd* featured Green's "Body and Soul," but it also included Duke's "Talkative Toes," with a lyric by Howard Dietz. Balanchine's former wife, Tamara Geva, "sang and strutted" the song, recalled Duke.[35] Several tunesmiths got their songs performed in *Shoot the Works*, which opened at the George M. Cohan Theatre on July 21, 1931. Duke's contribution was "Mu-Cha-Cha," which he wrote with Jay Gorney. Harburg provided the lyric.[36] Duke's fame continued to expand, so much so that in July the *New York Times* could title an article simply "Duke Writing Play Score." The composer, "remembered for his songs in last year's edition of 'The Garrick Gaieties,' will write the music for 'The Gay Divorce,' a musical comedy which will be presented by Tom Weatherly. . . . Edward Eliscu is writing the lyrics." A famous film actress was to star.[37]

On April 15, 1932, the Boston Symphony performed Dukelsky's *Epitaph* in a program that also included works by Stravinsky and Brahms. In a letter published in the Symphony's *Programme*, Duke explained that he wrote the work in the summer of 1931 as a belated tribute to the memory of Serge Diaghilev, who had died on August 19, 1929. Based on a 1921 poem by the Russian Osip Mandelstam, Duke claimed it gave him "curious insight into the emotional paradox of Diaghilev's life—the life of a Siberian who adored Italy and died in Venice. In the poem it is the presumably Italian swallow that dies on the snows of Russia—and it is to Russia that Diaghilev's heart belonged, even if his mind was that of an embittered Medici." The score called for a piccolo, two flutes, two oboes, English horn, two clarinets, bass clarinet, two bassoons, double-bassoon, two horns, two trumpets, three trombones, tuba, kettledrums, xylophone, two guitars, piano, and the usual strings.[38]

Dukelsky described the organization of the work:

> Musically ... there is a vaguely Italian flavour in one or two episodes, in juxtaposition to the Northern-Russian feeling that prevails in the composition as a whole. After a slow introduction (D), the women's voices are heard in uncertain, halting phrases. The first episode depicts a theatre in St. Petersburg, just emptied after a performance and already plunged in the peculiar gloom that prevails an empty theatre. Then the noise, the bustle outside, the coachmen, the furs of the "Venuses of the North" are described by the poet. The music becomes more strongly marked and has the quality of the Petersburg "chanson de faubourg." This gradually dies out and the soloist is heard in a lyrical monologue (G-sharp minor) which, thematically, is in sharp contrast with the purely "epic" tone of the early passages. After an orchestral outburst (based on the first subject, now in D major), the chorus brings the work to a close with a prayerlike chant "a cappella"; this is based on the "chanson de faubourg" episode, completely transformed and now assuming an almost religious peacefulness. The Epitaph ends *pp* on a D minor chord.[39]

A critic found the work "quite indigestible. Written to a quasi-ironic poem memorializing the death of Diaghileff, the music seems doubly ironic, having little relation to the text. It offered an opportunity, however, for some expressive singing by the soprano soloist, Adelle Alberts. And the Cecilia society chorus, trained by Arthur Fiedler, performed the difficult choral sections of the program admirably."[40] Prokofiev informed Dukelsky in June that when he first read the manuscript, "written on jazz paper, I was overcome by a feeling of disgust and put it aside. Koussevitzky regards the *Epitaphe* with a kind of well-meaning encouragement, so if you really give it so much significance, then I'll look at it more attentively."[41]

Following the performance, tragedy struck. Adelle Alberts died in childbirth a short time after the opening, and Dukelsky became deathly ill on the day of the performance. Instead of going to a doctor in a Boston hospital, he went to his mother in their flat in New York. She quickly summoned a doctor, who identified diphtheria. The house they lived in was quarantined, and Vladimir spent several weeks recuperating. To occupy his time, he wrote several "languorous, magnolia-scented songs to Mikhail Kuzmin's 'Voyage in Italy.'"[42]

Once he recovered, Duke, his visitor visa having expired, sailed on the *Morro Castle* for Vera Cruz, Mexico, needing a foreign country to obtain a quota number and from where he could reenter the United States as an immigrant and become eligible for citizenship. He found the town "ugly" and "barren" and so hot that breathing "was out of the question." He passed his time "swigging crystal-cool Carta Blanca beer" until catching a night train to Mexico City. The trip scared him out of his wits. Peering out his window, he discovered that "we were traveling in the sky, taking sharp curves in order not to hit the moon and stars, over an abyss of what looked like 100,000 feet." But Duke loved Mexico City and behaved like a typical tourist. He ate the food, admired the architecture, floated through the gardens of Xochimilco, climbed the cathedral, and drank pulque, tequila, and nanche, which he called "sheer ambrosia."[43]

He quickly met some of the cultural elite of the city. Carlos Chavez, born in 1899, began piano studies as a child. In the early 1920s, he traveled in Europe to learn about modern musical developments, and he lived in New York City for several years before returning to Mexico to found the Mexican Symphonic Orchestra and become the director of the National Conservatory. Duke described Chavez as looking like his music: "wiry, angular, nervous and aggressively functional." They dined together frequently, and Chavez promised to perform *Zephyr and Flora*, which he called fresh, young music. Duke found Chavez's secretary, Carolina Amor, "as troublesomely pretty as her name." Whether a romance developed between them is not known, but later Duke would dedicate a composition to her.[44]

Composer Silvestre Revueltas, also born in 1899, also studied in the United States. In 1929 Chavez invited Revueltas to become assistant conductor of the Mexican Symphonic Orchestra, and he and Chavez spent the rest of their lives promoting Mexican music. Duke found Revueltas's compositions "Mexico-hewn, perhaps more genuinely so than the sharper, wittier, better-made music of Chavez." Music aside, Duke could not refrain from commenting on the Indian wife of Revueltas. She had "the beautifully shaped slim legs of the women of her race and a sad, melodious speaking voice." Duke also saw a "mediocre bullfight" and a burlesque show that "defied description."⁴⁵

His quota number obtained, he returned to New York, where "I could have kissed the 'sidewalks of New York,' so great was my joy at walking them again, and even thought of writing a modern version of the affecting old ballad." He was obviously upset when learning the *Gay Divorce* was going into rehearsal with music by Cole Porter, but impresario Billy Rose hired him at fifty dollars a week to review all the manuscripts that poured in for a revue to be called *Corned Beef and Roses*. The show never opened. During the two months he labored for Rose, Duke spent his evenings working on a revue to be called *Walk a Little Faster*.⁴⁶

About this time, Duke composed a popular song that in time would make him even more famous. While having drinks at Tony Soma's famous establishment known as West Side Tony's with among others Dorothy Parker, Robert Benchley, and Monty Woolley, someone cried out, "Oh to be in Paris now that April's here." In the phrase, Vernon detected a title for a song, and the party repaired to a piano upstairs where he wrote "April in Paris."⁴⁷ Harburg, who had never been to Paris, later wrote the lyric after reading travel brochures of the city, and the song was added to the revue *Walk a Little Faster*.⁴⁸

Late in his life, Harburg recounted his collaboration with Duke:

> I liked Vernon's facility. He was fast and very sophisticated, almost too sophisticated for Broadway. *Walk a Little Faster* had some very smart stuff in it. In fact, that's when I bounced out of the bread-and-butter stage into sophistication. My light-verse background popped up to reinforce me, and I could write much easier with Vernon than I could with some of the others. It was light, and airy, and very smart.
>
> Vernon brought with him all of that Noel Coward/Diaghilev/Paris/Russia background. He was a global guy with an ability to articulate the English language that was very interesting. A whole new world for me. He could drive you crazy, and he could also open up a new vista. Maybe it was a little bit chi-chi and decorative, but with my pumpernickel background and his orchid tunes we made a wonderful marriage. Maybe we were a strange mixture. We didn't compromise with each other. I applied the everyday down-deep things that

concerned humanity to his sense of style and grace, and I think it gave our songs an almost classic feeling, along with some humor. We came together at a certain point, and for a while it was fine. He satisfied my sense of light verse and the need for sophistication.[49]

Walk a Little Faster premiered in Boston to a positive notice by H. T. Parker: "Modernisms abound in Mr. Duke's music. He has confided it and Mr. [Conrad] Salinger has scored it . . . for a jazz, rather than a theatre orchestra. Being a modernist, Mr. Duke makes bold rhythms. . . . Nor does Mr. Duke hesitate at modulations that might grate on the more innocent Berlin or Kern. Yet when need is, he can write a nostalgic, quasi-sentimental melody. . . . 'April in Paris' is worthy, in place and kind, of that city in the spring."[50] The show opened in New York in December, ran for five months, lost money, and was poorly received. Overlooking "April in Paris," Walter Winchell identified "Where Have We Met Before?" "So Nonchalant," and "Speaking of Love" as quality songs, but most of the music was "nothing to set your tootsies tapping."[51]

Duke recalled that Evelyn Hoey performed "April in Paris" in a beautiful set of a Left Bank Paris café, but she suffered from laryngitis and was barely audible. After the second performance, Duke and his brother, "dejected and resentful of the critics' indifference, sat in the Times Square Childs' restaurant, Alex consoling me to the best of his ability, when in stormed Harburg, disheveled and obviously in a rage." He threw Bob Garland's negative review on the table, insisting that "April in Paris" was fine for decadent Europeans but not for Americans. He left in a huff, claiming that the song should have been a saucy jingle.[52]

Obviously Harburg's reaction was premature. Biographer Isaac Goldberg told Duke that he thought the song was one of the finest compositions that had ever graced an American musical. If he had his way, he would make a study of it compulsory in all harmony courses.[53] According to critic Samuel Steatton,

> "April in Paris," a song from one of the last season's revues, has been called one of the finest light songs to have been sung on our stage during the past ten years. This particular Vernon Duke chanson is mentioned because it revealed the hitherto unknown possibilities of a supposedly overworked form and turned it into a frame full of

resiliency and verve. It is the ability of Duke to "revert" to Dukelsky when writing popular tunes that results in middle sections that are as catchy and appealing as the usual eight bar stroke of genius that is characteristic of the Tin Pan Alley school.[54]

Duke wrote in *Passport to Paris* that "Goldberg was especially appreciative of the Duke side of me, rather than the Dukelsky one; as I suspected, most of the 'serious' new music left him cold—mine, possibly, included." But Goldberg greatly admired *Walk a Little Faster* and was appalled at the way Duke's score was treated by the New York critics. He wrote to Duke on December 13, 1932: "From scraps that I read here and there in the Gotham (Goddamn) press, I gathered that they had been stupid—that is the 'mot juste'—with your music. It is nothing new. I shall be glad, as a public service, and not alone as a service to you, to write to one of the newspapers."[55]

In January 1933, Goldberg submitted an article to the *New York Evening Post* entitled "Dukelsky into Duke." He considered

> it important for our lighter musical stage that talent such as Duke's should not, at this point in his development, pass insufficiently appreciated. The man has an individual gift that makes him stand out in company of those who have made of our musical comedy something more than the dull routine it once used to be. In fact, I do not hesitate to say that he is the most important personality to come to our stage since Kern and Gershwin and Porter were followed by Rodgers, Youmans and their fellows, and that, if he is not allowed to find his place in contemporary revues, musical comedies and even comic opera, the loss will be, to us and to him, artistically considerable.

Duke acknowledged that Goldberg "did very handsomely by me," but he could not resist noting that Walter Winchell had crowned him the greatest composer, superior to even Gershwin and Porter.[56]

Through his newspaper columns and radio broadcasts, Winchell had become America's premier gossiper. He would combine unrelated events and individuals in a fragmented sentence or in one breath—the marriage of an actor with a drought in Africa, for example. Being mentioned by Winchell, no matter how trivial the reason, would acknowledge a person's existence and imply that he or she was somehow important.⁵⁷ In his column in October, Winchell reported that Duke was "courting a Park Avenue Russian baroness."⁵⁸

Far more important than being mentioned by Winchell was being appreciated by fellow songwriters. While waiting in the publishing offices of Max Dreyfus, Vernon encountered

> a white-haired, bird-like little fellow who said in a high-pitched voice: "You're Vernon Duke, aren't you? Let me shake your hand—I'm Jerome Kern." We shook hands and I murmured something indicative of my profound respect for the dean of America's show composers, who interrupted me to say: "You may think it odd and I'm not in the habit of saying such things, but I'm crazy about your music—it's new and it's fresh. Believe it or not, I'm under your influence. Good day to you."⁵⁹

Certainly new and fresh at the time was Duke's "This Is Romance," with Edward Heyman providing the lyric. Published in 1933 by Harms, it was quickly recorded that year by the Nye Mayhew Orchestra, the Ray Noble Orchestra, Ben Bernie & All the Lads, and by Hal Kemp the following year, and by Georgie Auld and Artie Shaw in 1940. Heyman's lyric does not equal the one he wrote for "Body and Soul," but as the Auld and Shaw Orchestras demonstrate, the song works very well as an instrumental. Walter Winchell called it "one of the tunier tunes."⁶⁰

By this time, Vernon, Alex, and their mother had moved from uptown to Greenwich Village, where they were burglarized twice, and then to West Fourth Street. Alex found work with an architect in Jersey City, and Vernon entertained fellow composers, including Bernard Herrmann, whom he remembered as a "torrential talker" oblivious of his appearance. He greatly admired Herrmann because of "'his overflowing love of music, his dogged determination to serve it as composer and conductor—in contrast to conductors' traditional tendency to make music serve *them*."⁶¹

At Carnegie Hall on April 4, 1933, Léon Barzin served Dukelsky well when he conducted the National Orchestral Association in a presentation of his First Symphony. As Vladimir remembered, the "audience and critics were surprisingly kind to that youthful piece."⁶² One critic, however, had mixed feelings: "His first essay in the form, it was characterized by cleverness and dignity in the handling of the rather intractable themes forming its ideational basis and by its skillful and effective employment of the orchestral idiom. This much, of course, was to be expected, for Mr. Dukelsky had had other music played here in which he demonstrated himself an experienced craftsman, and an ingenious tonetaster, if not precisely a deep or original musical thinker." But anticipating an early masterpiece, the critic found "it revealed none of the qualities the ear sought in it, nothing to encourage the listener in any belief in Mr. Dukelsky's special capacity for thinking and feeling deeply and truly."[63] In May, however, Dukelsky received good news from Prokofiev, who had returned to the Soviet Union: "Your 2nd Symphony was performed in Warsaw a few days ago, broadcasted and approved by a group of young composers in Moscow."[64]

Also in May, Dukelsky and several other like-minded individuals issued a manifesto that began with: "We, the undersigned, have united to form a Composers' Protective Society to reinstate the composer to his rightful place in the world of music." Each orchestra was encouraged to provide $1,000 annually to commission a work from a representative American composer and to hold an annual festival of modern music. Twenty-nine composers signed the manifesto, including Bernard Herrmann, George Gershwin, and of course Vladimir Dukelsky. The manifesto was published in the *New York Times*.[65] By July the society had added twelve more composers to its membership, including Johnny Green. Dukelsky, Henry Cowell, Harold Morris, and Bernard Wagenaar formed the executive council that was to direct the society during its period of organization.[66]

Dukelsky, however, needed Duke to keep food on the table, so he and Harburg submitted four songs to Lee Shubert for the new edition of the *Ziegfeld Follies*. Bobby Connolly was to direct, Fanny Brice to star. She was first seen in the *Follies of 1910*, and beginning in 1916 she starred in seven *Ziegfeld Follies*. The cast also included Eve Arden, Buddy and Vilma Ebsen, June and Cherry Preisser, Everett Marshall, Jane Froman, Patricia Bowman, Willie and Eugene Howard, and the Ziegfeld Girls. Vernon wrote:

> Most revues are disorganized in the early stages, before the unnecessary material gets weeded out and the whole vehicle starts taking shape, but in the *Follies of 1933–34* sheer chaos reigned triumphantly.

After weeks of quarrels, tantrums, firings, hirings, Connolly's disappearances, Lee Shubert's dreaded entrances, money and tears flowing, stagehands fleeing, we got off to an unpromising start in Boston. . . . True Fanny stopped the show, as was her habit, but faulty cues and backstage mishaps stopped it too—often. We expected a real lambasting from the critics, but to everyone's surprise they loved the show.[67]

The revue, however, needed work, and John Murray Anderson summoned Duke back to the *Follies*. In Newark, New Jersey, it was "revamped, redesigned, rewritten and, in part, recast" before it opened at the Shubert Theater. "Showmanship and taste, previously absent from the production, were now in abundant evidence, and it was fascinating to watch a singing and dancing Phoenix emerging from the ashes. Murray restaged 'What Is There to Say' unrecognizably and brought genuine poetry to 'Water under the Bridge,' a weird 'mood' song Harburg and I wrote for Everett Marshall to sing and Patricia Bowman to dance."[68]

The *Follies* opened on January 4, 1934, at the Winter Garden in New York City and is best remembered as the venue in which Fanny Brice introduced her "Baby Snooks" character.[69] According to a critic for the *Stage*, she blatantly stole the show: "Through it all Fannie Brice shines like a naughty deed in a jaded world. . . . Meanwhile Vilma and Buddy Ebsen are swell dancers. . . . Betzi Beaton is so pie-eyed every night that she can hardly do her act—and you can almost believe it. Willie Howard is grand. There are other points in the show, but when we recall Fannie Brice's Minsky number, we forget what they are."[70] Brooks Atkinson of the *New York Times* praised the show, or rather performers Brice and Eugene Howard, "whose combination is extraordinarily cheerful. For Miss Brice and Mr. Howard are well met in the theatre—both racial in style, both given to the rolling, roguish eye, and both mighty good company." Vilma and Buddy Ebsen and former Metropolitan Opera star Everett Marshall "helped to make this the best edition of the 'Ziegfeld Follies' the Shuberts ever put on the stage."[71] It ran for 182 performances before going on the road. On March 16, 1935, at the Shubert Theater in New Haven, it became the first Broadway musical to be entirely recorded, although the touring company had dropped or rearranged some of the original sketches and production numbers. The two-hour show was recorded on forty-two blank 78 rpm disks, each lasting about three minutes. With two recording turntables, the completion of one disk was immediately followed by the beginning of another.[72]

The revue would be the last time Duke and Harburg would work together, but twenty-five of their songs were eventually published.[73] "Suddenly," "What Is There to Say?" and "I Like the Likes of You" survived the show, and Duke considered their "Water under the Bridge" as "the first of the 'out of this world' (not heavenly, just plain uncommercial) tunes for which I achieved considerable notoriety; I don't want to call myself a prophet, but the odd harmonic structure of the piece, written in 1933, has all the earmarks of postwar 'bop' [jazz] conceptions." Duke could not get the song published, but in 1934 he recorded it with vocalist Bonnie Lake and clarinetist Ralph McLane. "I'm Mad about a Man about Town," with his own lyric, is on the reverse side of the record. This is the first recording by Duke of any of his works.[74] Another first came in late March 1934, when he and Kay Swift were interviewed by Francis C. Healey on a radio program called *The Songwriter Looks at Art*.[75]

In April, Duke told Elizabeth Borton of the *Boston Herald*, "The two idioms which I write are as different as work and play. Jazz is easy for me—that is just recreation for which I happen to get paid." And paid well, added Borton, "for he has had success on Broadway in more shows than one—the latest being the *Ziegfeld Follies* of this year." Duke was equally frank when he admitted, "If somebody commissioned me to write a song praising American buckwheat, and offered me money for it, I would write it. The greatest musicians and artists, after all, earned their living by what they did. They were so resourceful that they could turn any chance necessity into a living art." He also reflected on Dukelsky, the composer:

> Music has been getting too clever. . . . Too many men are writing music for 10 flutes, or for 40 percussion instruments. Or they write something that does not sound musically "inevitable," or that sounds as if the composer had said all he could say. There is a lack of music that bursts out of an inner reservoir full to overflowing with feeling and energy. . . .
>
> I am trying to return to the romantic music, and I think that I am approaching it more in this ballet [*Jardin Public*] I am doing, than in anything I have written up to now.

> I formerly wrote with great facility—with superficial verve. Now I feel much more deeply, and I find it harder to express myself. Also, I will not write now, until I feel that I have something worth saying.[76]

Borton described Duke as "a handsome young man with very pink cheeks and an appearance of heathy, plump youth which he loathes. He wants to seem 40 and have gray hair and a look of having done something spectacular in the way of suffering or accomplishment." She also noted that he was a "Stage Door Johnny," who can often be found "sitting in the wings during rehearsals, keeping time occasionally with his cane . . . and dropping an attentive eye toward every shapely ankle on its way by."[77]

Without lifting a finger, the "Stage Door Johnny" got one of his songs accepted to a show. In late 1934 John Murray Anderson phoned him about a revue he was staging called *Thumbs Up!* Anderson needed a song that presented a nostalgic evocation of Manhattan in the fall. Duke had such a song but warned that it moved from key to key, making it hard on the singer. When he mentioned the title, "Autumn in New York," Anderson suggested Duke immediately hop a cab for 15 Park Avenue. There the song was interpolated into the score by Jimmy Hanley and Henry Sullivan.[78] Duke had written the song in Westport, Connecticut, in the summer of 1934 without a commission for a particular show. The revue ran from December 1934 to May 1935, but critics failed to mention the song.[79]

In retrospect, Dukelsky probably would have preferred the critics ignoring his ballet *Jardin Public*, which he had completed in January 1934.[80] He had to wait a year before he received a commission to present it. The ballet is based in part on *The Counterfeiters* by André Gide, who wrote to him in January 1935:

> I am happy to learn that you have not abandoned your beautiful project. To help its success, I gladly agree to forego my "royalties" for the ballet's performances in America. The title that I already indicated to you, "Jardin Public," seems excellent to me and I hope you won't hesitate to use it. It would be best to indicate: "after a page from André Gide's novel *The Counterfeiters*, and to reproduce said page "in extenso" in the program, which would serve to explain the ballet.[81]

Ballets Russes de Monte Carlo (the successor to Ballets Russes) and now directed by Col. Wassili de Basil (whose real name was Vkoskresensky) staged the ballet. Choreographed by Léonide Massine, who had worked with Dukelsky on *Zephyr and Flora,* and set in a continental park from dawn to night, the ballet mixed tragedy and comedy.[82] It opened at the Chicago Auditorium in March 1935 and was a disaster. The score was to be published in Paris but had to be copied by hand, and it arrived in Chicago with mistakes. It reached the theater in time for only one rehearsal. Dukelsky recalled that his "music, fairly dissonant in the first place, sounded like Schoenberg married to Varese and caused me to run out of the theater—then to return, panting and wishing I had stayed away. There were two or three highspots, applauded to the echo, but the total effect was one of a hopeless mess."[83]

Despite the disappointment, Duke remembered Chicago as being "pretty wonderful in the thirties; it was out to beat New York, and nearly did, artistically speaking." Costume designer Jean Lurcat and Duke "did a lot of sight-seeing when not rehearsing, ate great food at Ernie Byfield's home atop of one of the Ambassador Hotels, marveled at the luxury of Lake Shore drive rubbing shoulders with the worst and most odoriferous slums known to man, took in ribald doings at Club 606, a close rival to Mexico's Teatro Garibaldi, saw a colored man shot at a North Side dive at 4 A.M., and stood in wonder before an electric sign reading 'Chez Paree.'"[84]

At the Majestic Theater in New York, the ballet was "spottily performed and spottily received," admitted Dukelsky, "although the music sounded better."[85] John Martin of the *New York Times* acknowledged that the dancers and the orchestra performed valiantly, but what emerged was "something less than impressive. It is couched entirely in terms of what used to be called smart modernism before the depression, and seems additionally empty and decadent at this time by the very fact that it indicates some awareness of the economic situation and can find nothing to say about it."[86]

Duke fared better in an article by James B. Reston in a September 1935 issue of the *New York Times*:

> Of all the fascinating characters on Broadway, none seems more interesting than Vernon Duke of that particular quarter of the street known as Tin Pan Alley. He is the Sir Arthur Sullivan of the Rialto,

and true Dr. Jekyll and Mr. Hyde. . . . Duke is Duke only when he writes popular music. . . . The rest of the time, he is Vladimir Dukelsky, and under this name he writes lofty symphonic pieces. There are some who predict a great future for him in the latter field, but most of the critics are inclined to believe his "April in Paris" will outlast the more erudite numbers.[87]

"April in Paris" would outlast the "erudite numbers," but so would another song he would soon write for a Broadway show. As he recalled in his autobiography: "The Shuberts, encouraged by the success of their first *Follies*, were busily preparing a second. Ira Gershwin was available for the lyric-writing job as George was working on *Porgy and Bess* with DuBose Heyward. When asked whom he would like for his music man, Ira suggested me—and Lee Shubert, not having done badly with me a year before, readily agreed."[88]

DUKE AT HIS VERY BEST
NEW YORK, 1935–1940

In September 1935, Samuel Chotzinoff of the *Stage* predicted that Vernon Duke, who would write the score for the *Ziegfeld Follies of 1936*, would soon "burst forth with something both original and mature. Here is a young man who is no stranger to serious music, the mechanics of which he applies in small doses to his lighter efforts. A touch of this procedure in a popular ditty is sure to lend it a sophistication that flatters the ear of the trained listener, and is not without its effects on the sensibilities of the untrained."[1] Then only thirty-two years old, Duke was unaware that he was about to ascend to an artistic plateau where he would write some of his best, if not always his most widely recognized, songs.[2]

To work on the show, Duke and Ira Gershwin moved into a house in Ocean Beach, on Fire Island, New York. Accompanying the two were Ira's wife, Leonore, librettist Moss Hart, and George Gershwin, who was often absent working on *Porgy and Bess*.[3] Lying off the southern shore of Long Island, Ocean Beach lacked electric lights and automobiles, and only two boats reached the island daily. It had become a colony of writers, composers, and stage personalities, which included dramatist Lillian Hellman, producer Billy Rose, and his wife, Fanny Brice.[4] Also vacationing on the island was Joan, a teenager whose "strong, nut-brown body" Duke first observed in a gleaming white bathing suit too small for her. He took a chance by inviting her to dinner and especially to the house where he and the Gershwins were staying. After hearing too "many good-natured cracks on the subject of cradle robbing," Vernon decided they should not see so much of each other.[5] He had more important affairs to attend to.

Duke recounted how he and Ira, men of radically different temperaments and work habits, collaborated on the island:

> Ira's writing methods were slow and soothing and very restful.... Our work sessions usually began with a family dinner with Ira and Leonore, joined by Fanny Brice or Ellen [sic] Berlin. After a long copious meal, the company would repair to the drawing room, which housed the piano, and hectic conversation would ensue; I, on tenterhooks, would be dying to get to the piano and persuade Leonore and her guests to go elsewhere for their energetic gossip. I would shoot expressive glances at ever-placid Ira, who affected not to catch their meaning and willingly joined in the conversation. After an hour or so of this, I, totally exasperated, would invade the piano determinedly and strike a few challenging chords. This time Ira would heed my desperate call, stretch himself, emit a series of protracted sighs, say something to the effect that "one had to work *so-o-o* hard for a living" and more in that vein, then interrupt himself to intone the magic word: "However..." This "however" meant that the eleventh hour had struck and the period of delicious procrastination was over. Ira, sighing pathetically, would then produce a small bridge table, various writing and erasing gadgets, a typewriter and four or five books, which he seldom consulted—Roget's *Thesaurus,* Webster's dictionary, rhyming dictionary, and the like—wipe and adjust his glasses, all these preparations at a *molto adagio* pace, and finally say in a resigned voice: "O.K. Dukie... play that chorus you had last night." After wrestling with last night's chorus for a half hour, Ira would embark on an ice-box-raiding expedition, with me, fearful of too long an interruption, in pursuit. There we'd stand in the kitchen, munching cheese and pickles, Ira obviously delighted with this escapist stratagem, I dutifully pretending to enjoy it too. Another sigh, another "however," then back to the piano. At 2 or 3 A.M. Ira would put away his working utensils and victoriously announce to Lee that he had completed four lines for the new chorus.[6]

At the end of the summer, the "Fire Islanders" took the ferry back to Long Island and dispersed. Joan went to Scarsdale to graduate from high school. George returned to his apartment on Riverside Drive and continued working on *Porgy and Bess*. Ira and Leonore settled in a new duplex on East Seventy-Second Street. And Vernon was off to his new apartment on West Fifty-Seventh Street, close to where his mother and brother were residing.[7] He and Ira, however, remained involved in the production of the revue.

Those hired by Harry Kaufman, the manager in chief of the production of *The Ziegfeld Follies of 1936*, included Duke, who composed all the songs, and Gershwin, who wrote the lyrics and although not credited contributed ideas and material for the sketches. John Murray Anderson directed, and Vincente Minnelli, who began his career as a designer for the *Earl Carroll Vanities* of 1931, designed the sets and costumes. Robert Alton arranged the dance numbers, and H. I. Phillips, Moss Hart, and David Freedman wrote the sketches.[8] Because the sketches were inflated anecdotes, Freedman claimed they were as difficult to write as plays. In a few pages they had to convey what a play did in three acts. And if the last line did not work, the sketch failed.[9]

In his Broadway debut, George Balanchine created the ballet sequences. Since he first met Duke in London, Balanchine had risen to prominence as choreographer of ballets, working with composers such as Prokofiev, Stravinsky, Debussy, Satie, and Ravel. And when he moved to the United States in 1933, he opened a ballet studio in New York.[10] Duke took credit for persuading Kaufman to hire Balanchine, claiming that for some time he had been "blowing Balanchine's horn as the greatest of all choreographers, and therefore indispensable to what was planned as the greatest of all revues." After "concerted screaming," as Duke put it, by George's agent and himself, they persuaded the choreographer to join the revue.[11]

Regarding the performers, Fanny Brice was the star, but comedienne Eve Arden, who had appeared in the *Ziegfeld Follies of 1934* and *Parade* the following year, had a large role. Already known for his work in six Broadway shows, including *Roberta* of 1933, Bob Hope was prominently featured.[12] Duke found Hope "a most engaging young man, with a freshly scrubbed, balcony-nosed face, rather self-effacing compared with our trio of female prima donnas and always worried about his waistline (so was I)."[13]

The original cast also included Hugh O'Connell, Cherry and June Preisser, the tap-dancing Nicholas Brothers (Fayard and Harold), Harriet Hoctor, and Gertrude Niesen. Niesen was not a Broadway performer but a radio singer under contract with the Columbia network. She chose to join the cast of the *Follies* because radio work prevented her from developing her acting skills. Experience on the stage would correct that neglect. Working with Anderson may also have been a factor in her decision, as was the opportunity to sing the songs of Gershwin and Duke.[14] But not everyone was happy with her decision. According to Duke, Niesen "found fault with everybody and everything." He also mentioned that the producers had signed "a genuine Paris importation, Mlle. Josephine Baker, originally of Harlem. La Baker, with a French count in tow, two beautifully groomed dogs of exotic appearance, and a large assortment of the best Vuitton luggage, received us majestically in her hotel suite."[15] Before relocating to Paris, Baker, as a member of the chorus, had appeared in the 1922 production of *Shuffle Along*.[16]

The cast consisted of seventy-five other performers, many being ballerinas who lived apart from the rest of the cast. Their captain, Evelyn Dale, told a newspaper reporter, "We must have mental, as well as physical co-ordination. A family spirit of affection, mental understanding, kindred tastes and purpose must be preserved." None of the ballerinas could stay out after midnight, which meant they never stayed out that late because the revue ended at 11:30. By emphasizing that her "girls have a fine standard of breeding and refinement," Dale may have implied that other members of the cast were lacking in these characteristics.[17] The curfew obviously "protected" the dancers, perhaps to their dismay, from the advances of "Stage Door Johnnies."

The show premiered at the Boston Opera House on December 25, 1935. Following the opening number came a series of sketches, dances, and songs. Boston audiences were especially privileged to see a sketch that included a dance created by Balanchine, costumes designed by Minnelli, and a Duke and Gershwin song sung by Judy Canova. As "Maw," she sang "The Ballad of Baby Face McGinty (Who Bit Off More than He Could Chew)" to her three bearded sons in a Kentucky cabin about a gangster modeled on Baby Face Nelson, Machine Gun Kelly, and Al Capone. Each stanza began with the lights coming up on a darkened cabin and recounted an event in McGinty's life. At age seven, he stole his grandmother's false teeth to get some gin. At twenty-one, he ruled St. Louis, holding up a bank every day and dealing in booze. He killed, raped, and murdered until arrested for not paying his income taxes. As the lights went up on the last stanza, the entire cast sang:

> So long, good-bye, McGinty—
> On one thing you were lax:
> You could get away with murder
> But not on your income tax.[18]

The performance, recalled Duke, although "imaginatively staged by Balanchine, was inexplicably dropped in Boston."[19] Ira thought it was "a stunner," but understood it was not cut because it needed work, which was the usual explanation. It was cut because "there was a more than usual amount of comedy; there were plenty of stageable songs and special material (because of production postponements Duke and I had been at it eight or nine months and twenty-five numbers were available). . . . But we had too much show with too many elaborate production numbers." Consequently, "unless you are Richard Wagner or Eugene O'Neill, overlength has to be considered. The Show Must Go On—but not too long after eleven P.M."[20] Also dropped from the show were "Please Send My Daddy Back to Mother," "I'm Sharing My Wealth," "The Knife Thrower's Wife," "Does a Duck Love Water?" "Wishing Tree of Harlem," "Why Save for That Rainy Day?" "Hot Number," "The Last of the Cabbies," "Sunday Tan," "I Used to Be above Love," "The Better Half Knows Better," and "Oh, Bring Back the Ballet Again."[21]

Elinor Hughes, theater critic for the *Boston Herald*, was less than enthusiastic about the production and its performers, although she was impressed with Gertrude Niesen's renditions of "Moment of Moments" and "Words without Music," songs she thought would become the most popular numbers in the production. But the show "must be cut, pruned and provided with more comedy. All this undoubtedly sounds like unkind carping, but with such an abundance of talents combined, it was only natural to expect something exceptional. . . . It is the mundane material of sketches and songs that disappoint." She ended her review by noting, "The celebrated Ira Gershwin, the even more famous Vernon Duke, and Moss Hart did a lot of lyrics, music and sketches, but it was an evening for the eye, not the ear."[22]

On January 1, 1936, the show opened on Broadway at the Winter Garden, but, according to Duke, it was marked by Josephine Baker's "unprecedented but, I fear, not unprefabricated triumph. The entire balcony was filled with her friends and admirers, and they made such a din at their idol's merest apparition, that no one, not even the audience-proof Fanny, could follow amidst the frenzied cheering accorded La Baker." Duke considered her a "woman of indefinable talents—she's no trained dancer, an inaudible singer, and certainly no comedienne in the American sense."[23]

Despite the competition, Fanny Brice remained the star, and her singing of "He Hasn't a Thing Except Me" stopped the show. The sketch opens with a forlorn Brice leaning against a lamppost. The lamppost walks off, and after the verse, Brice sings:

> I give you His Highness
> A pain worse than sinus.
> Though I felt all hopped up
> The minute he popped up,
> It's easy to see
> He hasn't a thing except me.

In the middle of the second chorus she stops singing and addresses the audience as herself, an audience that was clearly familiar with her history of singing about men. If she ever met a man like the one she has been singing about, no telling what she would do. The conductor raps impatiently. Fannie gets back into character.[24]

Ira considered Fanny

> one of the most versatile and accomplished personalities in our musical theater. In this particular *Follies*, for example, she put over this torch song, and did a wonderful burlesque of modern dancing, following her singing of "Modernistic Moe." In the skits she played Baby Snooks; then a tough Tenth Avenue girl, then the most elegant English drawing-room matron in "Fawncy, Fawncy"; then a Bronx housewife who has misplaced her winning Sweepstakes ticket; then a starlet in a satire of Hollywood musicals—all exquisitely and incomparably executed.[25]

According to a critic, however, little had been done to improve the revue. It consisted of a "mosaic of pageantry, dancing spectacle, girls and a modicum of comedy. And the girls are beautiful." The paucity of comedy was no fault of Fanny Brice, who was everywhere in sketches, burlesques, and "in song she is just about the stoutest prop the show has." The reviewer acknowledged, "Ira Gershwin's lyrics are saucy and witty. Vernon Duke's score is pretty but not spectacular."[26] If the show offered nothing but Fanny Brice, wrote Brooks Atkinson of the *New York Times*, "most of us would feel sufficiently grateful." He thought the songs by Duke were "probably all right," and "Gertrude Niesen sings most of them with a cloudy voice suggesting an oboe with a cold, and probably that is all right, too."[27]

Duke insisted that the "second Shubert *Follies* was a better show than the first, thanks to Minnelli, Balanchine, and Anderson." Yet somehow, "perhaps owing to the performers, the score didn't come off too impressively in the theater." But he was most impressed with Fanny Brice, especially in "The Gazooka," in which she appeared as "Ruby Blondell," a cross of Ruby Keeler and Joan Blondell. The Gazooka was a dance that parodied the Carioca, the Continental, and other film-created dance crazes, and was announced as done in "Techinquecolor" and on "Widescope Screen." Duke remarked that Gershwin and David Freedman were eighteen years ahead of their time and "proved a regular pair of Nostradamuses in this opus."[28]

Although all the music was billed as Duke's, it was really Dukelsky and Balanchine who created three ballets for the revue—"Words without Music," "Night Flight," and "Five A.M." The first was written for dancer Harriet Hoctor and was reminiscent of the ballets Balanchine choreographed for Diaghilev in which modernist movements were expressed in a modern art setting. Dukelsky's score was a symphonic arrangement of his song "Words without Music."[29] As part of the performance, Gertrude Niesen sang the song (the verse: *Tranquillo*, the refrain: *Molto expressivo*) and probably did justice to Ira's melancholy lyric:

> Words without music
> Smoke without flame—
> Charming phrases
> That sing your praises
> And call your name.[30]

Because he had previously worked almost exclusively with his brother, George, whose music usually lacked heartache, Ira demonstrated considerable flexibility in fashioning lyrics to Duke's lush harmonies and melancholy melodies.[31]

Influences from Debussy and Ravel emanate from Dukelsky's score for "Night Flight," the ballet reflecting recent flights by Charles Lindbergh and Amelia Earhart.[32] One review noted that Hoctor was "the spirit of flight silhouetted against the black shadow of a great wrecked plane."[33] Another mentioned that she hovered "like a released and almost transparent soul over an aeroplane's grim shadow . . . a triumph of ballet technique and genuine imagination."[34]

In "Five A.M." the music and the choreography departed from the traditions of the Broadway musical. The orchestra score produced sounds of a big city with syncopation and blue notes, reminiscent of Gershwin's *Rhapsody in Blue* and his tone poem, *An American in Paris*. It also exhibited influences of Prokofiev, Debussy, Scriabin, and Rachmaninoff. To the music Balanchine fashioned a *ballet d'action* in which the dance expands on Ira's lyrics.[35]

The scene opens with Baker, playing a young woman—clearly a prostitute—surrounded by a crowd. As her guests depart, she turns off the lights and reflects on her evening out:

> Five A.M. And I am home again. Five A.M.
> Five A.M. My time is my own again. Five A.M.
> Through with the night I slave in,
> I'm in my haven at last.

Baker falls asleep and in a Balanchine choreographed dream sequence, four men, one after the other, come out of the shadows to dance with her. They treat her like a queen, lifting and swaying with her, until the music becomes fragmented and the dream turns into a nightmare. When Baker opens the door of her apartment, one of the shadowy dancers is seen, but he disappears. Baker completes the song and the dance sequence.[36]

The mostly white audience sat in silence, shocked that the four adoring male dancers were white. Not only had Balanchine and Dukelsky introduced a new form in their ballet, but they and Gershwin had also shattered a taboo.[37] Instead of commenting on the ballet, however, most critics focused on Josephine Baker. John Anderson wrote: "In sex appeal to jaded Europeans of the jazz-loving type, a Negro wench always has a head start. The particular tawny tint of tall and stringy Josephine Baker's bare skin

"I CAN'T GET STARTED." CHAPPELL & CO., 1936. Author's Collection.

stirred French pulses. But to Manhattan theatre-goers last week she was just a slightly buck-toothed young Negro woman whose figure might be matched in any night club now, whose dancing & singing could be topped practically anywhere outside France."[38] Other critics were less critical but barely so. Brooks Atkinson concluded that "Josephine Baker has become a celebrity who offers her presence instead of her talent. They have given her a ravishing setting, effulgent gowns or practically no costume at all, which is an improvement, but her singing voice is only a squeak in the dark and her dancing is only the pain of an artist. Miss Baker has refined her art until there is nothing left in it."[39] The first audiences "found her a little disappointing," noted Ira Wolfert. "But that may very well be provincial Broadway's fault. She is an exotic belle with racy eyes and a sharp face that can fill with wild, streaming fury. Her voice is soft and thin—something like a cracked bell's muted clap."[40]

Although the three ballets by Duke and Balanchine certainly deserve recognition, the *Follies of 1936* is best remembered for one song, "I Can't Get Started with You." That it was placed in the second half of the revue, next to the last song sung, suggests that no one thought it had a chance of becoming a hit, even though it was introduced by Bob Hope. In the sketch, Hope and Eve Arden in evening clothes are standing on a street corner. She hails passing cabs, but none stops. Hope brags about how famous he is, but Arden is clearly not impressed. The orchestra now introduces the song, and Hope sings the verse and the choruses. By the time he finishes, Arden has warmed up to him. Hope plants a long kiss, and she calls him marvelous. That is all he wanted to know. Hope jauntily exits and the stage goes black.[41]

When Fanny Brice came down with laryngitis, the show was closed on February 3 and 4, only four days after it had opened. She rejoined the cast on the fifth. And on the twenty-ninth, she and select members of the cast performed sketches and sang songs in *The Ziegfeld Follies of the Air*, a weekly CBS broadcast that would continue for the next three months. Al Goodman and His Orchestra provided the music.[42] Apparently the show served to introduce new songs, "You, Only You" being presented in an April broadcast. It was written not by Ira and Vernon but by Fred E. Ahlert and Joe Young.[43] In early May, due to arthritis of the leg, Brice again withdrew from the show, forcing it to close for several months.[44]

In June, Harry Kaufman ordered Vernon to write some new songs for the show when it reopened. He and lyricist Ted Fetter (Ira had left for California) would have first crack at incorporating them, provided they were as good or better than those provided by their competitors. But behind their backs, Kaufman bought five pieces from publishers and immediately put them into rehearsal. Although Vernon's contract clearly stated that no interpolations would be allowed unless approved by Ira and himself, friends persuaded him not to rock the boat.[45]

The *Follies* reopened on September 14, with a recovered Brice and with Bobby Clark replacing Bob Hope and Gypsy Rose Lee stepping in for Eve Arden. Evidently they formed the new team that presented "I Can't Get Started." Josephine Baker, Gertrude Niesen, Hugh O'Connell, Harriet Hoctor, and the Nicholas Brothers also left the show, but a surprise replacement was Jane Pickens of the Pickens Sisters, a trio mostly heard on the airwaves.

A reviewer for the *New York Times* noted she had learned "that lyrics sometimes make sense: often enough, at all events, to give the audience the benefit of the doubt." The show could not be called new, but the new materials were "generally up to the mark," including the exquisite "Midnight Blue," by Edgar Leslie and Joe Burke and sung by Pickens, and "Harlem Waltz," "Ridin' the Rails," and "You Don't Love Right," by other lyricists and tunesmiths.[46]

Ira told Vernon in October 1936 that he was "terribly happy about the Follies. Moss [Hart] wired it's one of the best revues he ever saw and who are we to refute him? So long as it continues to do over 28,000 [gross dollars per week], it's the best revue ANYBODY ever saw."[47] The contract stated that no cuts in royalties would occur as long as the gross remained over $28,000. But a short time later, Ira received a telegram from Kaufman, claiming that Vernon had agreed to a 50 percent cut in royalties. Vernon received a similar telegram stating that because of high overhead the show would have to close unless the authors agreed to the cut and claiming that Ira had agreed to it. A 5 or 10 percent cut was not unusual, but 50 percent was catastrophic for those who relied on royalties for their livelihood. Because Vernon and Ira each thought the other had agreed to the cut, they fell for the deception and accepted the new terms.[48]

On October 21, Vernon wrote to Ira about the swindle, labeling Kaufman "not only an ass, a horse's ass but also a cheap bitch" but insisting that "this was not a usual example of Duke tantrums, as I have given this matter much thought." He wondered why Ira had accepted the cut, "because by standing pat we would have won the battle." He was outraged that he still received a cut in royalties even though the gross for the second week was over $28,000. Vernon apologized for his "Kaufmania," but had to present one more example of the man's ruthlessness. Will Irwin had four tunes in the show and was playing the piano at rehearsals to earn some extra money. Kaufman insisted that he rehearse for nothing, because he had given him a break by interpolating his songs. Irwin protested and was told he was an ungrateful son of a bitch and would never work for him again. Apparently, for Irwin there was little Vernon could do, but his lawyer persuaded Kaufman to end the royalty swindle under threat that all of Vernon's materials would be withdrawn from the show. Kaufman also agreed that the show would be billed "Music Mostly by Vernon Duke."[49]

The show closed in New York on December 19, but in January 1937 it went on the road to several cities in the Midwest and South. After a few weeks in Chicago, it arrived in Cleveland in April and in Washington, D.C., in May. Except for his high praise of the sketches featuring Bobby Clark and Fanny Brice, a reviewer for the local D.C. paper was less than sanguine: "Vernon Duke wrote the music of the 'Follies' and Ira Gershwin the lyrics. And any one aware of what he has been humming the last few months will find very little that is familiar to the musical score of the show." Beyond a few recognizable songs, "words and music are not up to previous 'Follies.'"[50] On November 11, Billie Burke canceled a performance in Greensboro, North Carolina, thus ending the road tour.[51] The show closed after 227 performances.[52]

Once his duties in the *Ziegfeld Follies* were completed, Ira wrote a few songs with Phil Charig, Vincent Youmans, Harry Warren, and others, but he was not sure he wanted to continue writing Broadway shows. He blamed the Great Depression for the sorry state of Broadway but also Hollywood for luring so many theater people to its wonderland. "Boy," he quipped on one occasion, "what the pix have done to the legit." Yet he too fell victim to its siren song, as did his brother, George.[53] The decline in the number of Broadway shows was in direct proportion to an increase in the number of movies produced after the advent of sound. Fewer shows meant fewer people were employed. And as the demand for movie musicals increased, increasing numbers of directors, choreographers, musicians, composers, and lyricists departed for Hollywood.

Ira and Duke would never again work together on a Broadway show, but they remained friends for life.[54] Their songs, moreover, would link them forever. Because it was customary for the sheet music of some of the songs of a revue or musical play to be sold in the lobby where the show was being staged, many attendees must have perused or bought copies. At the Winter Garden, customers had their choice of "Island in the West Indies," "Words without Music," "That Moment of Moments," and "I Can't Get Started." And once a song was published, performers were free to experiment with its rhythm, harmony, melody, lyric, and mood. At a recording studio on January 18, 1936, Hal Kemp's "sweet band" recorded two songs: "That Moment of Moments" with a fine arrangement and sensitive vocalization by Bob Allen and an up-tempo version of "I Can't Get Started," with Skinnay

"I CAN'T GET STARTED." VICTOR C28-7 36208. Author's Collection.

Ennis singing it as a rhythm song in the lighthearted, whimsical way it was presented in the *Follies*.[55]

This was just the beginning of the transformation of "I Can't Get Started." In February, John De Vries, sometime songwriter and friend of jazz musicians, bought the sheet music at a performance of the revue. He dashed off to the Famous Door on 52nd Street and turned the music over to members of a jazz band led by trumpeter Bunny Berigan. They and increasing numbers of jazz artists found something unique in the song, something more than a typical upbeat show tune. As demonstrated in Berigan's great solo, it had depth and poignancy. Within a decade of its publication, it had been recorded by numerous jazz musicians, including trumpeter Dizzy Gillespie, saxophonists Charlie Parker, Lester Young, and Ben Webster, clarinetist Artie Shaw, and pianists Teddy Wilson, Art Tatum, and Lennie Tristano. Jazz and pop vocalists also recorded the song, including Billie Holiday, Ginny Simms, Kay Starr, and Lee Wiley.[56]

At the same time Duke was writing songs, Dukelsky's ballet *Jardin Public* opened at the Covent Garden in London to mixed reviews. In July 1935 a critic wrote that the composer "has provided a descriptive score in accordance with the precepts of smart modernism. His contemporary polytonal harmonies are not obtrusively acrid, and as he co-operated with M. Léonide Massine in adapting the scenario from a fragment of Andre Gide's 'Faux Monnayers,' the music ably fits the action."[57] Another reviewer agreed: "The alternating humour and pain of Dukelsky's music are integral with the action."[58] Other critics were not so sanguine: "Perhaps the exceptional cacophony and general silliness of the music is apt to prejudice one against what virtue there may be in the choreography," wrote one.[59] The worst notice claimed, "It is not that melody is eschewed and thematic material of value entirely absent; this music lacks almost everything that is desirable in any type of ballet."[60]

Consequently, choreographer Léonide Massine and Colonel Wassili de Basil, director of Ballets Russes de Monte Carlo, urged Dukelsky to eliminate some of the harsh and strident sounds and replace them with lush tunes. Insisting that *"Jardin* was orchestrated more dexterously than the Diaghilev *Zephyr,"* Vladimir nevertheless admitted that "the orchestration failed to adequately underline and intensify the musical thought." He sought the advice of George Gershwin, who suggested a session or two with Joseph Schillinger, who at the time had revolutionized the art of composition teaching and the study of orchestration.[61]

Schillinger and Dukelsky went through the scores of a cantata and *Jardin Public*, page by page: "Schillinger sought to determine, first of all, whether the musical thought was 'orchestrable'; the next step was to hear a passage on the piano and ascertain that the orchestration interpreted the music properly.... Both works were given a new orchestral dress.... Were it not for Joseph Schillinger, I would still be faced with: 'What happened to your music? It sounded so well on the piano!'" The improved ballet opened at the New York Metropolitan Opera House in April 1936. George Gershwin was in the audience as were critics. One noted, "The score is sound ballet composition, and there are attractive melodies in it." Another called it "fatuous."[62]

In the spring of 1936, de Basil and his troupe, Massine, and Dukelsky sailed for Europe. Vladimir was to assist in the final changes of *Jardin Public* before it opened in Barcelona and reopened London. What Vladimir remembered of Spain was that he gained weight and that the orchestra entered a sequence at the wrong time. He gained more weight in Paris but also found the time to arrange some of John Field's piano pieces into ballet music.[63] Field was an Irishman who lived in Russia during the early nineteenth century and was known as the "Irish Chopin." In his adaptation, Dukelsky added some introductions and counterpoint and called it "Field Day." This may be the first indication of what would be a growing interest in recovering the works of forgotten composers. Before leaving the States, he had copied by hand Field's Variation on a Russian Theme in A Minor, which contains harmonic peculiarities, strange modifications, construction irregularities, and the whole tone scale.[64]

The work of the moment, however, was *Jardin Public*, which in June reopened at Covent Garden. It was an improvement over the first version, concluded a critic, and Dukelsky "provided a descriptive score in accordance with the precepts of the modern musical atonalists, but his music is not obtrusively acrid, and in the quieter moments it is particularly effective."[65] Three other commentators stated the opposite. It was composed of "such poor material that patching has only made it seem worse," wrote one. "And Dukelsky's music, extremely modern and extremely ugly, has no redeeming feature at all, not even in the scoring."[66] Another said, "I like it as little as I liked the old." The third complained, "The music of M. Dukelsky is extremely poor stuff, with a sense of effort about it from the first bar to the last. Only too obvious the effort is simply to be odd, to produce something so cacophonous that it will be talked about, even if in the least complimentary terms."[67]

In Paris things looked up. He was happy to see Boris Kochno, who now was collecting jazz records and who was impressed with Dukelsky playing jazz. Vladimir was invited to dinner parties where he played and socialites sang while seated with him at the piano. He became reacquainted with Serge Lifar, who had danced in *Zephyr and Flora*, and Uncle Ilya, whom he had not seen since Constantinople. Dukelsky had been sending him money for two years.[68]

It was Duke, however, who returned to the United States. When the SS *Normandie* docked in New York in mid-1936, he was hardly ashore when his arrival was announced in the *Boston Herald*: "The active Vernon Duke—who hides under the name of Vladimir Dukelsky when he wishes to write serious music, returned from Europe a few days ago."⁶⁹ Late that year Duke and lyricist Ted Fetter wrote some of the songs for *The Show Is On,* directed by Vincente Minnelli. Songs by the Gershwins, Rodgers and Hart, Hoagy Carmichael, and others were also included. The great jazz trumpet player Bunny Berigan was to have a role.⁷⁰ The opening at the Shubert Theater produced a positive review from the *Boston Herald*: "For 'The Show Is On' Mr. Duke has written 'What Has He Got?' a catchy song paying tribute to the Fred Astaire–Ginger Rogers craze; the music for 'Cassanova'—both the songs done by Gracie Barrie and the ballet music; a pleasant sentimental ballad, 'Now,' sung by Miss Barrie and danced by Paul Haakon and the chorus; 'Sway Britannia,' a comic song for Bert Lahr; the 'Epilogue' for the entire company, and the score of 'Tragedian.'"⁷¹

The latter, subtitled *A Ballet of the Barnstormers,* Duke called "a curious bit of Americana." Because of the complexity and daring of the music, it was signed Vladimir Dukelsky, but "Ironically, the one Dukelsky interpolation was bounced out of the show. Another casualty, a tragic one, was the failure of the late Bunny Berigan (to whom I owe the ultimate success of 'I Can't Get Started') to put his 'Jam Session' finale across. It just didn't work in the theater."⁷² The revue was the last one Minnelli would direct on Broadway. He soon departed for Hollywood to make a movie.⁷³

After its opening, Duke boarded the SS *Kungsholm* for a twenty-eight-day cruise of the West Indies. He went alone and wanted to remain alone but was introduced to a "rather mousy, provincial matron, obviously bent on some fancy hell raising." He deeply regretted spending the night with her, because she would not leave him alone when he disembarked at St. Thomas, St. Lucia, Jamaica, and other islands. At Trinidad, Duke got drunk with some Yale men, who understanding his predicament provided him with a sweater with a "Y" on it and a bandage over one eye. Thus disguised, he and his new friends evaded the matron and "indulged in some fairly dangerous escapades."⁷⁴

Back in New York, Duke wrote to Ira about the possibility of finding work in Hollywood. Ira's response was to the point: "It's a bad place to take a gamble on unless they definitely want you. . . . The fact that you are in New York is worth 25 to 50% more on your price when they get around to you. And if your next show is a hit there will be plenty of offers. And don't send

IRA GERSHWIN AND VERNON DUKE, BEVERLY HILLS, 1937.
From Duke, *Passport to Paris*. Reproduced with permission from Kay Duke Ingalls.

songs on approval. Hold out." Ira mentioned that Jerome Kern was ill but on the road to recovery, and "All of us are well, Lee, George, Moss."[75] On July 11, 1937, however, George Gershwin died at the age of thirty-eight from a brain tumor. The musical community was shocked.[76]

After attending George's funeral in New York, Ira returned to Los Angeles to work on the music George was preparing for *The Goldwyn Follies*, an early Technicolor film. Needing help on the movie, Ira contacted Duke.[77] And soon after arriving, he witnessed the power of Samuel Goldwyn. About to go into production was a ballet, *An American in Paris*, which George Balanchine, making his film debut, and cinematographer Gregg Toland had prepared. Sets and costumes were ready, the shooting schedule was set, camera angles were prepared, and the choreography was designed. But Samuel Goldwyn found everything too arty, and the ballet was canceled.[78]

The importance of Duke in finishing the film was reported in the *New York Times*. Out of the voluminous George Gershwin files, he "salvaged the tune for another *Follies* song, 'Love Walked In' which he arranged and harmonized; two other songs, 'I Was Doing All Right,' and 'Our Love Is Here to Stay,' had refrains but no verses; Duke supplied these, and Ira Gershwin, of course, did all the lyrics." The *Times* noted, "The music for two ballets, 'Romeo and Juliet,' . . . and 'Water Nymph,' were especially composed by Duke to fit the steps executed by Ballanchine [sic] and are (historical note) the first ballets expressively created for the screen."[79] The ballets cost about $100,000 each to produce.[80]

To differentiate between the two families in *Romeo and Juliet*, Dukelsky wrote for the Capulets and Duke for Montagues. The Capulets dance *en pointe* to a classical refrain. The Montagues tap dance to a jazz beat. At one moment a ballerina rushes a tap dancer and knocks her over, but the two sides reconcile, and the two dancing styles fuse.[81] Looking back on the ballet, Duke, in the vernacular of his time, labeled the Montagues "jazz addicts" and the Capulets as "longhairs." Romeo was a "hepcat" and "Juliet was distinctly on the 'square' side." Duke, however, was not pleased with Goldwyn's drastic editing, which nearly obliterated the point of the ballet.[82]

He and Goldwyn did share a love for *Water Nymph*. The ballet came the closest to those created by Balanchine for Diaghilev, and the score by Dukelsky could easily have been written in the 1920s or early 1930s. The choreography, designed for Vera Zorina, William Dollar, and members of Balanchine's American ballet company, clearly exhibited the influence of modern dance.[83] The ballet, recalled Duke, "with wonderful sets by Richard Day and Zorina's superman beauty, not to forget the pretty music, was a 100 per cent success. . . . The sixty-piece orchestra, admirably conducted by Alfred Newman, was a help, too."[84]

Thanks to the $9,000 earned from *The Goldwyn Follies*, the movie composer "hit on the idea of letting the fairly solvent Duke pay for Dukelsky, the pauper," and put some of his "Goldwyn eggs in the *St. Petersburg* basket," a cantata begun in 1932.[85] In early January 1938, the *New York Times* announced that a new work would be offered by Vladimir Dukelsky, better known as Vernon Duke: "But if Jekyll Duke has his revues, Hyde Dukelsky has had his big and serious scores played by the Boston and Chicago orchestras."[86] On January 12, *The End of St. Petersburg* finally had its premiere at Carnegie Hall. Unfortunately for Dukelsky, it was presented with *The Mass of Life* by Frederick Delius, clearly the favorite of Olin Downes of the *New York Times*: "Mr. Dukelsky's score is not of the same value, but it received a long and vigorous applause" and the conductor "repeatedly brought the composer on stage with him to bow acknowledgements." Downes found his style "peppery" and "ultra-modern" and wondered whether classical music was "really native with the composer or whether, turning from Broadway to the august precincts of Carnegie Hall, he felt it incumbent upon him to impress the wiseacres and write in terms of the epoch of Schoenberg and Stravinsky."[87]

Three other critics compared the composer with the tunesmith. Oscar Thompson wrote: "The music is glib and glacial . . . though ingeniously contrived. . . . Vernon Duke is nowhere in evidence in this music. Perhaps it would have had more sympathy and spontaneity if he had not been quite so rigorously excluded."[88] To Samuel Chotzinoff, "Mr. Dukelsky's alter ego, known as Vernon Duke, is much more expert in setting words to music. Mr. Duke's harmonies too are happier than Mr. Dukelsky's. Notwithstanding the modernism, the climaxes, the skillful orchestration of 'The End of St. Petersburg,' I find the same composer's lowdown ditty 'April in Paris' a more genuine product."[89]

Elliott Carter insisted that "Dukelsky's popular songs have absolutely no connection with his original and imaginative serious music in either style or content. In this he is linear and dissonant and frequently violently rhythmic, fond of a dry, unresonant orchestration. . . . The 'End of St Petersburg' contains some of the best music by this composer since he wrote his exquisite 'Zephyr and Flora' for Diaghilev."[90]

Dukelsky was disappointed that Prokofiev, who had smuggled the work into the Soviet Union, was not present.[91] But in a January 14 letter, Prokofiev congratulated him on his other success, although it was "in the realm of prostitution," perhaps a reference to his Hollywood achievements. He mentioned that *Leningrad*, the Soviet title of *The End of St. Petersburg*, could not be performed in Russia because only the classics were allowed to be played. He and his wife would arrive in New York in February.[92]

While in the United States, Prokofiev turned down an offer from a Hollywood music studio at $2,500 a week. He wanted to be with his music and children in Moscow, but he also wanted to return with things unavailable in the Soviet Union. In his autobiography, Duke poked fun at his longtime friend and critic: "The list was imposing, and we went to Macy's department store, another sample of capitalist bait designed by the lackeys of Wall Street to be swallowed by oppressed workers. Although he wouldn't admit it, Serge enjoyed himself hugely in the store—he loved gadgets and trinkets of every description." His departure to the Soviet Union separated the two men for the rest of their lives: "Thus, in the course of one fleeting year, I lost my two best friends in music: George Gershwin, Duke's creator, and Sergei Prokofiev, Dukelsky's protector."[93]

Duke was soon to experience another loss, this one professional rather than personal. He got the opportunity to write the music for the stage version of *Serena Blandish*, adapted by S. N. Behrman. According to Duke, "Berry, as everyone called him, said that I was the one right man for the job, speaking two musical languages as I did and possessing the necessary 'cosmopolitan' outlook." The producer, however, reneged, citing previous commitments and the stage version never got off the ground. Duke admitted in his autobiography that "*Serena* turned out to be the first of my long list of unproduced musicals." Vincente Minnelli, however, made plans to make a movie of the work, and according to the *New York Times*, Duke was to write the music. Minnelli hired Sam Harris to produce with him. Playwright S. J. Perelman was to write a "colored" version that would star Maxine Sullivan, Ethel Waters, and Cab Calloway. But Cole Porter, not Duke, was to compose the music.[94]

In a letter to Ira Gershwin, Duke offered some of the details of the fiasco: "Vincente was caught in so many lies that he actually apologized profusely for behaving so badly.... Cole Porter has declined to do the score and Perelman, upon taking the next train back to Hollywood, announced that he could now go back cheerfully to hating the colored race which he had done previous to the 'Serena' entanglement.... My score will, therefore, be switched to something less nebulous and in the near future I hope." He closed his letter by asking Ira to tell Ginger Rogers that he was "entertaining her mother to the best of my ability and that we've become very friendly."[95]

Later in the year, Duke again wrote to Ira. Concerned about his lack of activity as a Broadway lyricist, Duke told him he was "too much of an admirer of your lyrical and other gifts not to get worried about your inactivity." He concluded his letter by emphasizing "that my one dream is to do another show with you; my other dream is to do another show with you. Am I on the black list or can I go on living in hope? Balanchine and I both pray for your return and for a grand re-union."[96] Ira, however, was committed to working on a film biography of his brother. "Not a studio in town but was after me for the life of George," he mentioned in his response. "First one, then the other, but at no time none. At Metro contracts were being prepared, money no object, when the war scare jumbled things up and suddenly the studios went cautious and presto! musicals disappeared from the face of the earth. So here I was stuck with a two year lease in this artificial, paper-moonish spot, of which, by the way, I'm very fond."[97]

Dukelsky went back to work and composed *Dédicaces* for piano, orchestra, and soprano obbligato. The Boston Symphony introduced the work in Boston in December 1938 and performed it in January at Carnegie Hall. The concert also featured Haydn's Symphony in B-flat, no. 102 and Tchaikovsky's Fourth Symphony, but the long review in the *New York Times* was largely devoted to Dukelsky's work. Based on a French poem by Guillaume Apollinaire, the composition is in three movements ("To the City," "To the Country," and "To the Sea") in which the piano plays as important a part as if in a concerto for the instrument. Pianist Jesús María Sanromá "gave a brilliant reading of the frantically difficult piano part, which reached its climax in a vehement cadenza at the start of 'To the Sea.'" Soprano Marguerite Porter "undoubtedly sang her music correctly, but it was so discordantly written, against a thin, bizarre accompaniment, that the true pitch was a matter of conjecture." Although the composition was "not destined for posterity, it displayed Mr. Dukelsky's true command of orchestral writing and his considerable, if misdirected, talents as a creator."[98]

In an article titled "A Dual Personality in Music," critic Daniel I. McNamara pointed out:

> Performances of symphony works usually are costly, not profitable, to the composer. Duke meets such situations with income from his popular music. Vladimir Dukelsky's expenses in connection with the Boston Symphony Orchestra's performances of his widely acclaimed "Dedicaces" in Boston and New York during the holiday season were met by Vernon Duke's profits from such songs as "April in Paris,"

"This Is Romance," "I Can't Get Started," "What Is There to Say?," "I Like the Likes of You," and many others.[99]

On March 7, 1939, the well-off Vladimir Dukelsky became an American citizen and Vernon Duke became his official name.[100] With his command of English and American vernacular and his knowledge of American music and institutions, he probably became as American as any first-generation immigrant possibly could. That he continued to sign his classical pieces as Dukelsky, however, indicates that he remained just as proud of his Russian heritage as he was of his American citizenship.

Later that year the American was stricken with appendicitis and spent several days in a hospital in Brooklyn, but soon he was off to Washington, D.C., to work on *A Vagabond Hero*. It closed in its pre-Broadway tryout and perhaps is best remembered for Duke's "I Cling to You."[101] Dukelsky fared better in early 1940 when his and Rebecca Clarke's works were performed at the New York Public Library to an enthusiastic and capacity audience. The performers included pianists Richard Singer, Zehman Goodman, and Kurt Engle; violinists Walter Eisenberg and Elsie Stein; cellists Jesse Forstot and Willi Gara; and sopranos Elizabeth Duehren and Meg Mundy. Mundy sang nine songs by Dukelsky, who was at the piano, and a piano trio performed a theme and seven variations also by him.[102]

Although Dukelsky was progressing creatively, Duke was foundering romantically. In late 1939, inspired by the marriage of George Balanchine and Vera Zorina and implored by his mother, Anna, to settle down, Duke had proposed to Joan, the teenager he had met on Fire Island and now in college. Joan accepted but on the condition she finish college first. To Anna, however, this was a bad choice, correctly pointing out that Joan was too young and emotionally unstable. Duke believed that marriage would change both of them for the better. Later, Joan wrote to Vernon that she did not think she would make a good wife but would marry him all the same. The engagement ended, and a few months later Joan married a lawyer. To cope with his loss, Duke admitted to inventing "sillier and sillier distractions," including a party given by one Mr. Vernon Duke to meet one Mr. Vladimir Dukelsky. Most of his guests were unaware of Dukelsky, which hurt the host's pride. The few ignorant of Duke caught on fast when he played some boogie-woogie.[103]

HILDEGARDE, VERNON DUKE, AND LEO KAHN. *Decca Presents Hildegarde in an Album of Songs by Vernon Duke*, 1940. Author's Collection.

Although the timing could have been better, about this time Duke received a letter from Sergei Prokofiev, written on April 5, 1940, mentioning he had heard that Duke was doing well and wondered what he had composed "in the way of music" or "in the way of tra-la-la? Is the tra-la-la still paying well? Have you gotten married, or are you still on the prowl for des petites demoiselles?"[104]

Whether the ballet *Raffles* Duke composed for a show called *Keep off the Grass* qualifies as "tra-la-la" music is debatable. But he wrote the work in three days, and Balanchine choreographed it for dancer Ray Bolger. John Anderson mentioned that "Mr. Bolger performs his astonishing footwork with the usual gangling precision, and is at his best in a 'Raffles' number, with music by Vernon Duke." It was Dukelsky, however, who later composed a series of what he called "fruity piano pieces," each glorifying an American city. He considered "New York Nocturne" the best of the lot. The Charlie Barnet jazz orchestra recorded the song.[105]

Also in 1940, Duke teamed up with cabaret singer Hildegarde and her pianist Leo Kahn. Hildegarde's glamour and reputation (she had numerous romances and never married) may have entered into Duke's decision to record with her. He called her "a tantalizing wholesome Milwaukee 'bachfisch'" in his autobiography. The two pianists accompanied the "bachfisch" on "April in Paris," "I Can't Get Started," "Suddenly," "What Is There to Say," "I Cling to You," and "Now," the most sensitive rendition of the lot. Duke was happy with the result: "It turned out a good album (Decca)—Dave Kapp supervising shrewdly, Hildegarde singing continentally and Leo and I playing 'a lot of piano.'"[106] According to one critic, Duke had "composed some songs that have reached the pinnacle of popular fame" and that Hildegarde "takes some of his selections and makes them into one of Decca's most pleasing sets."[107] Whether she and Duke became romantically involved is not known, but later in the year Walter Winchell noted that Duke's present "Juliet" was one Frances Ronald.[108]

The recording, however, was only part of a very exciting 1940. Although Duke and Al Stillman wrote the entire score for *It Happened on Ice*, only two of their songs remained when the show opened— "Long Ago" and "Don't Blow That Horn, Gabriel."[109] Far more successful was a show originally called *Little Joe*. The libretto, written by Lynn Root about African Americans, passed through several hands before reaching Duke, who admired the work but felt insufficiently knowledgeable about the subject matter to write the music. Duke claimed, however, that his "colored" maid convinced him that he could, indeed, write the score, and soon after joined the production team.[110] Duke pleaded with Ira Gershwin to join him, noting that the libretto is "utterly fascinating" and claiming to have written a "stupendous score," when in fact he had written only a few songs.[111] Ira had read and liked *Little Joe* and thought it had a good chance to succeed, but he was committed to another play. He told Vernon that Johnny Mercer or Yip Harburg would be excellent choices.[112] The producers considered Harburg, but he had no interest in the project. Harburg acknowledged that Duke "couldn't write bad music, but he was a concert composer. . . . His domain was writing these smart, charming, sophisticated songs. When he brought the show to me and wanted me to do it with him on Broadway, I felt he was wrong for the music and I turned it down. And he got mad at me and never talked to me again for a long time."[113]

Duke, however, got to collaborate with an outstanding lyricist, John Latouche. The composer of the enormously popular "Ballad for Americans," Latouche, as explained in the *Boston Herald*, was "a poet who loves people, hates the traditional 'ivory tower' of poets, breaks all the rules about how poetry should be written, believes heart and soul that it should express the great masses of people in our democracy. He believes with equal passion in democracy itself and in America." He was also short, good looking, intense, effervescent, twenty-five, married, and an excellent cook. Duke was described as "tall, handsome, sophisticated, suave, charming of manner, imperturbable, unmarried, and thirty-six." The two men shared a love of the theater and good food. They often met to produce excellent cuisine. The newspaper even published two of their recipes, "Patlijan Karne Yaruk" and "Yablquchni."[114]

Because Latouche was a southerner from Richmond, Virginia, he, George Balanchine, costume designer Boris Aronson, and Duke headed south to absorb African American culture. After a brief stay in Richmond, Vernon and John ventured to Virginia Beach "to imbibe the 'atmosphere,'" as Duke put it, "although there wasn't much to imbibe... except highballs." Becoming "saturated with southern talk and Negro spirituals," they decided to ignore "pedantic authenticity" and write their own kind of "colored songs." They returned to New York with a rough draft of the score.[115] Their songs included "Cabin in the Sky," "Honey in the Honeycomb," "Do What You Wanna Do," "Love Turned the Light Out," and "My Old Virginia Home."[116]

If the songs were not "authentic," Balanchine sought to make the dances reflect at least in part the people being portrayed. He hired Katherine Dunham and her African American dance troupe. As a graduate student, Dunham studied anthropology at the University of Chicago and conducted fieldwork in the Caribbean. Later she studied both classical and modern dance and developed a style that combined African, Afro-Caribbean, and Latin American dance with that of black Americans.[117] Dunham recalled working with Balanchine, who initially insisted that he was the choreographer: "But watching us in our own classes and training and the company's use of their bodies, he finally felt that we should work together, which we did."[118] He and Dunham created five ballets, three of them featuring her troupe: *Egyptian Ballet, Lazy Steps,* and *Boogy Woogy*.[119]

ADVERTISEMENT FOR THE BROADWAY PRODUCTION OF *CABIN IN THE SKY*.
Brooklyn Daily Eagle, October 31, 1940.

Her dancers executed unconventional movements in ways that advanced the narrative of the story, but when some of the white producers sought to add tap dancing to the show—insisting that is what the audience would expect of an all-black show—Balanchine, Duke, and Aronson convinced them otherwise.[120] Duke probably oversaw the productions of the ballets in which Domenico Savino, Charles Cooke, Joseph Livingston, and Nathan Van Cleve created the orchestrations. At times, a Haitian and two Cuban drummers augmented the arrangements. Max Meth conducted the orchestra.[121] Although his songs may have been "conventional," the music Duke wrote for the ballets had to conform to the dancers' rhythms and the stories they told.

Duke, Latouche, and others were given the task of persuading Ethel Waters to join the cast. After her success in *Mamba's Daughters* of the preceding season, she wanted to remain in dramatic roles. Although they "sold that wonderful woman on our play," recalled Duke, she was widely known to be difficult to work with. Duke claimed that he got on her good side by kissing her hand in lieu of "good morning" and "be seeing you."[122] In fact, with Waters, Duke met his match. She insisted on changes in the libretto, added lines to her dialogue, vetoed the casting of a famous actor, and got a Duke song replaced.[123] Dunham recalled that "Balanchine and Vernon Duke wanted to open the show with the black choir singing a Russian dirge. I think it would have been wonderful. Ethel Waters hit the ceiling." It was replaced with a spiritual.[124] With its name changed to *Cabin in the Sky*, the show was about to open on Broadway when cast and crew concluded that something was missing. Waters needed a song to uplift the spirits of the character she was playing, so Duke dug up an old song he had written with Ted Fetter called "Fooling Around with Love." The title was changed to "Taking a Chance on Love," and Latouche reworked the lyric.[125]

"TAKING A CHANCE ON LOVE," MILLER MUSIC, INC., 1940. Author's Collection.

"PRESENTING THE SONGS OF VERNON DUKE AND JOHN LATOUCHE." Miller Music, Inc., 1940. Author's Collection.

A correspondent described the rehearsals:

Pit a threesome of turbulent Russians against a tempestuous cast of Negro players from Harlem and what have you got? Well, in this instance . . . the result is a lingual ruckus approaching bedlam. At least half a dozen times at each rehearsal of Cabin in the Sky, Ethel Waters, Todd Duncan, Rex Ingram, J. Rosamund Johnson, Katherine Dunham and her dancers have paused in puzzlement while the argumentative trio of Muscovites disputed a difference of opinion in their native tongue. An articulate combination, when George Balanchine, who is staging the production, Vernon Duke (née Vladimir Dukelsky), who wrote the music, and Boris Aronson, who designed the scenery, air their respective views. The Russian vowels and consonants fly as thick as borscht.[126]

The "Muscovites" finally got it right. As recalled by Duke, "After the opening, having kissed every member of the cast, cried with Ethel and slapped Max Meth, the frenzied conductor, on the back a dozen of times, Balanchine, Zorina and I repaired to '21' and sat in a happy haze, drinking Pommery Greno of the right year, to be joined at 2:30 A.M. by Vinton, his eyes shining, who waved the ecstatic Brooks Atkinson's review."[127]

"Perhaps 'Cabin in the Sky' could be better than it is," he wrote, "but this correspondent cannot imagine how. For the musical fantasy . . . is original and joyous in an imaginative vein that suits the theatre's special genius. Lynn Root began it by writing an extraordinarily fresh book. . . . For it would be difficult to prove that the book is happier in style than George Balanchine's lyrical direction or the excellent performance by a singularly well-chosen Negro cast." Atkinson had "never heard a song better sung than 'Taking a Chance on Love.'" Ethel Waters "stood that song on its head last evening and ought to receive a Congressional medal by way of reward."[128] Much of the success of the song—indeed, all the songs—must be attributed to John Latouche, insisted Ira Wolfert: "Mr. Duke taught us something about popular composers we never knew before—the lyric writer is important. . . . Mr. Duke, a top-ranking composer for many years, lost his touch completely when he parted company with his lyric writer [Ira Gershwin]. He tried a number of others, but nothing happened until he found Mr. Latouche."[129]

Not all the reviews were positive. Left-leaning publications complained about the stereotyping, Ralph Warner of the *Daily Worker* being the most vociferous: "Truly the slave holders love to watch their own conception of the Negro come to life." But Warner, aware that Latouche was a leftist, pointed out that his lyrics "do not suffer from this fault. . . . He has written several excellent sets of words to the less than exciting music of Vernon Duke." Warner probably knew that Duke was an anticommunist. Alvah Bessie of the *New Masses* told his readers that the show was "the usual Broadway chauvinism and restates the usual assumption that Negroes are charming clowns whose main interests in life are sex, religion, gambling, and personal ostentation in clothes." Ironically, the black press was generally pleased with the show. It ran for only 156 performances, but Miller Music published ten of its songs and Waters recorded four of them.[130] Duke proudly noted that the songs were "authentic, immediate hits—something that never happened to me before or since *Cabin*."[131]

DUKE SERVES HIS COUNTRY
NEW YORK AND PALM BEACH, 1940–1945

While Vernon Duke, proud resident of the New World, was composing some of his best songs, the Old World of Vladimir Dukelsky was falling apart. In 1936 the Spanish Civil War broke out. In 1939 Germany attacked Poland, and the Soviet Union invaded Finland. Great Britain and France declared war on Germany, and France fell to Germany the following year. Through newspapers and the radio, Duke, like most Americans, was well aware of the monumental events taking place in Europe, and probably, like most Americans, he was adamant that the United States should remain neutral. But as the United States began to shift to a war economy, the Great Depression wound down, and in 1940 Congress passed the Lend Lease Act, which was implemented early the following year. It shipped supplies and material to China, the Soviet Union, and Great Britain.[1]

As a former resident of London, Duke was eager to provide whatever assistance he could to Great Britain. On August 6, 1940, he, George Balanchine, Vera Zorina, and Anton Dolin (the dancer from *Zephyr and Flora*) presented "Pas De Deux—Blues" at the Winter Garden as part of an All Star Dance Gala for the British War Relief.[2] Duke and Balanchine played pianos, and Balanchine choreographed a dance for Zorina and Dolin.[3] John Latouche, too, was concerned about the war, and with the assistance of Duke and Balanchine he wrote "Fog," a song-poem, as a melodrama for speaker and musical accompaniment. "Fog" referred to the London fog that often shielded the city from German bombers. On February 22, 1941, at the Carnival for Britain, it was presented at Radio City Music Hall as a vehicle for Zorina. The money raised also went to the British War Relief. In April, English actress Gertrude Lawrence recited the work with Duke at the piano on the radio program *Friendship Bridge to England*.[4]

Despite the war, Duke and Latouche went about their everyday Broadway business and were, according to Robert Francis, "the hottest team to hit Tin Pan Alley since Rodgers and Hart." They were also "the wildest pair of opposites ever to be attached to each other."[5] Even their clothing drew comments. "Duke is a fashion plate," noted George Ross, but Latouche "wears clothes in casual style." When Duke described him "as having the appearance of an unmade bed," John retorted, "You look like a beautiful job of embalming."[6]

He and Latouche were in such great demand, recalled Duke, that they "could now write their own tickets. We wrote two of them which was a mistake—although the first of the two was nearly a winner."[7] *Banjo Eyes*, starring Eddie Cantor and based on the comedy *Three Men on a Horse* by George Abbott and John Cecil Holm, dealt with a greeting card poet who knew more about horses than was good for him. After an absence of ten years, Cantor wanted to return to the Broadway stage and initially sought Rodgers and Hart to write the score. Their lack of interest resulted in an August hiring of Duke and Latouche. They had only two months to write the music before rehearsals began. Once the libretto had been completed, conferences were held in Cantor's suite in Essex House.[8]

Latouche, however, often failed to attend, prompting Duke and a friend to conduct on one occasion a search that ended at the Stanton Griffs estate in New Canaan. Latouche persuaded the searchers to remain overnight, and in the morning Duke and Latouche went to work. As recalled by Duke, "Johnny, pouting disagreeably, produced a pad and a pencil and we began wrestling with a rhumba Cantor intended to sing to one of the race horses in the play. I played a chorus; Johnny made a face. I tried another; he shook his head disdainfully." The third rhumba resulted in Latouche suggesting that things would be better if Duke had less agility and more ability. A fracas followed, but "peace was restored and we all went back to New York with a fourth and final rhumba for Eddie Cantor's horse."[9]

The show opened at the Shubert Theater in New Haven on November 7, 1941, to a capacity crowd.[10] It featured ten songs by Duke and Latouche. After performances in Boston and Philadelphia, it began a New York run on December 25 at the Hollywood Theatre, but four of their songs were dropped.[11] It received a positive review from Brooks Atkinson: "As a musical comedy 'Banjo Eyes' has all the appurtenances of a big, noisy show. . . . Vernon Duke has written a vibrant score of metallic music and John Latouche has done some witty handsprings for lyrics." He found especially entertaining "I'll Take the City" and "We're Having a Baby, My Baby and I," with the lyric by Harold Adamson.[12] Duke was particularly pleased with "A Nickel to My Name."[13] The latter two songs would outlast the show, which closed on April 12, 1941, after 126 performances.[14]

The other show Duke and Latouche had been simultaneously working on, *The Lady Comes Across*, initially starred British actress Jessie Matthews, with whom Duke toured the town.[15] It premiered in New Haven on December 11, 1941, just four days after Japan attacked the U.S. naval base at Pearl Harbor, Hawaii.[16] The show, however, must go on, and on it went long after dancer Ray Bolger had withdrawn and Joe E. Lewis and Mischa Auer had joined the cast.[17] Matthews vividly remembered the chaos in the production:

> Most musicals have to be beaten into shape. *The Lady Comes Across* was very nearly battered to death. The script had to be changed and they'd left it a little late. Rehearsals had started. In the original script I was cast as an English girl who gets mixed up in a spy ring. Each morning new pages of dialogue were handed to me, and we looked to see who was left in and who'd been cut out. Spies came and spies went, actors were sacked and scenes deleted. This does work in film-land, but in the theatre constant changing spells disaster. I was still a spy-catcher, I still had to master the odd sentence in French, German, and Swedish, but I hadn't a clue whom I was supposed to catch.
>
> Organization was non-existent. The book of the play was hacked to pieces and none of the joins met. We got through three directors and two producers before the show limped off to Boston for its try-out.[18]

Some of the critics who saw the show at the Shubert Theater thought its premise had promise, but the story became increasingly dull as the music advanced and the plot only served to feature the songs. After a ten-day run, it was on to New York.[19] On January 9, 1942, three days before it opened,

Matthews disappeared and was replaced by Evelyn Wyckoff. Her courageous efforts could not prevent a highly negative review by Brooks Atkinson:

> As the men of letters for the occasion, Fred Thompson and Dawn Powell have scribbled off a highly superfluous book about a dream and a spy hunt. Vernon Duke and John La Touche [sic], who have been beating a steady retreat all season from their gifted music and lyrics for "Cabin in the Sky" last year, have turned out their most uninspired score to date. And George Balanchine, the choreographist, has done something special in the way of draining the joy out of musical stage dancing.[20]

Duke thought the play was full of good things, in particular Balanchine's choreography of "Tango" and "Polka" and the dancing of Gower Champion and Jeannie Tyler in "Lady." He also was fond of "Summer Is A-Comin' In" and "This Is Where I Came In," the latter "sung by siren-voiced, callipygous Wynne Murray," as Duke put it.[21]

After the opening, Duke and Balanchine "took a bevy of dancing beauties" to a Russian nightclub and proceeded to drown their "fears in quantities of vodka, accompanied by caviar, knife-throwing Caucasian sexagenarians, and a faded blond in a *kokoshnik*, left over from *Chauve Souris*, who sang chorus after chorus of 'Kirpitchiki,' the saddest post-Revolution Russian song written. I heartily recommend it to those who cry with difficulty; this song is a powerful tear-jerker. George and I wept on each other's shoulders between encores."[22] Weeping must have continued when the show closed after three performances and lost $80,000.[23] But the success of one song may have softened the blow. In early January, a newspaper announced that on the thirtieth Duke would be playing "A Nickel to My Name" at President Roosevelt's birthday ball at the Waldorf-Astoria.[24] By this time, Jan Savitt, Benny Goodman, and Bob Chester had recorded the song, making it a best seller.[25]

Duke then headed south, his departure prompting a newspaper to whimsically announce that the composer of "A Nickel to My Name" had recently left for Florida with eight trunks.[26] The United States had now entered World War II, and at Palm Beach Duke attended charity balls and war benefits. Even though there was not much war talk, "a number of 'eligible' young men appeared in spiffy uniforms at dinner parties and civilians began wearing an apologetic look, especially if they were of draft age."²⁷ Duke found the time to work on a violin concerto that was to be performed by Ruth Posselt in Boston sometime in the future.²⁸

He wrote to his mother about buying a house for her near Sarasota, where the air would be better for her asthma. She, however, had no intention of leaving her new apartment in the East Thirties. When she greeted him on his return from Florida, Duke was shocked: "She had always looked younger than her years, had a healthy color and a sturdy frame. I now beheld a gray-haired, emaciated woman, unmistakably sixty, her wonderfully kind eyes burning feverishly in the pale, haggard face." She died a short time later.²⁹

"Her memory will sing in my heart as long as it beats," Duke wrote in his autobiography. "And it's the small, everyday things I'll always remember—the way she started every sentence when speaking English with 'so that,' for which Alex and I chided her unmercifully, her artless admonitions to 'listen to me while I'm still here,' her refusal to indulge in even the smallest luxuries, her selfless and unreasoning love for her sons and her intense suffering at our slightest setbacks—these are the things that tug at my throat and will never leave me."³⁰

Another loss was pending. On June 22, 1941, Germany had invaded Russia, and Duke, like all expatriate Russians, hoped simultaneously for a German defeat and the end of Joseph Stalin:

> Most of us, especially those with some post-Revolutionary experience, knew how Utopian such wishful thinking was, but there existed another possibility, stemming from the new Russo-American friendship, which was based, of course, on our "all-out" help, without which the land of my birth would undeniably have been crushed. We all felt that with a closer *rapprochement* between the two countries, the Russians would eventually regain their freedom and a few of the civil liberties unheard of alike in Soviet Fairyland and Hitler's Playground.³¹

There was always music. Sometime in 1941 or 1942, he composed *April in Paris Fantasy* for clarinet and orchestra. With Ralph McLane on clarinet and John Green conducting the orchestra, it was broadcast over the radio in 1942. "Now you all know the tuneful songs written by Vernon Duke," the announcer proclaimed:

"April in Paris" from *Walk a Little Faster* is one of his melodies. And that song has won an enduring place in the field of modern music. Yet how many can place the name Vladimir Dukelsky? Well, they are one and the same person. . . . Under his real name of Dukelsky, Vladimir has written many thoughtful works before. He commands the genuine respect of musicians everywhere. Now we offer the interesting spectacle of the wedding of the two talents and personalities. Vernon Duke has made the "April in Paris Fantasy" you hear next. It is a concert piece for clarinet and orchestra, and it has all the charm of a popular song with the refinement of good musical writing.[32]

Soon after the United States entered the war, Duke attempted to enlist in the Navy but was rejected because of defective vision. But in August 1942, the month the Germans were defeated at Stalingrad, a friend with contacts with the Coast Guard helped him enlist as a coxswain, or petty officer third class. At boot camp on Ellis Island, his bad eyesight was clearly apparent on the firing range, and later in a training program he demonstrated that military strategy was not his forte. Boot camp, however, was a learning experience, not all of it bad:

> Making up my bunk according to the rigid rules of the Bluejacket's Manual, eating ice cream and pork chops off the same plate and tying knots were other problems; as were saluting with the proper dash, squashing one's G.I.-issue hat until it assumed the devil-may-care "salty" look, putting on "leggin's" and switching from dress to undress uniform in two minutes' time. The enlisted men were youths in their teens and early twenties, and I didn't mind being called "Pop" and actually enjoyed leading a "boot's" life; the strenuousness of my new duties was a good antidote for the gnawing despair caused by Mother's passing. I obeyed the rules, "rose and shone," caught the drift of sailor talk, the one recognizable feature of which was interpolating a certain four-letter word as frequently as possible, and even became popular with my "shipmates" (I never saw a ship in my two and half years in the Coast Guard except at a distance), who thought me a "character" but "pretty regular" withal. I, in turn, liked the rough

kids, who scoffed at anything except "liberty," drinking and picking "dames" . . . but they had healthy faith in a "square deal" and in an American way of life.³³

"Pop," however, was still a Broadway composer with the wherewithal to bypass drinking and picking up dames. On his first liberty, he checked into a hotel on East Thirty-Fifth Street. He took a pine-scented hot bath, donned civilian pajamas, and flopped into a triple size bed. Later he went to the Hollywood Theatre where "Cantor was still drawing full houses, and bumped into Cole Porter, who surveyed me in my tight dress blues from head to foot and whined: 'Vernon my boy—what did they do to you?'" At a party after the show, Duke played some songs, and lyricist Howard Dietz promised to add a lyric to one of them. He also gave him a book by John Cecil Holm to read. They agreed to collaborate on a show based on it, Duke's military duties permitting.³⁴

At the home Dietz and an MGM vice president shared on lower Fifth Avenue and at a summer place in Port Washington, Long Island, Duke and Dietz wrote songs for a musical to be called *Dancing in the Streets*. As Duke recalled: "My 'detail' in Brooklyn allowed me most of Saturday and the entire Sunday off, and week ends at the Dietzes' became a regular feature of my life and something to look forward to." Moreover, "Chatting with Greer Garson or Sylvia Ashley or Tanis Dietz by a swimming pool and partaking of spiced viands—after standing in a chow line to 'Come and get it'— . . . was very good for the morale, and the stomach as well. *Dancing in the Streets*, a gay tale of wartime Washington, was 'writing itself'; we'd dash off a song in the afternoon and exhibit it to the Dietzes and guests in the evening. Then back to the barracks I'd go, to my lowly duties in the daytime, canteen and service dances at night—two or three of these a week as a rule. As my shipmates insisted, I had a 'good racket.'" *Dancing in the Streets*, starring Mary Martin, opened at the Shubert Theater in Boston on March 22, 1943. Duke thought Martin was "delicious," Bob Alton's dances "fresh and energetic," and "Indefinable Charm," with a "unhackneyed lyric" by Dietz, one of his best ballads. The show received lukewarm notices and closed in Boston.³⁵

Also in March the film adaptation of *Cabin in the Sky*, directed by Vincente Minnelli, was released. On the insistence of producer Arthur Freed, three "Southern songs" by Harold Arlen and E. Y. Harburg were added—"Happiness Is a Thing Called Joe," "Life's Full o' Consequence," and "Li'l Black Sheep." Moreover, most of the original cast had been replaced, although Ethel Waters remained and was the star of the movie. Only four songs by Duke and Latouche were retained from the play, one being "Taking a Chance on Love."[36] According to a critic, the song "has worn well in three years, but it was sung so refreshingly and with such plaintive feeling by Miss Waters that it sounds like a brand-new number."[37] Reviews of the picture itself were mixed. The *New York Times* considered the film "as sparkling and completely satisfying as was the original stage production." To the *Wall Street Journal*, the movie "somehow fails to fully capture either the inspired sincerity or the broad and spontaneous humor of its stage predecessor."[38] That year Minnelli also directed *I Dood It*, starring Red Skelton and Eleanor Powell, which included a cameo appearance by Scott Hazel playing "Taking a Chance on Love." Probably because it was a movie performance, she eschewed interpretation for pianist fireworks.

In 1943 Dukelsky's violin concerto, completed in early 1941, had its debut. As recalled by Ruth Posselt's daughter, "Both my parents had been close to the work from near its inception and had collaborated with Duke on changes and improvements for the solo and orchestral parts." On March 19 and 20, with her husband, Richard Burgin, conducting, Posselt performed the work with the Boston Symphony.[39] She "gave a superb account, in technic and musicianship, of what must be a very difficult piece," wrote a critic. "Her tone throughout was lustrous, clear and of tropical warmth." Nevertheless, there were moments when the music sounded "fabricated rather than inspired, but on the whole the composer has produced a striking vehicle for virtuoso fiddlers." Following the performance and probably basking in the applause, the composer, attired in his Coast Guard uniform, joined Posselt on stage.[40]

Shortly after returning to his barracks and donning his bluejacket, Duke was "shipped" across the Hudson to the Barge Office at the Battery. His duties consisted of "pushing little flags across a large wall map of New York, which had to do with the movements of Coast Guardsmen assigned to pier duty." He asked and got a transfer to a downstairs office where he became a signal receiver: "This meant sitting for hours with a pair of earphones and getting fire signals in one ear and ship signals in the other; the din was at all times terrible and completely antimusical." From there he went on pier duty,

> WHILE MOST of Manhattan's night spots are breaking all cash register records, three well-known clubs are floundering and may droop within the fortnite . . . Here's a busy month for a genius—Vernon Duke . . . Currently in the Coast Guard, where he has charge of a nine-piece band at the Brooklyn barracks, his score for Metro's "Cabin in the Sky" was heard for the first time by the public in the world premiere at Dallas, March 11 . . . this week the Boston Symphony Orchestra will present his violin concerto, billing the composer under his concert name, Vladimir Dukelsky . . . Next week, "Dancing in the Streets," starring Mary Martin, opens at the Shubert Theater in Boston—the score is by Vernon Duke . . . Sudden thought: Every time you start to kick about the 48 points, just remember the kick you get out of the 48 stars . . .

"BUSY MONTH," *St. Louis Star and Times*, March 22, 1943.

inspecting cargo transports, especially those flying foreign flags including those from the Soviet Union, for "inflammatory stuffs." Apparently a "gold braid" suspicious of artists in uniform transferred Duke to Peekskill for some "advanced training." Again, Duke benefited from the experience. By marching, performing calisthenics, and crawling under barbed wire, he shed fifteen pounds, "acquired bulging muscles and was ready to punch anybody who dared called me a 'boot.'" Narrowly being assigned to a vessel voyaging between the Port of New York and Alaska, Duke was ordered to Brooklyn Barracks at the foot of Columbia Street.[41]

There Duke persuaded his commanding officer to allow him to form a band on his own time, and he set about rounding up musicians, one being a saxophone player named Sid Caesar. Duke remembered him as "a big, hulking lad of nineteen, who wore a sour expression on his not unhandsome face and whose brown hair was uncombed."[42] Caesar remembered Duke as someone who needed his help: "Vernon was very nearsighted and was too proud to wear his glasses. He couldn't do close order drill. He couldn't tell his left oblique from his right. Our friendship began when I told him to hang on to the collar of my uniform to help him march in the same direction as the rest of the men." Once Caesar learned what the officers on the base knew—that Duke was a Broadway composer—he assisted him in forming the band. The success of weekly dances led to the addition of sketches that made fun of the cooks, drivers, and the commander himself. Duke worked on the arrangements for the sketches, and soon the band was booked into venues off the base.[43]

After serving as best man to Sid Caesar in his marriage to Florence Levy on July 17, 1943, Duke was transferred from Brooklyn Barracks to Rahway, New Jersey. His sleeping quarters were in the gunner's shack where ammunition was stored. Fear about being blown apart resulted in insomnia, and his commanding officer saw to it that he engaged in no musical nonsense. Duke was certain that his "military duties at Rahway did even less for the war effort than those I performed in Brooklyn." He also came down with sinusitis and spent considerable time in the sick bay. Finally sent to a hospital, he was advised to seek a medical discharge. That he did, and in late December 1943, after eighteen months of service, he was discharged.[44]

Although now a civilian, Duke could hardly refuse a request to "report" to Coast Guard headquarters in Washington, D.C. Because the Coast Guard wanted service personnel, not civilians, to manage their musical shows, the head of public relations coaxed him back into the service in the Temporary Reserve. Offered a commission as a lieutenant junior grade, Duke thought he was too old for that rank and asked to be commissioned a lieutenant commander. With the promise of considerable free time to pursue his musical career, Duke settled on the rank of lieutenant.[45]

As his commission was being processed, Duke wrote the songs for *Jackpot*, which premiered at the National Theater in Washington, D.C., on January 5, 1944. Produced by Vinton Freedley, with lyrics by Howard Dietz and the libretto by Guy Bolton, Sidney Sheldon, and Ben Roberts, it told the story of three Marines winning a girl at a war bond rally.[46] Jay Carmody of the *Evening Star* was only slightly impressed: "Its dancing is designed to delight the eye. The production is lavish and alert to the pretty surprise of color. But despite all these, until some way is found to give it the sparkle of life, 'Jackpot' stands as one of those beautiful promises that the theater does not always keep, a very melancholy thing."[47]

It opened at the Alvin Theatre in New York on January 13.[48] Apparently Duke had not read the *Evening Star* review, because everyone "thought *Jackpot* a cinch after its provincial showings and a big New York advance reported by the box office." He took Sally Horan, "one of the town's better-looking career girls," and the president of Condé Nast to the opening. It was an evening he never forgot: "After the first ten minutes, my guests began to wilt along with the rest of the audience—ten more minutes and I began wishing I were dead; the jokes that made out-of-town customers cry with laughter were falling flat with a dull, sickening thud, until the actors were playing to masses of raised eyebrows and no applause."[49]

According to a critic for the *World Telegram*,

> With every number it sounds as though Mr. Duke had got a melody that was very good, but didn't know how to develop it melodically, with any rhythmic or tonal carry-through. After from four to eight bars the melody may break abruptly into a queer, unrelated theme in another key, of an octave lower and flatted so the singer seems to be talking rather than singing. Or Mr. Duke will take a melody like some recent popular song and then go off into something that sounds like an eccentricity by Eric Satie or Darius Milhaud.[50]

"No one expects a great deal of musical comedy books these days," wrote Lewis Nichols of the *New York Times*, but this was "one of the feeblest in quite a time, so sleepy that it goes far below any possible expectation." Duke's music was "probably no better than average, but 'Sugar Foot' is destined for fame, and 'I Kissed My Girl Goodbye,' 'What Happened?' and 'One Track Mind' are the best of the others. Howard Dietz has written the lyrics, although not to a uniform excellence."[51] None of these songs lasted beyond the sixty-seven performances of the show. After reading a review in the *New York Journal*, Duke, Freedley, and Dietz got drunk at the Harvard Club. Vernon was especially crushed by the bad notices, fearing they would negatively influence an appreciation of his upcoming *Tars and Spars*.[52]

Duke had been selected to write the score for this service musical. More than in any other show he had been associated with, he was given considerable authority. He prepared a list of Coast Guard enlisted personnel he sought to recruit, which included dancer/choreographer Gower Champion, actor Victor Mature, and comedian Sid Caesar.[53] Still stationed at Brooklyn Barracks, Caesar was stunned one day when informed he had been transferred to Coast Guard Barracks, Biltmore Hotel, Palm Beach. He soon boarded a train for Florida and was met at the station by Duke, who explained why he had been transferred. Thus, in a few days, Caesar "went from the cold and dismal Brooklyn port to balmy and swanky Palm Beach. One day I was fixing toilets in Brooklyn, the next day I was rehearsing with a big movie star like Victor Mature and a choreographer like Gower Champion. It was a charm. I knew in my bones that the show would be a hit."⁵⁴

All members of the cast were Coast Guard personnel, including the young ladies of the chorus who were personally selected by Duke. He unabashedly admitted that during the selection process he had enjoyed observing "a few dozen of the prospects' legs, now that their owners, having shed their Molyneux-designed uniforms, looked like any other female beach-combers. Selecting the chorus was a tough job, as some of the prettier candidates were allergic to stage appearances, some of the hopelessly unattractive ones were, on the contrary, dying to get into the show."⁵⁵

Finally, his commission came through, and in Miami Duke was sworn in as a lieutenant. He returned to Palm Beach "in natty officer's grays, the entire cast of *Tars and Spars* saluting like mad, their mouths open in amazement. 'Say, that isn't you, Duke?' Caesar gulped and added quickly, 'Beg pardon, sir.' Everybody laughed." The show opened at the Paramount Theater, Palm Beach on March 29, 1944, and according to Duke it was a hit, with Caesar, "laying them in the isles and grabbing the notices." Duke claimed that he and Dietz wrote some good songs, in particular "Arm in Arm," "You Gotta Have a Reason to Be a Civilian," and "Palm Beach."⁵⁶ On April 5, the show opened in Miami for a week before going on a national tour.⁵⁷

On June 6, 1944, Allied forces landed on the coast of France, and his beloved city of Paris was liberated in August. Duke must have celebrated the events with considerable libations, but soon he was hard at work on *Sadie Thompson,* based on a play that was based on the story "Rain" by W. Somerset Maugham. The setting is on an island in the South Seas in which a missionary seeks to reform a prostitute but with tragic results. The title character in this grim but familiar story had first been played on stage by Jeanne Engle, followed by a silent film version staring Gloria Swanson in 1928, followed by a sound version with Joan Crawford in 1932, followed by a stage revival staring Tallulah Bankhead in 1935.⁵⁸

It was rumored that either Gertrude Lawrence or Marlene Dietrich was being considered for the lead.⁵⁹ But Ethel Merman got the role. She rehearsed the new songs at her Central Park duplex with her accompanist Lew Kessler, Duke, Dietz, and director Rouben Mamoulian. As recalled by Duke, "Mamoulian, a fine director, had a rather pontifically highbrow, Moscow

Arty approach to Maugham's immortal strumpet which I thought somewhat misplaced." Duke was also concerned that the missionary was given songs, believing that "the hypocritical cleric would be best characterized as 'songless,' like the villainous whites in *Porgy and Bess*." Because of Mamoulian's success in directing *Oklahoma,* however, Duke gave in.[60]

Rehearsals began on September 18, 1944, but Merman differed with Mamoulian regarding how her character should be interpreted and was dissatisfied with Dietz's lyrics.[61] Merman considered her husband, Robert D. Levitt, better suited for the task. Dietz refused to back down, and Ethel quit, but he admitted, "The show would have been a perfect vehicle for Merman and there is little doubt that had she played Sadie it would have been a hit, but my pride which went before the fall couldn't take it."[62] Some of the songs written with Merman in mind were dropped.[63]

Now starring June Havoc, the show opened in Philadelphia, and according to Duke, "the book was excellent, the staging uneven to a degree, the casting ditto and the music, bereft of the Merman bombshell specials, good in spots and much too heavy in others." Business was fine the first week, but "took quite a dive the second." Yet the production was good enough for it to open at the Alvin Theatre in New York. Duke recalled fainting from exhaustion at an opening party at the apartment of Gypsy Rose Lee and listening the following day to the reviews read to him by a friend over the phone.[64] If he heard the one by John Chapman, he may have again collapsed: "Vernon Duke's score is heavy and dull and of scant variety. What George Gershwin could have done with the *Sadie Thompson* set up! Or Vincent Youmans! . . . It's unfortunate that so ambitious, expensive, intelligently planned, and accurately cast a show should lack the score to make it come alive."[65] To another critic, "'Sadie Thompson' is neither a play nor musical. Its dialogue, which follows closely enough to the original, is serious, and its performance is serious. But since the evening is musical, the story must be interrupted for song and ballet, which are not so serious. The mood of the story is lost in the orchestra, and the music is overwhelmed by the story." Vernon Duke "has turned out a long score. Unfortunately, it is not a distinguished one, there being—in the Broadway sense—only a few numbers of engaging quality. One is 'When You Live on an Island,' another 'Fisherman's Wharf.'" Regarding the lyrics, Dietz did not apply "his sharpest pencil in that department."[66]

Other critics presented opposite assessments. Although the subject matter was hardly the stuff of a musical, claimed one, all those participating in this production, "met all the difficulties involved with signal success. 'Sadie Thompson' is a very stirring contribution to the current theater."[67] Another considered "Sailing at Midnight," which stopped the show, superior to "April in Paris."[68] And Burton Rascoe placed the show in a class with *Oklahoma*. He was surprised at the quality of the show because "Duke had never before given me any indication that he could write a melodious tune. . . . Yet, in *Sadie Thompson* Mr. Duke has written a musical score that is not only full of heavenly sounds, pulse-quickening and ear-caressing but, in every instance, designed to interpret the text, elucidate character, further the action, and contribute to the harmonic unity of the production." [69] Duke thought the show "could be diagnosed as a mild success or a flop *d'estime*; it turned out to be the latter." But one of the songs from the show, "The Love I Long For," was recorded by Harry James. It shot up to number two on the record best-seller list where it remained for several weeks, and a decade later it had earned Duke $9,000 in royalties.[70]

By the time Lieutenant Duke arrived in California in early 1945, the war was winding down. He had been sent to Hollywood to keep an eye on the filming of *Tars and Spars*. Columbia Pictures had purchased the film rights for $50,000, in part through the efforts of Milton Bren, who was the producer but also a lieutenant commander in the Coast Guard. Bren hired Sammy Cahn and Julie Stein to write a new score, but, claimed Duke, "the picture turned out to be a Class C musical, chiefly notable for misusing Alfred Drake's great talents. . . . There was no connection whatever between our fresh and uninhibited little revue and Bren's flat-footed essay in musical flagwaving."[71] Propaganda movies, however, soon ceased production. On May 4 and August 14, 1945, Germany and Japan surrendered, respectively.

Happily reunited with Alex and Mona in their small house in Westwood, Duke enjoyed his outings in the Hollywood Hills, dinners with Ira and Lee Gershwin, drinks with Herb Spencer and Eddie Powell, both working for Twentieth-Century, and his heated arguments with some of Hollywood's elites. As he noted with some irony, "My last Coast Guard mission accomplished, I was promoted to lieutenant commander and 'mustered out' shortly afterwards."[72]

DUKELSKY REEMERGES
NEW YORK AND PARIS, 1945–1951

By the time Lt. Vernon Duke retired from the Coast Guard, composer Vladimir Dukelsky had published an article in *Music Publishers Journal*. He proudly announced that significant progress had been made in composers receiving recognition and getting their works performed since the founding of the Composers' Protective Society in 1933. The success and achievements included the rise to prominence of Copland, Harris, Schuman, Bernstein, Barber, and Menotti. Lesser known composers, such as Wallingford Riegger, Walter Piston, Theodore Chanler, Paul Bowles, Bernard Herrmann, Harold Morris, Elie Siegmeister, and Lukas Foss, had written significant works. Bernard Herrmann, Jerome Moross, and Aaron Copland had been monetarily rewarded, and opportunities for radio commissions and performances had increased. The Critics' Circle Prize for the best new composition of a season had been founded, and young composers such as Leonard Bernstein had been asked to conduct. Bona-fide composers such as Kurt Weill and Bernstein had participated in Broadway shows.[1]

Dukelsky also toyed with the idea of founding yet another society. He contacted "mellow-voiced" Rose Dirman about performing concerts of unfamiliar music with him: "Miss Dirman, one of our best oratorio singers, was agreeable and after two months' research we announced two really corking programs."[2] To critic Olin Downes, "The excursion presented much that was of interest, and material that would profit the inquiring singer." The many composers represented included Carl Heinrich Graun, Félicien David, Prokofiev, Nikolai Medtner, and Charles Ives. And there was "a group of five Victorian songs by the modest and gifted Mr. Dukelsky. We would fain that they had come earlier on the program, which began tardily." The songs, "requiring sound and varied musicianship, were given intelligent and musicianly advancement by Miss Dirman and her collaborator."[3] A week later the second concert offered songs not presented in the first, including those of Michael Cavendish, Schubert, Dvorak, Schoenberg, Alban Berg, Alexander Abramsky, Anatole Alexandrov, Vasily Nietchaiev, Lev Schwartz, Paul Hindemith, Paul Bowles, Elie Siegmeister, and Dukelsky.[4]

Proceeds from the concerts were to fund his projected Society for Forgotten Music. Vladimir explained his vision to a reporter from the *New York Times*:

> I have long been considering a society for producing fine music that was always neglected or that has been forgotten. . . . Much fine music has thus been lost to the public because artists won't perform it, saying that it does not suit their voice, their style, or the taste of their public. It is such music that I want to produce—and to have published. These concerts, which will, if possible, be an annual feature and will be given in other cities also, will be a step in righting this bad situation and will serve to sound out the public's reaction to the idea. I, myself, am a composer, and I don't like the idea of my music being forgotten a few years after I am gone.[5]

He may or may not have liked how his Second Symphony was performed at Carnegie Hall on April 30, 1945. As conductor Léon Barzin explained to the audience, the performance was a "public rehearsal." He stopped the orchestra several times to correct errors and imbalances, but as noted by a critic, "This appears to have been a wise move on Mr. Barzin's part, for it put the orchestra players at their ease and allowed the audience to share in the exploration of a new score." If interruptions hindered the critic from assessing the symphony as a whole, he did not admit it. He found it "a lurid and dramatic work which never quite achieves its objectives. It is heavily orchestrated, brassy, discursive, and its moments of genuine musical impulse and inspiration are separated by unimaginative and seemingly purposeless episodes."[6]

Dukelsky also composed a concerto for cello and orchestra. Cellist Gregor Piatigorsky performed it with the Boston Symphony Orchestra on January 4, 1946. A critic for the *Boston Globe* claimed that Duke and Dukelsky collaborated on the work. Not particularly serious, it nevertheless possessed "tunes, bright colors in the orchestra, a really beautiful slow movement and a rousing finale." He thought it "a good thing, this rapprochement between Mr. Dukelsky and Mr. Duke. Each has something to offer the other. Were they to pool all their resources, there is no telling what brilliant results might come about."[7]

Piatigorsky repeated the work at Carnegie Hall on January 9. Sandwiched between Bach's D Major Suite and Brahms's Fourth Symphony, it was "put in a rather hard place," wrote Olin Downes. "These works, it is true, did not make it entirely easy for Mr. Dukelsky, especially as he does not cling to the beaten path in his difficult and brilliantly sounding score. The score requires virtousity of a high order of the orchestra, and superior conducting, as well as temperament, technique and mettle on the part of the soloist." Downes liked "most of the concerto, in spite of its gadgets. For there are genuine lyrical themes, gay themes in dance or march style, invention when the style is not forced or affected. But why all the gadgets? The arsenal of 'modern' effects, harmonic, orchestral, rhythmic, is used as if Mr. Dukelsky wanted to assure us that he had as many tricks up his sleeve as any of them. . . . The result is often brilliant and warmly colored, but sometimes artificial and even, as of today, old-fashioned."[8]

In June producer Nat Karson, whose *Nellie Bly* with Eddie Cantor had flopped the previous season, rounded up S. J. Perelman and Al Hirschfeld to write the libretto and Duke and lyricist Ogden Nash to compose the music for a show to be called *Sweet Bye and Bye*.[9] The plot concerns a meek tree surgeon in the next century who inherits a fortune. Duke not only had to write the songs, noted a critic, "but he faces the odd task of writing an additional score with mood sounds representing the year 2076. . . . Duke's background research now is foreground investigation as he decides what probably will be the influence of radar, television, the atom and other futuristic influences on music."[10]

That Duke had concerns about the libretto was recalled by Hirschfeld late in his life:

> Boris Aronson did marvelous sets, based on kind of Braque or Matisse arbitrary shapes like a jigsaw puzzle. The opening curtain, and the thing spreads apart, up and down, and you're taken into the future. Aronson had a marvelous conception. I don't think Vernon really

understood what we were up to. I remember one evening—he had had dinner with some people the night before—he said he had told them about the script. And he said to them, "And they say it's a satire of advertising and of the future. Have you ever heard of anything so stupid?" Sid and I looked at each other and realized, we're in trouble! Because he didn't really get what we were trying to do. He didn't have a satirical point of view on it.[11]

Sweet Bye and Bye opened in New Haven on October 10 in a state of chaos. Gene Sheldon, a vaudeville mimic, was completely out of his element in a musical comedy and was eventually replaced by Eric Rhodes. Dolores Gray, recalled Duke, stopped the show with "Round About" and "Just Like a Man" and was a tower of strength, but even she could not carry "a show as incurably sick as ours was." Things got even worse in Philadelphia. The local orchestra leader, claimed Duke, furious at not getting a New York job, incited the pit musicians to make mistakes, drown out the singers, and end each song with a discord.[12]

The previews held at Forrest Theatre resulted in negative reviews, causing dissension and pettiness among Perelman, Hirschfeld, Nash, and Duke, who were staying in adjoining rooms in the Warwick Hotel. Perelman was outraged when he overheard Duke on the telephone boasting that he was assisting with the libretto. Perelman retaliated. Standing by the doorway where Duke could hear him, he placed mock calls to Walter Winchell and Leonard Lyons, claiming that Hirschfeld, who played the piano, was helping Duke with the music. Duke was duped and told Nash, "These fellows are insane. They're out to crucify me." When Nash confronted Perelman and Hirschfeld, he learned about the hoax and told them to stop picking on Duke, who was not in good health.[13]

After a week at the Forrest Theatre, the show moved to the Erlanger, "probably the most sinister theater in the world, situated in a street chiefly noted for cheap furniture stores," recalled Duke.[14] Although Perelman considered the show too sophisticated for out-of-town audiences, he was convinced it would succeed in New York. Hirschfeld thought the music the weakest part of the production and was especially critical of Duke putting five harpists in the orchestra to suggest futurist music.[15] Duke thought the libretto was extremely funny when read by Perelman, but when translated to the theater, "all the fun evaporated." Following the horrors of World War II and the invention and use of weapons of mass destruction, audiences were not "in the mood to look ahead, the prospects being as bleak as they were." The show closed permanently in Philadelphia. The best thing that came out of the experience was the friendship Duke formed with Nash, "the finest human being I was ever privileged to know and the freshest lyrical talent in this country since the death of the one and only Lorenz Hart. An old hand at the Gentle Art of Making Enemies, I can only marvel at the fact that Ogden hasn't a single enemy in the world." Duke mentioned that Nash inscribed his copy of *Many Long Years Ago* with "So it goes, or, All for the Best / Christ got a gospel by St. Luke / I got a score by Vernon Duke."[16]

On November 18, 1946, Leonard Bernstein conducted Dukelsky's *Ode to the Milky Way* at the City Center in New York City. The two had met a few years earlier, the Russian being nettled that the young man was now a favorite of Serge Koussevitzky. In time, however, "On getting to know Lennie I developed a real fondness for him and a sincere admiration for his gifts, but he is a narcissist and so was I in my youth, and two self-lovers seldom get along on first acquaintance."[17] A ten-minute work for full orchestra, *Ode* was performed on a program of music composed by veterans of World War II, including Samuel Barber, Alex North, and John Lessard. In the program notes, Duke wrote: "The Ode can perhaps be described as a kind of musical monologue—the unspoken thoughts and yearnings of a man stretched out on the deck of a transport and looking up at the Milky Way." In fact, the transport was the United Fruit Line passenger ship on which Dukelsky had cruised the West Indies. Wrapped, as it were, in "uncelestial gloom" and coming so soon after the *Sweet Bye and Bye* disaster, he feared the audience's reaction, but the "applause came thick and fast, sounding sweet to my unbelieving ears. The critics, instead of administering the customary shellacking, sang soothing choruses of praise and thought it 'the best by far, of the new works on the program.'"[18]

Dukelsky had hopes his Third Symphony would be performed in the United States. The three movements were about twenty-three minutes long, and several conductors were considering it for the coming season.[19] Dukelsky, however, was terribly disappointed that the Koussevitzky Music

Foundation, which he thought had commissioned it, turned him down, dedicated as it was to the memory of the conductor's recently departed wife. This led to a rupture with Koussevitzky, who had told him he had too many works to perform that season.[20] Later, when Dukelsky asked the conductor to explain why his supposedly commissioned symphony would not be performed, he received a curt letter. Although moved by the dedication, Koussevitzky pointed out that a board of the Foundation had rejected the work. That Dukelsky was a close friend of his wife meant nothing to those making the decision.[21]

Better news came from Europe. Dukelsky's ballet *Le Bal des Blanchisseuses* was well received when performed by the Ballets des Champs Elysées in Paris in December 1946.[22] Librettist Boris Kochno wrote to Vladimir on the nineteenth: "It is a spectacle of rare beauty, and notwithstanding its novelty and a certain strangeness—friends and non-friends both adore our 'Bal.' During the last performances we were *forced* to repeat the *coda* of the Finale. . . . 'Le Bal des Blanchisseuses' is a theatrical event of first magnitude."[23] Visiting Paris at the time was a critic for an English newspaper. She called the music "swing" and admitted not being "terribly fond of these modern ballets. If dancing is supposed to be the poetry of motion, this was prose . . . and Cockney at that."[24]

The ballet was performed and well received in several other cities on the continent and in London in 1947, "whose critics, probably not realizing that Duke was also Dukelsky, whose *Jardin Public* they had crucified, actually liked my lighthearted score."[25] Although a critic for the *Stage* erroneously labeled the music "ragtime," he loved the ballet and noted that the music allowed the choreographer to create the "right note of joie de vivre."[26]

The right note was also hit in New York in September, when the League of Composers presented a concert dedicated entirely to American artists. The CBS Symphony performed the works of Johann Peter, Charles Ives, Walter Piston, and Vladimir Dukelsky, whose Concerto for Cello and Orchestra featured cellist Maurice Bialkin.[27] For this concert Dukelsky was considered an American composer.

Some of his American compositions were included in his and Ogden Nash's *Musical Zoo*, in which the songs of Duke were based on the poems by Nash. As the flyleaf explains, "If you hum while you waltz, try 'The Mouse';

if you can't carry a tune, you can flicker with 'The Firefly'; and if you're the operatic type, 'The Sparrow' is especially recommended. But be sure not to miss a single bar, for these songs will suit your most ridiculous mood, be it as wistful as 'The Seagull,' pompous as 'The Rooster,' or busy as 'The Ant.'"[28] "By all standard methods of computation," wrote Mimi Wallner of the *New York Times*, "the 'Musical Zoo' should be a glowing masterpiece." It was, therefore, "somewhat of a mystery that the 'Musical Zoo' is not an inspired production. True, the settings as a whole have competence and charm, and occasionally, as in the case of 'The Pigeon' and 'The Mouse,' true felicity and insight. . . . But it is sad indeed to this reviewer that an Ogden Nash book, whose praises might be shouted from the rooftops, can only evoke a whispered and uncertain cheer."[29] Its poor sales might best be attributed to the melodies being too sophisticated and unconventional for most people to play or sing.

By this time, Dukelsky had departed for Europe "to 'cash in' on my unexpected success there." The Paris he returned to was mostly unchanged. He was again "the Dukelsky of Diaghilev days. . . . I had an odd feeling that both Serges—Diaghilev and Prokofiev—were here in Paris, as immortal, as real as the city herself." A few changes were welcomed: "The girls were better-looking and had sturdier, shapelier legs—a result of the new vogue for *les sports* and bicycling during the occupation. . . . Paris was even more virtuous than before with the closing of the brothels; the concierges seemed friendlier and the taxi drivers cleaner. . . . The book hunting was still in full flower on the *quais*, the fishermen still fished for nonexistent fish, and Paris dogs still made with the charm and seldom talked back to their owners." The French, however, did not appreciate his "April in Paris," because the two French versions of the lyric were of "deplorable banality." The tune, moreover, was "too special and fancy for the French, who lean more towards the *ginguette* style in their popular music."[30]

Dukelsky contacted friends he had met in the 1920s, many of them living in the same flats, including Paul Gilson, who persuaded Duke to collaborate with him on a cantata. Once the lyric to *Paris Aller et Retour* was submitted to him, he and a friend departed for the Riviera to compete the work. As recalled by Dukelsky, they "took a few melancholy trips—to Monte Carlo, unspeakably depressing and decadent, the Casino, the Hôtel de Paris and the café across the square all looking as if they had gout and didn't care who knew it." But Cannes was "as pretty and well-scrubbed as ever," and he knew of "few places lovelier than Cannes Harbor."[31]

Back in Paris, he finally founded the Society for Forgotten Music, not just to acquaint the public with a large number of unknown works but also to unearth educational materials that would help students in their search for broader and richer repertoires. Excluding the Middle Ages, the Renaissance, and early Baroque, the Society concentrated on the vast literature from the seventeenth through the nineteenth centuries.[32] With scouts in Paris, London, Vienna, and Milan, the Society gained access to many neglected treasures. In a period of two years, it would enlist 250 paying members, present fifteen concerts and two radio series, and end up in the black.[33]

Years later Dukelsky reflected on the collecting process. Researchers must question the opinions of historians and lexicographers, who have relegated various composers to that of "also rans," but they must also keep in mind that not everything their "discovered" subjects wrote should be recovered. The question to ask is whether a particular work has stature? Does it hold up as music of worth?[34]

While in Paris, Dukelsky initiated a festival of Gershwin's music sponsored by the U.S. State Department. He wrote to Ira Gershwin in early July that he had inaugurated the festival with a forty-minute broadcast. Mentioned as well was his recently published article in the Russian literary magazine *Novosselye,* in which he "devoted a great deal of space to George and his unique place in American music annals."[35] Ira responded in early October, delighted and appreciative that Dukelsky had initiated the festival. He hoped his Third Symphony would get the reception and publicity it deserved.[36]

It had its premiere in Brussels on October 10, 1947. The concert also included works by Beethoven, Arthur de Greef, and Benjamin Britten. Dukelsky considered it a stimulating program and was happy about the way his music sounded, but broadcast over the radio, it was not reviewed in any newspaper. In Paris in February 1948 his symphony and cantata *Paris Aller et Retour* were also broadcast, and both were well received by listeners and critics. Henri Sauguet wrote: "His Symphony displays nervous and vigorous writing, brilliant and powerful orchestration. It's a strong work, a work of lyrical beauty." Dukelsky noted, "The cantata came in for its share of praise, too, and was so highly thought of by [Roger] Desormiere that he gave a public performance of it a year later.... The *Blanchisseuses* were garnering fresh triumphs all over Europe, including England." Greatly pleased with these achievements, Dukelsky sailed for New York.[37]

Shortly after his arrival, Duke wrote the score for *The Angry God*, a film made in Mexico about the god Colima, who tried but failed to win the love of a beautiful Indian maiden who remained faithful to the man she loved. Only fifty-seven minutes long, it was released in March 1948. That Duke failed to mention the movie in his autobiography implies he was unhappy with the product. He could not have been pleased with the advertisement (and its spelling), which shouted, "*See*: Blazing Volcano in Furious Eruption. *See*: Witchcraft at Work with a Native Beauty a[t] the Stake. *See*: The Mad Frenzy of Mystic Rites." It included, however, "Song of Our Love," which he and Harold Rome had written for a never-produced musical about the whaling village of Nantucket, Rhode Island.[38]

Dukelsky kept busy. In May 1948, he founded the New York chapter of the Society for Forgotten Music with generous help from Sydney Beck of the New York Public Library and other idealistic music lovers.[39] And in early June 1948, he was elected president of the American branch of the society.[40] After only three months in New York, Dukelsky returned to Paris where he organized a concert of American music, which included the works of Walter Piston, Wallingford Riegger, David Diamond, Morton Gould, Charles Ives, and Edward MacDowell but not those of Vladimir Dukelsky. He did not consider himself a typical American composer of serious music, "although I'm as proud as the next fellow of my American citizenship." He had proven his "bona-fide Americanism" in his Broadway output, and because he had "a successful ballet on the boards," he decided to step aside in favor of his colleagues. The concert was presented on July 2, a few days after he had returned to the States.[41]

On December 12, 1948, Dukelsky accompanied soprano Rose Dirman at a concert sponsored by the Society for Forgotten Music at the New York Public Library. She sang three songs by Carl F. Zelter, with the words by Goethe, during the first half of the concert and three songs by Hector Berlioz after intermission. The program also included works by Heinrich Biber, de

Tremais, and Bedrich Smetana.[42] On March 6, 1949, at the same venue and for the same organization, Dukelsky accompanied soprano Nancy Chase on three songs by Friedrich Hebbel and three by Karol Szymanowski. Included in the program were compositions by Sergei Taneiev and J. N. Hummel.[43] And in late October 1949, he accompanied baritone Joseph Bell in a concert for the Society at Carl Fischer Hall in New York. Featured were the compositions of Luigi Manzi, G. Bononcini, Pietro Pignatta, Michael Cavendish, Adolphe Adam, Clara Schumann, Stephen Foster, Émile Paladilhe, Charles T. Griffes, and Sidney Homer.[44]

By this time, record producer Ahmet Ertegun had commissioned Dukelsky to write the background music for a recording of a Walter Benton poem. After World War II, Benton became a well-known poet who published in several prominent journals. He wrote *This Is My Beloved* in 1943 in the form of a diary. Rather erotic for the time, it became a best seller. Why Dukelsky accepted this undertaking is not known, but it may have had something to do with Benton being the offspring of Russian immigrant parents who had migrated to the United States in 1913, when Walter was six. After Montgomery Clift and Tyrone Power turned down offers to narrate the poem, John Dall, who recently had appeared in Alfred Hitchcock's *Rope*, accepted. The poem was issued on Atlantic's first 33⅓ long-playing record in March 1949. The composition was performed by a twenty-eight-piece orchestra and sixteen voices, the music augmenting what each scene emphasized. For example, to the words "I burst inside you like a screaming rocket," the music screams.[45] In another scene, the narrator explains why he is looking at her:

> Only because I want to remember this—
> > the musty glasses and the checkered tablecloth,
> > cigarette butts, burnt matches, spilled beer and
> > > crumpled napkins.[46]

Because most of the poem is about Benton in, on, or about the body of his lover, Lillian, this scene is unique and called for a completely different accompaniment. Suddenly, a walking bass line is heard, followed by a moaning clarinet. Duke, of course, always insisted that he never infused his classical music with jazz. A reviewer of the album was not impressed, claiming that Dall sounded like a "sophomore in bad need of a shower." But the music was superior to the text and was conducted with zest by Lehman Engel.⁴⁷ Another critic wrote: "The whole thing strikes me as uncomfortably pretentious, like a Hollywood spectacle making with big ideas—and that goes for the words and music."⁴⁸ In his autobiography, Duke admitted that *This Is My Beloved* was "a rather florid and stylistically questionable record of a tragic love affair."⁴⁹ Dall soon found himself involved in his own "a tragic love affair" in the film noir classic *Gun Crazy*. Duke courted actress Temple Texas, Richard Widmark's girlfriend in *Kiss of Death*.⁵⁰

While in Paris in the spring of 1949, Dukelsky, unhappy about how the album was being promoted, wrote to Ertegun. Why had there been no advertisements "in *Variety, Newsweek, Life, Time,* etc.? . . . I am frankly astounded at the total lack of a *single* detail of the propaganda campaign in your letter. Not one clipping!"⁵¹ Dukelsky was in Paris because Paul Gilson and Nino Frank had asked him to compose the music for a French play based on the life of Milord l'Arsouille, who in reality was Charles de la Battut, the bastard son of an English peer and a French mother. Set during the period of Balzac, George Sand, Delacroix, Victor Hugo, and other amorous French artists and intellectuals, Vladimir was fascinated with the costumes the actors would wear: "Pictorially speaking, can you think of prettier clothes than those worn in the day of the Good King Louis Philippe? . . . Having paid obeisance to Romantic *floraison* of the first half of the nineteenth century in my first stage work, *Zephyr and Flora* . . . , having written the Pushkinesque *Entr'acte* for Balanchine, how could I refuse to help to transplant my favorite period to the contemporary musical theater?" Dukelsky and his lyricist, Francis Claude, wrote one song after another during June, "in a creative frenzy the like of which I had never experienced." He considered the score the best of his career. The two writers of the libretto completed the first scene of which Vladimir and Francis approved but then took the story in a new direction, imbuing it with "a nightmarish 'existentialist' overtone not at all in keeping with the romantic bravado and amorous songfulness of our contributions."⁵²

Much of his "creative frenzy" Duke attributed to an American studying voice in Paris with whom he fell madly in love. He took this chance because "there is nothing easier than to fall in love in the very special Paris June, when the whole city aches with romantic longing; all you need is a girl." The girl, Estelle, was "blond and pretty in a Campus Queen way, complete with sweater and skirt, socks and sneakers; probably a throwback in my mind to Joan, who was the classical American college belle." Although he was forty-five, his proposal was accepted, but she insisted on "*no* full-scale love-making prior to marriage" and that she spend the summer studying music in Rome.[53]

After Duke returned to New York, he received two letters from Estelle, one stating that she was remaining in Rome and calling off the engagement. Their age difference and music being her only true love was her explanation. The other letter was sent to Duke by mistake. Written to her mother, it contained disparaging remarks about him. Duke retaliated with a six-page, single-spaced letter countering her criticisms. It began, "I cannot thank you enough for your last two letters. These two effusions made me dislike you so thoroughly that it will now be a simple matter to get you out of my system once and for all." It ended with "I asked Marchese Roi and Baron Lanfranchi to look you up in Rome—so just try to add the Marchese and the Baron to your collection of Princes and Dukes and drop this one Duke from that valuable list."[54]

The rejection, however, hurt Duke deeply. Admitting that it took him a year to get over it, he wrote:

> At forty-five, adjusting one's entire world to the idea of marital existence is not simple; having effected such an adjustment—*before* entering into marriage—it's doubly difficult to readjust oneself to the "confirmed bachelor" status. Some of my friends insisted that it was not I but merely my pride that was hurt; they were right to some extent.... Nevertheless, pride played but a small part in my emotional downfall; by falling in love with Estelle, absurd though my love may have been, I got away from my own self and learned to like this selfless state. With Estelle abruptly stepping out of my life, I was free to face myself again, and self-contemplation is hardly a substitute for love.

Music, however, "came to my rescue, as it had so often in the past."[55]

In September 1949, Dukelsky attended the Yaddo Festival in Saratoga Springs, New York, in which Nancy Chang sang and Dean Dixon conducted six of his songs based on A. E. Housman's *Shropshire Lad*.[56] A review in the *New York Times* noted that even though the "song cycle hardly probed the depths of . . . the tragically touching poem, it was invariably proficient in its workmanship."[57] In early October, Dukelsky spoke during intermission of a concert broadcast by the CBS Symphony. Bernard Herrmann conducted his *Ode to the Milky Way* and two other works.[58] In mid-month, Dukelsky accompanied John Creighton Murray in a performance of his Violin Sonata in D Major at Carnegie Hall.[59] Again, the *Times* offered a lukewarm appraisal: "Mr. Dukelsky's Sonata, with the composer at the piano, proved an effective vehicle for the young violinist's flair for dramatic flourishes and for his ability to sustain a melodic line. The music was most appealing in the melodious, unforced slow movement. Otherwise it tended to become academic in the development of its clear-cut themes."[60] In March 1950, pianist Barbara Denenholz premiered Dukelsky's *Three Caprices* at Carnegie Hall.[61]

By this time, Dukelsky's relationship with the League of Composers had become strained in part because he was not invited to become a member of its board. In mid-1950, he wrote to Nicolai Berezowsky, congratulating him on becoming the chairman of the League and explaining the problems he had with it:

> For several years now I refused to attend the League's functions because of the simple fact that Mr. Aaron Copland presided over its destinies. I have attempted to co-operate with Mr. Copland in the past as you know and found him not merely hopeless, but totally objectionable.... I never quite understood why it seems impossible for any musical organization in this country to exist without the guidance of Mr. Copland; and I am happy to see that at last one of them is finally freeing itself of his yoke.

The dislike may have resulted from Serge Koussevitzky of the Boston Symphony performing Copland's Third Symphony but not Dukelsky's Third.[62]

The following year Dukelsky quit the League of Composers, his hostile letter of resignation blaming the entire organization for neglecting his music. The resignation prompted longtime friend Nicolas Slonimsky to lecture Dukelsky on protocol: "As you well understand, everyone has suffered rebukes, undeserved neglect, and ingratitude.... But I cannot imagine, in my wildest nightmares, that I should advertise the fact that I am not appreciated. This is the worst publicity that anyone can spread, for the question immediately arises: if nobody wants him, he must be no good." Slonimsky considered him "one of the luckiest composers now living in America, and lots of composers who get performances might look at you with envy. You are the only symphonic composer in America who makes money writing music."[63] The money, however, came not from Dukelsky but from Duke, especially from the royalties from his popular songs.

In 1950 Duke's agent asked him if he would be interested in writing the score for *Casey Jones*, based on the mythical railroad hero. Sammy Cahn, who was to write the lyrics, wrote to Duke in September, announcing that he would be in New York in early October and predicting that their meeting "will result in both pleasure and profit for us." He mentioned that he had called his brother, Alex, but had only spoken with his wife. She had great hopes Duke would come to California in the near future.[64]

Cahn met Duke in his apartment and was taken aback by his dress—he wore a handkerchief in his jacket sleeve and a huge carnation in his lapel. What impressed him most, however, was his library. Books were everywhere, "in the hallways, in the bedroom, in the bathroom. (A composer of popular songs who read *books*—most unusual, damn near subversive.) He was, I have to say, the most talented composer I ever worked with. Most popular songs are written in four eight-bar sections with a bridge—a departure—in between.... Vernon Duke had more variations in the bridge than anyone I ever knew."[65]

Vernon described the lyricist as "a small, fidgety man with a black mustache and a supercharged personality. He expressed his joy at meeting me, 'a man he always admired from afar,' as he put it; the adjective he used continually in connection with my person and gifts was 'great,' which was a nice adjective after reading so many less nice ones used to describe my music." Duke and Cahn wrote a half dozen songs for *Casey Jones*. Sammy was an "immensely industrious worker, and had enough humility and capacity for self-criticism not to be content with everything he wrote," noted Duke. He would write a lyric Duke thought fit nicely one of his tunes, but then he would take another tack and they would write several variations on the same theme, Cahn always assuring Duke that he was doing "great." Although the show was never produced, Cahn persuaded Duke to join him in Hollywood to work on a picture: "It was my turn to say, 'Great!' because I was sick of New York, which was seemingly as sick of me, and because I wanted to be with my 'new' family—Alex, Mona, and Natasha, their daughter—again, after five years."[66]

DUKE AND DUKELSKY BECOME ONE
LOS ANGELES, 1951–1969

The Los Angeles Vernon Duke moved to in early 1951 was not the city it would become. Founded in 1771 by Spanish colonizers at the American Indian village of Yaanga, it remained a provincial backwater surrounded by cattle ranches and vineyards until well into the nineteenth century.[1] It gained international recognition by hosting the 1932 Olympics, but during the Great Depression, Los Angeles was noted mainly for its film industry. Of all the cities where Duke lived—Kiev, Odessa, Constantinople, Paris, and New York—only Los Angeles lacked a true urban identity, resulting in it being labeled "suburbs in search of a city" and "the fragmented metropolis."[2]

Its first freeway, the Arroyo Seco Parkway, had opened in 1940, but the freeway system that would eventually grid the city was still in its planning stages, and the smog that would envelop the Los Angeles basin was not yet a health hazard. The city had experienced rapid economic and population growth during World War II, but its population numbered slightly less than two million at its end.[3] Many residents had come from other states seeking work in the arms industries. Others came from Europe.

Refugees from the Russian Revolution had begun settling in Los Angeles, especially in Hollywood, in the 1920s. Many were from the old aristocracy: military officers, engineers, scientists, professors, lawyers, doctors, members of the clergy, businessmen, musicians from conservatories, and actors from imperial theaters. Although most came to the West Coast from

Siberia and China, others arrived via Odessa and Constantinople. They established restaurants, art clubs, cafés, aid societies, the Orthodox Church, and even a bookstore on Sunset Boulevard. By the end of the 1920s, perhaps 950 Russians lived in Hollywood with another 550 scattered over the rest of greater Los Angeles.[4] Vladimir's friend Nicolas Slonimsky was there, as was the less friendly Stravinsky. Soprano Nina Koshetz, whom he had met in New York, lived in Hollywood and appeared in several movies. Pianists Sergei Rachmaninoff and Vladimir Horowitz settled there, as did film composer Dimitri Tiomkin. Russian actors and actors from parts of the Russian Empire became familiar faces in American films, but only Yul Brynner became a star. Most were character actors, including Gregory Ratoff (who also directed), Mikhail Rasumny, Lewis Milestone (who also directed), Anatole Litvak (who also directed), Vladimir Sokoloff, Mischa Auer, Michael Chekhov, Maria Ouspenskaya, Feodor Chaliapin Jr., and perhaps the best known, Akim Tamiroff.[5]

Duke met some of these actors and directors as well as other émigrés and therefore was not entirely cut off from his Russian culture. But his move to Los Angeles may be seen as the last sharp turn in his life, the final stage in his exile from Russia. In his autobiography, he acknowledged that he was not just an American but also a Californian and would not live anywhere else:

> I still cling to the idea that, in direct contrast with New York, California "is a good place to live but not to visit." A short stay in the L.A. area won't yield much to an observant visitor. The place looks like a watered-down Riviera on a large scale, the gas stations are more impressive than the palms, and the natives are very clean and big-framed and look as if they spent their entire lives eating health foods, drinking fruit juices, and getting a tan by speeding in shiny convertibles with the tops down. The weather is so uniformly good that it deprives people of their major topic of conversation; the distances are so great that no one in L.A. has ever been known to "drop in" on a friend, who usually lives ten miles away; the nightlife is of no particular distinction or variety and offers nothing that hasn't been seen already in New York or Chicago with fancier trimmings; most disappointing of all, people who are busy with studio or office work

go to bed at 10 P.M. and get up at 6:30 or 7 A.M. A stranger with a car has little to do after ten but to go boozing or take in a film. A stranger without a car is a dead duck! However, to know the place is to love it.⁶

Vernon even had high praise for Hollywood, where he would venture from time to time for its atmosphere, which he called bucolic. Gone was the Garden of Allah with its Fitzgeraldian phantoms, but the hospitable 1922 period piece Chateau Marmont remained. A Victorian ice cream parlor and an Edwardian beer garden were doing a rousing business. Villagers book-hunted at Pickwick or Larry Edmunds. The notorious Hollywood Boulevard was not notorious, and the side streets were cozy and well scrubbed.⁷

Duke stayed with his brother, Alex, who was employed as a film scenic artist at Metro-Goldwyn-Mayer, before moving into a small house in Westwood.⁸ He probably attended his brother's tempera show, held at the Landau Gallery on La Cienega Boulevard for two weeks in July 1952. His paintings consisted of musicians, often depicted in a satirical way, and impressions of the movement and color of the ballet.⁹ Duke joined a small community that revolved around UCLA. The university then enrolled only about 14,000 students, many of them veterans. But it was developing a first-rate music department. Three members of the famous Roth String Quartet would soon become part of its faculty, and the fourth would join the Los Angeles Conservatory of Music.¹⁰

Above the university lay the Hollywood Hills where a record producer took Duke to a cocktail party shortly after his arrival. There he met more men with beards than without, discussing Thelonious Monk, the jazz author Hugues Panassié, and the 1921 Brunswick blues recordings. Told by the "cats" that canyon living was "the craziest," he considered buying a house in the hills. But he quickly concluded that driving up the curving roads congested with "souped-up jalopies with scatologically percussive mufflers" was not for him, especially after receiving a traffic ticket on one of his forays.¹¹

A more positive encounter with the law occurred after he was robbed of his television and hi-fi equipment. One of the two police officers sent to investigate was an amateur songwriter who shyly asked Vernon if he would listen to a song he had written. The officer returned the next day with his recorder and played a pretty good "pop" chorus. Duke found "something touching about the young man's earnestness and modesty—and I took his song to a publisher; the lyrics weren't bad either. The weary publisher didn't buy." The event stayed with him, and "every once in a while, I'm seized with a sudden desire to turn off the phonograph, junk the radio, shut out the television, and invite the humble Pan of the Police Force to dust off his artless old flute and regale me with a few poor but *living* notes of music."[12]

Duke's fame accompanied him to Los Angeles, where he became the subject of an extensive article in the *Los Angeles Times* in early 1952. When reporter Leonard Wibberley arrived, Duke was in his kitchen, developing an oyster soup with a meat base and three varieties of pepper: "The yellow stuff is Turkish sauce. . . . It goes excellently with fish—I'm planning tuna. Food interests me as much as music. It demands harmony, contrast, drama, and high tonal quality. Indeed there is a close connection between the national dishes of different countries and their musical history." The interview, however, was not about food but about music, in particular about the branch of the Society for Forgotten Music that Duke was introducing to Los Angeles. Music lovers, he insisted, only wanted to hear the same compositions over and over again. But why go to a concert of Beethoven's Fifth when you have an excellent recording of it in your home? How many new concertos and sonatas do you hear? Duke's objective was to make the public aware of the hundreds of pieces of music in all forms by many composers that have been completely forgotten or perhaps had one performance and then were ignored for a century or two. To Wibberley's suggestion that perhaps they laid an egg, Duke said, "Not so. . . . They may have been indifferently performed at the premiere. Or they may have been given bad notices by biased critics. Or they may have been written by someone who was out of favor at the time." Many neglected composers were unable to earn a living with their music, lacked influence, or failed to find patrons. One of the examples he offered was the sixteenth-century composer Don Carlos Gesualdo. The several pieces of his music the society uncovered contain modern harmonies. Unfortunately, he "killed his wife and her lover, which gave him a black eye, but he was a magnificent musician."[13]

When it came to administering black eyes to conductors who dared to reject his compositions, Duke seldom held back. On February 15, 1952, he wrote to Dimitri Mitropoulos complaining that for thirteen years he had written to him about performing his Third Symphony but had heard nothing from him: "That I'm sure constitutes a record of some sort and it is also something of an achievement because no one in the course of my varied and rather noisy career has treated me in this fashion." Even if the conductor disliked his music, Duke sought to be honored with a reply: "I know all about conductors' busy schedules, their being pestered by charlatans and amateurs, but no one, not even my worst enemy, would call me either a charlatan or an amateur."[14]

Mitropoulos failed to respond, but his friend Nicolas Slonimsky, upon receiving a copy of the letter, had much to say: "Your letter to Mitropoulos stunned me into temporary silence.... Your whole letter sounds as if you do not expect Mitropoulos to do anything about your music, but just want to blow off some steam. This is the most frustrating thing to do. It shows... your [sic] being unfairly excluded from a profession to which you rightfully belong."[15]

Ignoring his friend's advice, Duke continued to argue with conductors. The very brief and noncommittal note that Robert Whitney of the Louisville Philharmonic sent him about performing one of his works produced wonderment: "In it you say you were genuinely impressed with my third symphony, yet you are returning it to the publisher. Is it because your orchestra isn't large enough or because you are not sufficiently impressed?" He had sent him the symphony "with the intentions of obtaining a performance." But if he could not include it, "How about my 'Ballade' for strings, tympani, and piano solo? This only takes about ten minutes to perform and was already done with success by Bernard Herrmann, Daniel Saidenberg, and Nicolas Slonimsky." Duke's request came to naught.[16]

Rejections, however, never prevented Duke from having fun. In Los Angeles he acquired new friends and linked up with old ones. He learned to drive to attend the parties of Vincente Minnelli, John Houseman, the Tony Duquettes, Edwin Lester, and especially to those hosted by Ira and Leonore Gershwin. Ira preferred small parties of five or six people, recalled Vernon, who were "known for their love of argument, and letting them loose in his drawing room; the feathers fly while Ira grunts contentedly, puffing on an aromatic Montecristo." On one occasion, Duke got into an argument with pianist, composer, arranger, actor, author, and self-deprecating neurotic

Oscar Levant. As they screamed at each other, Leonore was about to send for help, but "Ira beamed delightedly, took the Montecristo out of his mouth, and said with a purr: 'Now, isn't that better than a stupid big party, where nobody knows anybody?'"[17]

Ogden Nash, another friend, toyed with the idea of working in Hollywood as a lyricist and asked Duke for help. In January 1952 Nash wrote: "I am more grateful than I can say for your continued loyalty and your efforts to open the gates for me, and I hope with all my heart that it won't be long before we can do some work together again." When Nash arrived in Los Angeles, Duke hosted a cocktail party for him that was attended by agents and producers. In February, Nash informed his daughter Isabel that Duke was "really working like mad to get me out of here." Probably because he was not yet well established in the city, Duke was unsuccessful in finding Nash work.[18]

Duke's own Los Angeles musical career, however, got off to a financially rewarding if troubling start. It began with Warner Brothers' *She's Working Her Way through College,* starring Virginia Mayo, Gene Nelson, Patrice Wymore, and Ronald Reagan. Duke asked the producer for permission to orchestrate his own music and to use only nine musicians, long of the view that a small orchestra provided a better sound for a musical. As Duke recalled, William Jacobs did not think "much of my revolutionary notion, frowned and sent me to his musical director (a titan in his sphere, owing to a positively titan salary he was getting) for a 'conference.'" It did not go well. The director insisted that a small orchestra would cost him his assignment and would force arrangers to go hungry. He told Duke to "go back to your room and compose some nice music, like a good little boy, and let me worry about orchestrations, eh?"[19] That he was making three thousand dollars a week perhaps lessened the humiliation, a condition not lost on Nicolas Slonimsky: "If you can arrange for me to ghost-write for you—or for anybody—I would be willing to fly to Hollywood for half your salary—or a quarter. Your affluence is certainly unique among musicians of any kind short of Heifetz."[20]

Duke was only one of several tunesmiths whose songs were performed in the movie, which is about a burlesque star who goes back to college. Even though "the story is weak," wrote one critic, "there is high entertainment value in the many musical numbers, including elaborate and skillfully executed dance routines." Among the tunes, especially notable was Duke's "Love Is Still for Free."[21] There were "nine solo numbers and production numbers sung and staged with lavish effect," wrote another reviewer. He thought highly of Vernon's "The Stuff That Dreams Are Made Of."[22]

Sammy Cahn probably got him his next picture, *April in Paris*, starring Doris Day and Ray Bolger. "The moment we were signed," Cahn recalled, "I went over to our office at the studio, which was inaccessible—Mr. Duke had filled it with flowers. I tried to dissuade him from his natural compulsion—the hanky, the carnation, and now that he was working, a big cigar—because, as I warned him, one day Jack Warner was going to see him on the lot and say, 'Who's the schmuck who thinks he's me.'" As it turned out, Doris Day, not Warner, presented the problems. Day told Duke and Cahn she was delighted with the songs when first presented to her, but a few days later they learned she hated them. Duke and Cahn rewrote the songs, but Cahn considered them inferior to the originals.[23] The title song is heard twice, and the other Duke/Cahn songs include "It Must Be Good," "I'm Gonna Ring the Bell Tonight," "That's What Makes Paris Paree," "Give Me Your Lips," "I Know a Place," and "I Ask You." Don Ward called the movie "conventional Parisian dream stuff" and considered the music of Duke and Cahn "fairly acceptable, but not nearly up to the good old title tune."[24] Edwin Martin noted, "The score makes easy listening, but other than the title tune, makes no great impression."[25]

Despite his Hollywood employment, Duke was still regarded as a Broadway composer, and in 1952 he was called upon to write the music for a show to be called *Two's Company*.[26] On May 16, producers Jimmy Russo and Milton Rosenstock, Charlie Chaplin, and Duke had dinner at the home of Bette Davis and her husband, Gary Merrill. Duke and Chaplin performed some of the sketches for the proposed musical, and according to Duke, Davis "absolutely howled most of the time and confessed that she had never enjoyed herself more." They also sang some of the songs, with lyrics by Ogden Nash, that would be suitable for Davis and for the show itself. Davis signed a contract a short time later.[27]

Born in Lowell, Massachusetts, Bette Davis had attended the Cushing Academy in Ashburnham, Massachusetts, and had known Duke's brother, Alex, when he was there. Her first Broadway show, a comedy called *Solid South*, ran for four weeks in 1930. She loved the East Coast and had long sought to do a play, but being terrified at the thought had turned down several offers. The three thousand dollars per week against 10 percent of the house gross probably made the decision a bit easier. Still, her Yankee conscience welcomed the challenge as she prepared "to sing, be sustainedly funny, perform bumps, grinds, struts, kicks, and shimmies, and dance the Black Bottom."[28]

Jules Dassin directed the dances and sketches, and Jerome Robbins created the choreography.[29] Rehearsals began in September 1952, and it opened in Detroit on Sunday, October 19.[30] Thus began a series of mishaps and problems. While singing her opening number, Davis fainted and had to be carried from the stage. She returned in five minutes, quipping, "You cannot say I did not fall for you" and managed to get through the performance.[31] The three succeeding performances, however, were canceled because she complained of having a cold and a throat ailment.[32] During a scene in Boston, a long string of beads she was wearing in a sketch satirizing Sadie Thompson, the lady of rather loose morals in the play of the same name, broke and scattered all over the floor. Her improvised "You see! Nobody ever gave Sadie anything that was any good" got a smile from the audience.[33]

Duke told a reporter that Davis might not be an opera diva but that she stays on note and he would rather work with her than almost all of the divas he had collaborated with. He also admitted that he had toned down his music in deference to Nash: "Ogden's lyrics are so special, so good, and so intellectual that for once I preferred people admire the words rather than the tune." The reporter thought "It Just Occurred to Me" and "Clear Blue Sky" would become hits and noted that Duke was trying to get Nash to join with him on a musical version of *The Man Who Came to Dinner.*[34]

That project never got off the ground, and *Two's Company* had difficulty taking off in New York. It was to open at the Alvin Theater on December 4, but the producers asked the drama critics not to attend until the fifteenth. More time was needed by John Murray Anderson, who had replaced Dassin, to polish the show.[35] As it turned out, a throat ailment of Davis prevented the revue from opening until the fifteenth.[36] The reviews were mixed. Mark Barron wrote that Davis has "a nice sense of stage comedy." Supporting actors "and the score by Vernon Duke and Ogden Nash do much to lift this revue out of the ordinary class."[37] Brooks Atkinson was

VERNON DUKE, ENGLAND, 1953.
Reproduced with permission from Kay Duke Ingalls.

impressed with the ballet dancers who "have more flair for the revue stage than most performers, especially if Vernon Duke and Ogden Nash are calling the tunes and lyrics. Like the revue as a whole, the music is uneven. But Mr. Duke never lets a ballet down, and Mr. Nash always has a word for it that is pithy or humorous."[38] "Round About" and "Just Like a Man" were borrowed from *Sweet Bye and Bye* and sung respectively by Ellen Hanley and Davis.[39] For ninety-one performances, Davis carried the show, but when she again became ill, it was closed. Because the audience came only to see Davis, no replacement was deemed possible. The show did reasonably well at the box office, but Nash was not pleased with the outcome. "I can't bring myself to contemplate any further theater venture at the moment," he told Duke.⁴⁰

Before the closing, Duke, in February 1953, sailed for Paris, where he had been commissioned to write a ballet to be performed at the Theatre Marigny in Paris.⁴¹ He also wanted to visit his aunt and uncle in Ljubljana, Yugoslavia. While on board the SS *Saturnia*, he learned that Stalin and Prokofiev had died, and on arrival in Naples he read in an American newspaper that *Two's Company* had closed. His first impulse was to return home, but he went on to Yugoslavia and had a very nice visit with his relatives, whom he had not seen since meeting with them in Constantinople. They wanted to hear all about his career and took him to recitals, two operas, and a concert performed by the Ljubljana Philharmonic. The remainder of his trip was uneventful, and he sailed home on the SS *Vulcania*.⁴²

On Long Island he saw a revival of *Cabin in the Sky*, which now included "Summer Is A-Comin' In" from *Lady Comes Across* and "Not a Care in the World" from *Banjo Eyes*. The dialogue was presented in standard English, and some of the music from the original production was restored. Juanita Hall, Nipsey Russell, and Josephine Premice took on the major roles, and Billy Strayhorn and Luther Henderson provided the two-piano accompaniment. During its weeklong run, the performances were sold out, and the show received positive notices.⁴³

Apparently it was during his stay in New York that he recorded an album called *Vernon Duke Plays Vernon Duke* at John Latouche's apartment. He played the songs on a strangely designed piano with an extra keyboard. By pressing a special pedal, every note was augmented by a corresponding note an octave higher. He included two of his most famous songs, "Autumn in New York" and "April in Paris," the latter sung by Huguette Ferly, and several lesser known songs, such as "Who's to Blame" sung by Dorothy Richards. As George Frazier wrote in the liner notes, Duke was a "real rarity in his field in his ability to interpret his own music on the piano. It is no secret that most composers of popular songs play their brainchildren as if they were trying to disown them. Vernon Duke, however, interprets his songs affectionately, excitingly, and never with any loss of values."⁴⁴

That year pianist Dick Hyman also interpreted his songs. Classically trained by pianist Anton Rovinsky, he drifted toward jazz at an early age and

VERNON DUKE PLAYS VERNON DUKE. Atlantic Recording Corporation, 1953.

even took lessons from the great Teddy Wilson. After World War II, he joined Benny Goodman's big band before forming his own trio and joining the New York staff of the National Broadcasting Company. *Autumn in New York* includes "Cabin in the Sky," "What Is There to Say," "Now," and "The Love I Long For," as well as Duke's more famous compositions. The renditions by Hyman are as complicated as Duke's harmonies and often reflect his classical training as much as his jazz background.[45]

Duke returned to Los Angeles, and in September 1953 he prepared to work on *Dilly,* adapted from the novel by Theodore Pratt. Jerry Lawrence and Robert Lee were hired to write the libretto, and Gala Eben was to produce.[46] Duke intended to write the lyrics with Lawrence and Lee, but he also wanted to work again with John Latouche. Duke persuaded him to join the team, but shortly after signing a contract, John left the show, explaining in a letter to Duke that he had heard Lawrence's lyrics, which were "witty and beautifully constructed. Added to your own baroque tendencies lyrically, I think you have a combination that outweighs my own misty creative efforts."[47] Duke responded on November 23, 1953, claiming that he had no proof that Lawrence and Lee had any aptitude for lyrics: "I solemnly swear that I will not write another line for 'Dilly.' . . . Johnny, we love you and we need you; need I say more?"[48] Latouche did not budge.

In January 1954, Duke hosted a party at his Westwood house honoring Gala Eben. Also in attendance were Beegle and Tony Duquette, the Arthur Freeds, Pat and Frank Lieberman, the Robert E. Lees, Nesuhi Ertegun, Leonore and Ira Gershwin, and Ella Logan, who was to star in the show. The party, written up in a society column in the *Los Angeles Times*, suggests that Duke had become a member of some of the city's elite.[49] Auditions began in July in the house of movie star Edward G. Robinson, but the show was never produced.[50]

By this time, Duke was regularly appearing on television and radio shows. In March 1954, he was a guest on *Leave It to the Girls*, a television show featuring a panel of women and one man. The show had evolved from serious discussions of the problems of career women to a more comedic routine about love, romance, and marriage. "Vernon Duke comes to the aid of John Henry Faulk," read an announcement.[51] That Duke was invited because of his reputation as a ladies' man seems probable, as does the probability that he applied his considerable European charm on the panel. He reappeared on the show in May, when he again defended men.[52] In September he joined singer Champ Butler and the first Mr. America on *You're Never Too Old*, a television program.[53] In May 1955, he appeared on Dave Garroway's radio show, along with Mary Pickford, Alistair Cooke, and Buddy Morrow.[54] At mid-month he was a guest on the television show *Musical Nitecap* at 11:30 P.M.[55] *Panorama Pacific* was his next stop.[56] The following year, when General Electric decided to bring back the *Colgate Comedy Hour*, it paid Duke $4,000 for fifty seconds of theme music.[57]

When not appearing on television shows, Duke was working on his autobiography, which he probably had begun shortly after arriving in Los Angeles. As meticulous in his writing as in his composing, Duke submitted many more racy pages than Little, Brown and Company could accept. According to a reporter, when Duke asked his publishers why they had cut two hundred pages, he was told, "We've been in Boston over 100 years and we expect to stay here."[58] Even in its reduced size, *Passport to Paris* is a tour de force, but its ending paragraph is especially significant: "I'm dropping the name of Vladimir Dukelsky and henceforth will sign all music that may still flow from my pen—regardless of its nature—as Vernon Duke. And having once obtained a passport to the Champs Elysées of Paris as Dukelsky, Russian, I shall humbly aspire to the more permanent Elysian Fields, the Elysium of Ancient Greeks . . . as Duke the American."[59]

Irving Kolodin compared Duke and Dukelsky to a couple who "shared the same roof (not the most uncommon thing among contemporary composers), even the same skin (which is not). Over the years it became apparent that Duke had as much esteem for Dukelsky as Dukelsky had affection for Duke. . . . And like some other couples in which such a 'supporting role' has become habit after years, the use of separate names had come to seem rather superfluous. So, as noted at the end of *Passport to Paris*, they have become one again and henceforth he will be only Duke."[60]

Passport to Paris received very positive notices. According to Francis Steegmuller of the *New York Times*, Duke was "an autobiographer of considerable perception and honesty; he chronicles not only the practical advantages and disadvantages of his musical duality, but also his awareness that the versatility may well be accompanied by some artistic disadvantages. With innumerable deft touches he illustrates the similarities and dissimilarities of the two musical worlds in which he has lived." Steegmuller was also impressed by the "extremely vivid evocation of scenes, moods, personalities and atmospheres found in the first half of the book—for, of course, the book breaks into two almost equally balanced halves." He was especially taken with the years "before the personality becomes so openly hyphenated; . . . but it is a tribute to the second personality, second in the sense of being openly two, that the spectacle of such fresh youth is given the vividness of such perspective."[61]

Claudia Cassidy of the *Chicago Sunday Tribune* called the book "gabby" but "frequently entertaining." It was "Duke's farewell to a man he had supported for decades, Vladimir Dukelsky." The "dressy wunderkind" may have "caught the caboose of the Diaghileff train with a ballet called 'Zephyr and Flora,' but 'April in Paris' made more money." Cassidy even mentioned the index that "will let the specifically curious pounce without prowling."[62] Duke claimed not to like writing about himself, another critic pointed out, but "he has managed to repress the sheer agony it must have been to write this 484 page autobiography." He knew everyone in the entertainment business, and name after name "drop out of this hefty volume like a cascade; names almost for the sake of names."[63]

Nicolas Slonimsky congratulated Duke: "Of all musical autobiographies, this is by far the most brilliantly written one, and probably the most honest one as well. Wagner's autobiography is dull and incomplete in its personal part; Berlioz was utterly untrustworthy; Rimsky-Korsakov wrote like a clerk. I had no idea that you possessed a literary talent of this magnitude."[64] That the book was so well written also surprised lyricist Howard Dietz: "I say 'surprising' in no patronizing sense, but in a spirt of admiration and wonder. You are not supposed to be a writer, and they ought to bar you from the union. What's going to happen to us writers when composers encroach and do it better?" He read the book and *War and Peace* in Bermuda, "so you can call it a Russian holiday."[65]

Duke complained to Ogden Nash in May that "not a single magazine has as yet come out with a notice of the book: not Time, Newsweek, the New Yorker, Atlantic, Harper's or the Saturday Review of Literature." He asked Nash to contact the editors of these magazines he knew and inquire into their silence: "I believe that these gentleman do not think me important enough as either composer or author, which might be their excuse, but I do not see how they can ignore new and exciting stuff of such figures as Diaghilev, Prokofiev, Gershwin, Balanchine, Cocteau, and so on."[66]

Dietz, however, praised the book in an essay in *Atlantic Review*: "It has erudition, unparaded application of his literary storehouse, style without pretense, and is a contribution to works in English by authors to whom English is a second language." The theme of the book is "a duel between his dual musical egos. . . . It is not unlike those ambivalent finales in the early Ziegfeldian or George Whitean revues featuring a contest between opera and jazz. Jazz wins in this life story as it was destined to from the day in Constantinople when Vladimir played the sheet music of a song called 'Swanee' by George Gershwin."[67]

In August 1955, after a considerable amount of "bombarding" conductors and producers, Duke finally got his Third Symphony performed. The concert, attended by 7,500 people, including Duke, came about largely by luck. The previous year, Duke had met Walter Hendl in Santa Barbara:

> We had a few beers and talked music, agreeing on most points. I showed him my symphony, to which he took an immediate liking

and . . . offered to perform it at Chautauqua New York the next summer! "Well, it's not the Boston Symphony, but beggars can't be choosers," I mused, my heart brimful with gratitude. My piece was, indeed, played at Chautauqua and played well; it received a substantial success and the (one) local critic wrote an approving notice.[68]

The following year, however, success proved elusive when Duke and Ogden Nash again teamed up, this time for a revue to be produced and directed by twenty-two-year-old Ben Bagley. Bagley had begun his Broadway career the previous year with the *Shoestring Revue* at the President Theater. A small but brilliant cast accompanied by two pianists cost about $15,000 and made a profit for its producers. The success of the show prompted the directors of the Phoenix Theater to employ Bagley to produce *The Littlest Revue* for their 1955–56 season. Bagley hired several tunesmiths and lyricists, including Duke and Nash, to write the music supporting sketches satirizing cultural topics.[69]

Although Nash was considerably older and considerably wiser regarding Broadway shows, Bagley was the man in charge, and on one occasion he provoked the mild-mannered Nash. When he cut the song "Blame It on Mother," Nash exploded, causing Duke to inform Bagley that he should be honored for being the only one to get Nash to raise his voice.[70] Of the sixteen songs presented in the revue, Duke wrote six with Nash and one each with Sammy Cahn and John Latouche.[71] Unlike many musicals that opened in a tryout town, *The Littlest Revue* premiered cold at Phoenix Theater on May 22, 1956.[72] Brooks Atkinson praised it for its "uniformly high standard of intelligence and humor."[73] Walter Winchell, however, thought the cast did their best "with too many listless tunes and sketches."[74] Another critic noted that "Duke is one of the best composers in show business, but none of the numbers makes much of an impression."[75] According to William Hawkins, "Most of the tunes have the slightly listless air of having been rejected from other scores."[76] The show ended on June 17, a week earlier than scheduled.[77] Ben Bagley gave up producing for the theater, and even though Nash and Duke remained good friends, they never again worked together.[78]

When the cast album was being produced in mid-1956, Nash somehow got his own section in the liner notes in which he poked fun at those involved in the production, including Duke. Because of his artistic integrity, "he refuses to recognize a time difference between Beverly Hills and New York; if you are waked up at two in the morning by a phone call from a man to whom it is still yesterday, that's Duke." When it came to Bagley, however, Nash was more caustic than witty: "Usually diffident and soft-spoken, he is a tiger when aroused, and few of his colleagues venture to cross him without a chair handy to thrust in his face."[79]

On August 7, 1956, two months after the show closed, Duke lost a very good friend, John Latouche, to a heart attack.[80] Early the following year Duke published a tribute to him in *Theater Arts*. The article briefly recounts his musical life, emphasizing that his poetry background was the key to his lyric writing: "Latouche's full-scale theatrical debut was with *Cabin in the Sky* (1940), the real beginning of his stormy career as one of America's most promising and most controversial lyricists." But he had his share of failures, including his and Duke's *The Lady Comes Across*. Although Latouche turned down many offers, fearing he would be forced to write lyrics, not poetry, his poetry was well displayed in his last work, *The Ballad of Baby Doe*. Duke considered it "an authentically American opera, possibly an American *Carmen*." Duke concluded his article by quoting a line from the opera: "'Your name will thin like a whisper in the wind.' Let's hope Johnny's will not."[81]

Duke wrote to Effie Latouche, John's mother, in March, mentioning that the editors of the journal had omitted several paragraphs about himself and John, probably because they were too personal. And they failed to include some of the photographs she had sent the editor. He sincerely hoped she liked what he said about John "because, believe me, it was heartfelt and certainly well meant." He had refrained from discussing anything about John's politics, even though the editor "kept asking me to stress the point that Johnny was never the radical so many people supposed him to be."[82]

As if timed to lessen the pain, the following month the Roth String Quartet performed a Duke composition at Schoenberg Hall at UCLA. The *Los Angeles Times* reviewed the concert:

> The contemporary work of the evening was the Quartet in C Major by Vernon Duke, written in 1956 and dedicated to the Roth Quartet. Mr. Duke, who usually publishes his serious music under the name

of Vladimir Dukelsky, was in the audience to witness the world premiere of his music, and it is safe to assume that the work was given an authentic reading.

The Quartet, a fairly short composition, is in three movements. In place of a slow movement, the composer wrote something of a lengthy introduction to the short and lively finale. The first movement suffered from a haphazard development and generally unclear form. Mr. Duke's musical idiom is mildly dissonant and sometimes reminiscent of Prokofiev in his weaker moments.[83]

At this point in his life, Duke had met hundreds of people, famous and unknown, but he had established few long-term relationships with men and even shorter ones with women, largely because his life had been in such flux but also because of his volatile personality. In his autobiography he wrote: "Through my entire life I was cursed, or possibly blessed, with a dual personality as lover as well as composer. I have desired and I have loved, certainly, but with two exceptions I never desired those I loved, never loved those I desired. . . . I've never been married and my stock answer when asked why not is, 'Because, should I be married to one woman, I'd be unfaithful to all the 'others.'"[84]

A year after the book was published, Duke met Kay McCracken, a soprano and protégé of former opera star Lotte Lehmann:

> Vernon Duke and I met in Santa Barbara, California, following a Music Academy of the West performance of *The Marriage of Figaro*, produced and directed by Lotte Lehmann. During the performance (I was in the chorus), Luba Tcheresky, who was singing Cherubino, told me there was a man in the audience she thought I ought to meet—she thought I was his "type," which was a bit offputting at that moment. I didn't recognize the name Vernon Duke, which shocked Luba, who scoldingly informed me as to the titles of his songs, which I did indeed recognize—I had grown up with "April in Paris," "Autumn in New York," "I Can't Get Started," et al.
>
> After the performance, Luba brought Vernon to the cast party, and on the drive there, Vernon told Luba he had seen a girl on the stage

he wanted to meet. She asked which one, and he said, "the big blond in the chorus." When I arrived at the party, with my Mother in tow, he pointed me out to Luba, and said, "She's the one." The remainder of that evening I spent sitting on the sofa between Maurice Abravanel (who had conducted the "Figaro") and Vernon Duke who carried on an animated conversation in French, very little of which I could understand at the time. I remember being fascinated by the whole situation, although trying to follow the conversation was almost like watching a tennis match on fast forward. I was instantly aware of the charm and erudition of this very handsome man, but could not understand his interest in me. However, at dinner the next evening I was won over.[85]

Vernon invited Kay, who still lived with her mother in Santa Barbara, to his apartment for a weekend in early September 1956. There she met several of his friends and Alex and his family. She wrote to him on the fourteenth: "You were a perfect host, and I must say that I loved every minute of my stay in L.A." If in Los Angeles for a music lesson, she promised to call.[86] Apparently she called more than once. On November 6 from New York, Vernon wrote: "I really miss you very badly—there was something wonderfully thrilling about our infrequent (also much too short) meetings and I'm looking forward hungrily to resuming them. Are you?"[87] She was and accepted his marriage proposal sometime later. Early the following year, Duke bought a house, his first, at 567 Almoloya Drive in the upscale neighborhood of Pacific Palisades.

In August 1957, Duke went to New York to work on *Time Remembered*, based on a play by Jean Anouilh that had opened in Paris in 1940. Translated into English, it was performed on the BBC in 1954 and then at the Lyric Theater in Hammersmith. Leslie Bridgewater composed the original music.[88] The American version starred Richard Burton and Helen Hayes.[89] Duke supplied the music for the first act of the play, and rehearsals began in late August.[90] It was not a musical but incorporated incidental music and two songs composed by Duke.

He wrote to Kay on September 25, noting how much he "loved every word of your card and just getting it gave me a wonderful lift. Just completed the orchestrating job—horrors! They want more music, I fear." He would be at the Hotel Taft in New Haven for a few days: "Please write often—even post cards will do."[91] On the twenty-ninth, Duke wrote to Kay about some of the details of their forthcoming wedding, but he also reflected on his decision to marry: "It's a very simple thing, really. I—at last—have someone to take care of, to live and work for. It's a dammed good feeling."[92] A day later he added: "The knowledge that we have a future together makes me wonderfully happy—and gives me the sort of serene contentment I've never experienced before."[93]

In New Haven *Time Remembered* "had a very smooth opening," Vernon told Kay. Hayes and Burton were superb, although Susan Strasberg, "perhaps through inexperience, wasn't altogether right." Stanley Grover "sang 'Ages Ago' extremely well." Vernon thought the play "a bit too subtle and crazy for out-of-towners," but his music, "completely subdued (when played under dialogue), was universally liked."[94] In New York the play ran for 147 performances and was well received by the critics. Brooks Atkinson raved about the "immaculately imposing" production, the "lush extravagance" of the scenery, and the "loveliness" of the costumes, but he failed to mention the music.[95] An album of the music of the play was later issued with Duke at the piano and Pete Rugolo conducting the orchestra.[96]

Because of Duke's work on the play, the marriage date had to be changed several times, but on October 24, 1957, gossip columnist Hedda Hopper enthused: "Strike me down if Vernon Duke hasn't at last succumbed to Cupid."[97] Initially Duke wanted his brother, Alex, who recently had stopped seeing a psychoanalyst, to be the best man, but worried about his phobia of big places, Vernon chose Tony Duquette instead.[98]

Taking his last chance on love, Duke, fifty-four, married McCracken, twenty-three, on October 30, 1957, at St. Matthew's Episcopal Church in Pacific Palisades, California.[99] The bride wore a light blue chiffon gown, shoes of matching shade, a sequinned Juliet cap, and pale blue gloves. White chrysanthemums and candles graced the altar, and soprano Luba Tscheresky sang Beethoven's "I Love Thee." Following the ceremony, a reception was held in the home of the Duquettes for about 150 guests.[100]

A short time later, bride and groom departed for San Francisco for the premiere of Duke's ballet, *Emperor Norton*. It is about a true San Francisco character affectionately tolerated by the city who in the 1870s considered himself emperor of America and protector of Mexico. Antonio Sotomayor originated the idea and designed the scenery and costumes, Lew Christensen choreographed the ballet, and Duke wrote the music.[101] According to one critic, "There was good material in this ballet, with deft comedy in the early scene and beauty of pattern and movement in the ballroom sequences. Further experience with it likely will result in tightening of certain scenes and closer integration." In a series of divertissements that culminated in a "riotous can-can," however, the music was "inseparable from Offenbach . . . even when spiced, as this score was, by Vernon Duke."[102]

In August a local newspaper reported that Duke was working on *Mistress into Maid*, the opera he had begun in 1929. Carl Zytowski of the University of California, Santa Barbara would direct the opera, which would have its premiere at the university on December 12 and 13. Duke would help supervise the staging during the rehearsal period beginning in September.[103] A romantic comedy set in Russia in the 1930s, it featured lovers from two families pitted against one another. A twenty-piece orchestra accompanied the soloists.[104]

About the same time, Duke began writing liner notes for the recordings produced by the Society for Forgotten Music.[105] In 1957 he had contacted Lester Koenig of Contemporary Records about another matter, when Koenig inquired about the possibility of recording some of the Society's music: "I began to sell the idea as eloquently as I could, which was unnecessary. Koenig was selling *me* on the idea! After this successful salesmanship, we rolled up our sleeves and went to work shaping the society into a recording venture." Contemporary's first recording for the Society included the F-sharp Minor Sonata by Jan Ladislav Dussek, a quartet by Felix Mendelssohn (written when he was only fourteen), the Second Quartet by Mikhail Glinka, and a few piano pieces by Dussek.[106]

Despite this success, Duke was puzzled that even though he was "one of the most over-recorded *tunesmiths*, I have had little or no luck in getting myself heard on a disk as a *composer*. This was not due to a lack of performances: The Boston Symphony alone, in the Koussevitzky Golden Era, programmed seven works of mine between 1928 and 1946. But the record companies' masterminds had their own system of pigeonholing and the hole allotted me was slightly south of respectability."[107]

In 1959, however, Stereo Records Contemporary Composers Series issued an album of his works. It consisted of String Quartet in C, Variations on an Old Russian Chant for Oboe and Strings, *Surrealist Suite*, and Three Caprices for Piano. In his liner notes, Nicolas Slonimsky noted that the latter were performed by Vernon Duke and "are lively pieces in a romantic style, almost Schumannesque in their imaginative tone-painting. The harmonies are modern, of course, and dissonances are treated as self-sustaining entities. The texture is translucent throughout, permitting the light of fanciful melody to pass in the interplay of colors." He also had positive things to say about *Surrealist Suite*, which Duke had dedicated to Salvador Dali in 1939: "Vernon Duke is Parisian *par excellence*, on the direct line of descent from the greatest spoofer of them all, Erik Satie. Like all good spoofing, Duke's music has considerable artistic merit; it is vivid and expressive of the spirit of the thing spoofed." Slonimsky also found similarities in his classical and popular music: "The two heads of the monster were not entirely separable, for there was a spiritual kinship between them. The lyrical élan of Duke's popular songs had a counterpart in the poetic melos of the symphonic and chamber music. Moreover, even in the popular field, the subtle harmonies and the greatly developed contrapuntal texture betrayed a musical mind tempted from infancy by sophistication."[108]

In 1961 Stereo Records produced another album devoted entirely to the music by Duke. He accompanied violinist Israel Baker on Sonata in D for Violin and Piano and in the liner notes commented on his other works: Etude for Violin and Bassoon, *Souvenir de Venise* (Piano Sonata No. 2), and *Parisian Suite*. Regarding the latter two, "Certain places affect me so much that I cannot help reacting to them in music—not *describing* them as Debussy or Ravel did, but actually *thinking* of them musically." Duke also took the opportunity to expound on the problems and disappointments faced by the composer:

> I know of nothing more frustrating than chasing performances. . . . What does it get you? Applause, prolonged just long enough for you to take a bow, for which you practiced so painstakingly, and walk off at a suspiciously lively clip for fear that the clapping may subside before you disappear into the wings. Two or three half-hearted notices may greet you in the morning. . . .

Mortified and stunned by the ensuing reaction, you begin to wonder—is it worth the bother? Why spend time, money, inhuman effort, why pull wires, flatter fools, cajole bores, antagonize friends—only to see the fruit of one's labors wither in a few tortured minutes in an antiquated concert hall? Worse yet, once played, your work bears the stigma of being shopworn because only world premieres are of interest to the performing fraternity.[109]

Regarding the rejections, Kay recalled how Vernon was "able to disguise his disappointment and immediately plunge himself into some other endeavor such as writing poetry, articles for magazines, 'serious' songs for me and other singers, and all the while kept up a prodigious correspondence. His library was a great source of pleasure and over the years swelled to nearly 15,000 volumes of music, books on music, English, Russian, and French literature, theater and costume, and books on Paris, the city he loved most of all." Kay was intimately involved in the creativity that went on in their house. She "typed the lyrics, sang the songs, auditioned the songs, helped coach the performers, provided coffee, drinks, lunches, and encouragement to any and all who appeared on our doorstep." And Duke's "facility at the piano and his vast knowledge of classical song literature made him a wonderful vocal coach and accompanist."[110]

André Previn also possessed great facility at the piano and had a vast knowledge of classical music. In 1958 he recorded *André Previn Plays Songs by Vernon Duke*. Like Dick Hyman, who had issued a recording of Duke's songs a few years earlier, Previn was a classically trained pianist who also played jazz. Like Hyman, Previn included "Cabin in the Sky," "The Love I Long For," and "What Is There to Say," an indication that they offered special challenges to pianists of similar backgrounds. Duke mentioned in the liner notes that he had hoped Previn would include "some of the obscurer items along with the bread-and-butter repertoire. I am pleased to say that he did just that: my own special favorites, *Round About* and *Ages Ago*, that have found but few admirers to date, because of lack of exposure, are among his best offerings in the present album." Duke considered

> the piano copy of a standard—or show tune—is merely the gem, the skeleton of what the composer intended; piano copies have to be

playable and simple in the extreme to be within reach of the buying public. Thus, I regard every recorded version of a song as legitimate *variations on a theme*—a time honoured musical form, as any purist will concede. In contrast with some of my colleagues, I especially appreciate those recordings of my light music that bring out unsuspected riches in my original, thanks to the performer's inspired meddling with it. I consider such meddling a compliment, not an imposition.[111]

Obviously he was pleased with Previn's "meddling."

Previn was also a member of an eleven-piece orchestra that in 1959 recorded *Barney Kessel Plays "Carmen."* This is a jazz version of Bizet's opera, and in the liner notes Duke clearly demonstrates his love of jazz and knowledge of the opera. He begins with a brief history of *Carmen* and concludes with an analysis of each act of the new version. "Is it 'respectful' as regards Bizet? Well . . . let's say it's full of love, rather than respect. Certainly, Barney's guitar "epigraphs" are as close to the original as possible, with only a slight harmonic deviation now and again. The airs, once intoned, are then in for a joyous and uninhibited airing, true jazz-fashion. The human voice is not missed, as it was in Petit's ballet; all the participants, including Previn's resourceful piano and Manne's melodic drums, sing away exuberantly, unhampered by a recitative's shackles."[112]

Duke also wrote articles for magazines, such as *Variety*. Published in January 1958, "Manors and Manners" is a condemnation of the "hustlers and the hucksters, the publicity-grabbing operators and promoters, the benzedrine brigade of show business." Labeling them "dollaristocats," he had nothing but contempt for their ostentation and pretension. They regard Europe "as a de luxe combination of Palm Springs, Las Vegas, and Miami Beach, with an assortment of foreign flavors and slews of unnecessary foreigners."[113] A year later, agents, of whom twenty had worked for him since the end of World War II, got similar treatment. He rued the time when the agent was "a rugged individualist, a character—the more colorful and less conformist, the better." Now, however, they had given way to "the bright boys (often referred to as 'junior executives'), assigned to clients by the cartel's masterminds, may specialize in entirely unrelated branches of the show game, yet look alike." Duke continued with a series of examples of how his agents often claimed to have found him work, but that work never materialized.[114]

Duke's article "The History of an Effort: The Society of Forgotten Music" traces the history of the society from his founding of it in 1947 to his move to California. He explained, "The average concertgoer and record collector usually thinks thus: 'If the music is forgotten, there must be a good reason for it. I know what I like, and I like what I know.'" Duke blamed the "moguls of the recording industry" for recording only compositions of famous composers that will sell. But "the true music lover cannot fail to realize that some of the indisputable masterpieces were forgotten shortly after they were created and gained stature only when resurrected many years later." He then identified a few of the compositions the Society had uncovered and noted that other works were in active preparation. Being "content in our fascinating field, we leave the lucrative game of re-recording classical best sellers to the 'major' companies. Remember, it took Shubert's *Unfinished*, now a symphonic evergreen, 37 years to get a hearing."[115]

In "The Plight of the Perishable Composer," Duke goes after the conductor who has become too powerful: "He browbeats his orchestra, hires and fires men at will, tells soloists what he expects them to play, threatens the trustees, and even builds his program without proper rehearsal." Even if a composer "should have the rare opportunity of having his work performed here in this country, the chances of a good rendition are poor. The composer is completely at the mercy of the conductor." Duke mentioned that he had to take his Third Symphony to Europe to have it performed after it was rejected by Koussevitzky. Neither did the composer escape his criticism:

> If modern music in America is not solidly on the map, insofar as popular acceptance goes, the fault probably lies in the ineffectual role played by the living composer. Determined to baffle or antagonize the auditor, rather than woo him, our note-scribbler, perhaps fearing physical mayhem, prefers to remain unseen and unheard as his own interpreter; the composer-virtuoso is now practically extinct.... With the exception of the prodigious Leonard Bernstein, one is unable to name a single American composer who is also a truly sought-after virtuoso or conductor.[116]

Although Duke overlooked that he was a composer who did not conduct, he did offer some suggestions for how beginning composers might get their works performed. Regarding the article itself, Duke complained to Ira Gershwin about its original title, "The Self Supporting Composer," being changed and about the drastic editing. The editor somehow replaced "conversion" with "conversation" in the text and mislabeled some of the photographs.[117]

That year Ira sent him a copy of his *Lyrics on Several Occasions*, in which he noted:

> You can count on the fingers of one hand, and perhaps the thumb and index finger on the other, the number of our theater composers whose melodic line and harmonies are highly individual. There is no question but that Vernon Duke must be considered one of these. Although "Words Without Music" is scarcely known—and therefore not in the class of "April in Paris," "Autumn in New York," "I Can't Get Started," "What Is There to Say?" and many others—it is an excellent example of Duke's distinctive style.[118]

The gift prompted an immediate response from Duke. He was mostly flattered by the references to him, but he could have done without Ira mentioning the incident in 1928 when he got into an argument with George Gershwin over the merits of various composers. "I was absurdly young," he explained, "also cocky and unkind. In the main, my estimates were fairly correct." In closing he mentioned that he had now been married for two years and in spite of their age differences, "we seem to be surprisingly happy." He was looking forward to working on *The Pink Jungle* as both composer and lyricist.[119]

A satirical look at the cosmetic industry, *The Pink Jungle* was a drama with music and a vehicle to give Ginger Rogers a change of pace. Duke had been friends with Rogers since 1930, and in the rehearsals he defended her against those who claimed she was inadequate and unexciting. Rogers, however, was critical of Duke's "Where Do You Go." He rewrote the lyric nineteen times before she finally settled on the original version. Rogers also did not care for his lyrics to "Tough to Be a Girl" and "100 Women in One." Because her singing was inaudible, Duke concluded that the greatest lyrics would not have made any difference.[120]

Also featuring Agnes Moorehead, Leif Erickson, and Maggie Hayes, the show opened in San Francisco in October 1959 and was to visit four cities before its Broadway debut in January 1960.[121] A reviewer thought the six Duke songs were "attractive and brightly clever" and the costumes "spectacularly arresting," but the show was top heavy with too much libretto.[122] Another critic noted, "It is a long, expensive and colorful comedy with music, having more complications than form. Undismayed by the weight of the production, Agnes Moorehead blithely steals the show." Duke's music was "only slightly more than incidental and not integrated too successfully."[123]

During what proved to be the show's last week, director Joseph Anthony told a reporter, "We are adding numbers. . . . We will have a charming dance—a waltz for Ginger Rogers—and we are also cutting. We have a lot to do yet before Broadway."[124] Anthony never got to Broadway, being replaced by Leslie Taking, who opened the show in Detroit without a run-through. Vernon told Kay, "Detroit is a *workshop* for us, and the notices (good, fair, or bad) won't matter until we hit Boston."[125] Duke found Detroit surprisingly clean, modern, and friendly except for the "ghoulish first-night audience!"[126] The show was sold out, and in a letter to Kay, he mentioned that it had really improved and will continue to get better and that he had "done the best job I'm capable of with the music and lyrics."[127]

The show moved to Boston, where it was to undergo revisions before opening in New York.[128] When interviewed about the difficulties facing the show, the librettist Leslie Stevens had much to say:

> Well, for Vernon Duke it was rewriting and re-orchestrating his music so that it could be handled by a 25-piece orchestra in the pit; it was adding more music so that the production could live up to its title, a comedy musical. . . . The over all problem is for all of us—actors, singers, dancers, choreographer, composer, and finally, author-director, who is myself—to continue to present 'The Pink Jungle' in transitional form, putting in new material as soon as it's sufficiently rehearsed, combining the old and about-to-be discarded with the fresh lines, tastiness songs and dances that are to be retained. Of course it would be easier to close down for a few weeks and do nothing but rehearse.[129]

The show closed for good in Boston.

A short time later, Duke returned to classical music. On February 18, 1960, at Schoenberg Hall at UCLA before a small but enthusiastic audience, he accompanied Kay as she sang arias in Italian, Russian, and French. She also performed some of Duke's classical songs, which the critic Mimi Clar found "too melodically vague to be of much interest. Of the several numbers composed by Mr. Duke, 'Loveliest of Trees' proved the most successful in its melodic development." She was impressed with his "sympathetic, capable accompaniment," which "served as a fine complement to Miss McCracken's vocal activity."[130]

That year Duke supervised the recording of three works by the Belgian composer Guillaume Lekeu (1870–1894) for the Society for Forgotten Music. He considered him "one of the most promising composers of the second half of the nineteenth century." His unfinished piano quartet was performed by the Baker Street String Quartet, the third movement of his Cello Sonata by Duke and cellist William van den Burg, and *Poèmes* by Duke and McCracken. In the liner notes, Duke mentioned that the three songs in *Poèmes*, written in 1892, were denounced by Rimsky-Korsakov as "'outrageous decadent nonsense.' In reality, these luscious and amply rewarding songs are no more 'decadent' than, say, Chausson or early Debussy. They could be embraced with profit by adventurous recitalists because, while highly meritorious as music, Lekeu's songs have strong audience appeal as well." Kay made her debut with this recording.[131]

Duke also promoted his own music, often unsuccessfully. He had written to Leonard Bernstein, conductor of the New York Philharmonic, in February 1959 about the possibility of a performance. Bernstein did not reply until November when he wrote: "I have finally gotten around to looking at your 3d symphony, and I find it very good indeed, but I wish to God I knew where and on what program I could put it in. If the opportunity should arise, be assured I have it in mind." A decade later, Duke questioned Bernstein as to why he had programmed so many great symphonies without much difficulty but not his. The symphony had been successful "wherever and whenever performed, but it is yet to be played in New York. How about it, Lennie?"[132] Bernstein never performed the work.

In promoting the works of unknown composers, Duke was more successful. At Judson Hall in New York in February 1961, he and Kay presented a recital of the songs by Heinrich von Herzogenberg, Paul Graener, Guillaume Lekeu, William Jackson, and others. As reviewed in the *New York Times*, "the works selected proved to be tasteful, competent, sometimes genuinely attractive, often of real historical interest." Although Kay McCracken Duke lacked a voice "of real polish or resonance," she had "a sense of style and projection. She knew how to sing simply and directly and that was effective. And she did everything with so much ease and assurance that she left a pleasant impression of enterprise and musical awareness."[133]

In 1961, Duke began a special series on the Los Angeles station KPFK. On December 4, it broadcast the Roth String Quartet with pianist André Previn performing Chausson's Piano Quartet in A.[134] The series continued well into the following year. On February 19, the station featured Duke analyzing the nineteenth-century Russian composer Mily Balakirev.[135] And on April 23, he probed the works of Guillaume Lekeu.[136]

While analyzing music, Duke was also writing poetry. The two volumes of verse in Russian he published in 1962 prompted a very positive response from the poet Vladimir Markov: "Composers who toyed with poetry were no rarity in Russia.... But when the composer appears with a printed collection of his verses, especially when he is not such a novice [in literature] it is a unique situation. Even more unique is the fact that his poetry is original, written with technical brilliance, happily festive, and goes against a mainstream of Russian poetic diaspora."[137]

As the volumes were being published in Munich, Duke was working on a book in English about the status of music in Europe and America. On April 2, 1962, during the writing, he paused to reflect on his life:

> When I look back on my many careers, I wonder why I went off in so many directions and tried to reach so many goals: I didn't reach any of them, in reality, and, as for my achievements, raised eyebrows is about the only thing they achieved.... I'm a Jack-of-all-Trades and a master of some—although my mastery is certain to be questioned by many.
>
> When I review my somewhat scarlet past, I'm struck by Fate's strange insistence on making me do things to which I was previously allergic—and to grow to like them.... In my first youth I hated popular tunes, the musical comedy brand especially; yet, if I am fairly

comfortably off today, it is because of my musical comedy catalog. . . . Baffled by anything mechanical, I cared little about recordings—only about my revenue from them; how could I guess that I would become director of SFM (Society for Forgotten Music) records. I hid my dislike of the marriage institution. . . . [But] behold the happy husband of Kay née McCracken, a young Montana girl of Scottish lineage and a wonderful singer.[138]

At the time, Duke was not in good health. He never had been. From his childhood diseases in Kiev to his sickness in Constantinople, his gastric fever in London, his diphtheria in New York, his sinusitis in New Jersey, and his appendicitis in Brooklyn, Duke came down with a variety of ailments. Los Angeles was no different. In April 1963, he told Kay that his colitis condition worried him and that he would probably go ahead with an operation. On the twenty-second he was admitted to St. John's Hospital and was operated on the following day. The operation was successful, and he remained in the hospital for five or six days.[139]

Duke was soon back to work on an operetta, *Zenda*. Director George Schaefer, interviewed in late June 1963, noted that the work had long been performed on the stage and filmed several times. "But I think we have a light-hearted, modern, humorous approach that will keep this from falling into the old operetta rut." He bragged that he got Vernon Duke "reinterested enough in the theater to compose the music. Don't need to tell you about his reputation."[140] It was to play for fifteen weeks in San Francisco, Los Angeles, and Pasadena before opening in New York.[141] The lyrics were provided by Leonard Adelson, Sid Kuller, and Martin Charnin. The cast featured Alfred Drake, Chita Rivera, and England's Anne Rogers. Rehearsals began in the NBC studios in Hollywood in July 1963.[142]

Based on *The Prisoner of Zenda* by Anthony Hope, the play is set in the mythical kingdom of Zenda. With plenty of swordplay, intrigue, and romance, it featured Drake in a dual role as the king and a visitor who resembles him so closely that they often exchange places. Even the wife of the king cannot tell them apart. But somehow everyone lives happily ever after. One of the problems of the play is that the dual characters Drake played could not appear at the same time.[143]

Its pre-Broadway tryout began on August 5, 1963, at the Curran Theatre in San Francisco and then opened in Los Angeles on September 24. Critic Philip K. Scheuer of the *Los Angeles Times* guaranteed that it would be a smash hit, even though the score "could probably have gained by the inclusion of some more whistleable 'April in Paris'—but reviewers always make this kind of observation after a first hearing." Some of the songs Scheuer found noteworthy included "Let Her Not Be Beautiful," "My Heart Has Come A-Tumbling Down," "Yesterday's Forgotten," and "Born at Last."[144]

Whether the cocktail party Vernon and Kay hosted in late October in their Pacific Palisades home for the members of the cast was to celebrate its quality or mourn its forthcoming end is not known, but on October 18 the *Los Angeles Times* had reported that *Zenda* would not open at the Mark Hellinger Theatre in New York. It would conclude on November 16 at the Pasadena Civic Auditorium. Still, the show grossed over a million dollars and made a profit.[145] Although New Yorkers did not get to see *Zenda*, they were privileged to attend a revival of *Cabin in the Sky* that opened in January 1964 at the Greenwich Mews Theatre. Duke wrote the music and lyric to a new song called "Livin' It Up."[146]

On January 10, 1964, Vernon appeared on Hugh Downs's morning television show to promote his new book, *Listen Here! A Critical Essay on Music Depreciation*. Longtime friend Nicolas Slonimsky saw the show and wrote to him the same day:

> You were your usual self-confident self (excuse the redundancy), but I noted also a new element of maturity (what a word!). You looked simultaneously like an elder statesman of music and a sempiternal playboy. You were of course glib and witty, and you easily dominated the scene. I was very much impressed by your playing—at last I could hear accompaniments compatible with the spirit of your songs. Most singers massacre "April in Paris," and most pianists mutilate the acidulously dulcet harmonies and neglect the implicit pedal point. So I had a good time with you on the screen of our second TV set in the kitchen which we watch at breakfast and lunch.
>
> Yes, I received your book, and I appreciated the dedication.... I fully expected to find brilliance and even erudition in which your opus

abounds, but time and again I had a gnawing pity that you wasted so much of your brain power and literary skill on long superannuated critiques, on such obvious matters as a rather spectacular misconception of the significance of Ornstein, or for that matter Stravinsky."[147]

The tone of the book indicates that Duke had not lost his penchant for controversy. Writing as the golden age of the Broadway musical was ending, he was highly critical of what was following it. Regarding the new shows, "The libretti are occasionally intelligent as well as entertaining; the sets good enough to grace the wall of a National Gallery; . . . the dancing is of so high a caliber that fanatical balletomanes who wouldn't be caught dead outside the City Center now do their slumming quite openly on Broadway." But something was missing—"*Music*, which is gradually being relegated to the role of a necessary but unimportant ornament. For we are entering the Era of the Musicless Musical. Most show composers no longer compose—they collaborate with three or four 'specialists,' whose names can be found on the program, if you can read the fine print. Show composing today is actually a *communal* effort."[148]

The chapter "The Deification of Stravinsky" got the most notice. The *Los Angeles Times* mentioned that "the author, with exhaustive documentation, dissects some of the contradictions of the composer's opinions and personality and attempts to deflate his eminent reputation." Deflation, in fact, was "the purpose of the entire book, and conductors, critics, composers, and current musical life in general get the full treatment. It makes amusing and lively reading; Mr. Duke writes with a caustic pen and it is hard not to agree with many of his conclusions, even when the shoe pinches."[149] In "Can a Heel Produce Great Beauty," Martin W. Bush also focused on the Stravinsky chapter: "Much of his personal goings-on are too awful to quote here. The book recounts his passionate greed for money, his venomous attitude toward all other composers, living and dead, his 'de-humanizing' of music in his own writings." If Duke sought to demystify Stravinsky, he certainly succeeded with this chapter.[150]

When the chapter was republished in *Listen: A Music Monthly*, Stravinsky, in a later issue, struck back. In "A Cure for V.D." he wrote: "The spectacle of a bad composer going sour is not new of course, and there is little new in the sourness of the very bad composer V.D.—to adopt his own system of initialing." Stravinsky went on to challenge Duke's charges point by point, and along the way he mocked his popular songs by creating fictitious ones: "March in Malibu," "Christmas in Caracas," "London in Leapyear," "June in Jutland," and "February in Fujiyama."[151] According to Kay, who was offended by the article, Duke found it amusing and called him "that son of a bitch." Duke responded to Stravinsky's response in an article he sent to the journal, but *Listen* closed down before it could be published.[152]

In "Dichotomic Dialogue," however, two characters, Duke and Dukelsky, discuss various issues, including Stravinsky whom they ridicule, but satire makes up only part of the article. The vehicle gives the author the opportunity to expound on a variety of subjects pertinent at the time, both characters bouncing ideas off each other. Part of their discussion is trivial, such as the dress of young women (too loud) and the Beatles (too much hair), but it matures when jazz is brought up. Gunther Schuller's advocation of "Third Stream" music, which combines jazz with classical music, was discussed. Dukelsky called it "Thirty-third Stream," and together they identified several classical composers who combined the two genres. Also analyzed were the two compositions that Charlie Barnet and His Orchestra performed right after the end of World War II that "fused" the two idioms. The duo listen to and comment on several jazz recordings as well.[153]

The real Duke continued to appear on radio and television shows. On December 17, 1963, the *Today* show saluted him with ninety minutes of his music and conversation. Rita Gardiner sang some of his songs.[154] Early the following year, he was interviewed on KBIG.[155] And he appeared on *Music Theater* with vocalist Martha Wright later in the year.[156]

While Duke continued to find the spotlight, Kay sought to find herself a spot in the classical world. In November 1964 she departed for Europe, intending to establish a career on her own. That they missed each other terribly is demonstrated in the numerous letters exchanged in the nearly two months Kay was away. She recounted her difficulties in getting auditions. He gossiped about friends, associates, and family.[157] In a long letter, Duke admitted he had a "pang of loneliness" and had hated to see her "go off to Europe alone." He acknowledged that she had made the decision with his "blessings" and hoped "with all my heart that you'll achieve what you set out to achieve—but we live in a pretty crazy world and achievement isn't any too easy even for those who deserve it as richly as you do." She was now, he confessed, "an *inextricable* part of me—which is both wonderful and a little scary." He concluded, "I'm keeping my fingers crossed—land that big opera job, dearest! We *must* be together soon. All my love."[158]

Duke got a long and most welcomed letter on November 14 and responded with a "fatter" one the same day. He was curious why Kay had not mentioned any auditions and wondered if she had an agent. He recommended that she contact three individuals, including Dean Dixon, if he was still on the continent. They might be able to provide her with useful information regarding the music scene. Although Dixon liked girls, "that doesn't mean that he would make a pass at you. . . . But a little harmless flirting—and above all, *flattery* might help." If Duke landed work on a film that might be produced in Paris, he would join Kay in Europe for Christmas. Duke mentioned a number of people he had interacted with, including his brother and sister-in-law, with whom he was having difficulties.[159]

Alex and Vernon's sibling rivalry had extended to politics. Vernon was a Democrat, or at least he had voted for Lyndon Johnson in the recent election.[160] Alex and Mona had agreed first with Senator Joseph McCarthy in his anticommunist hysteria and later with Senator Barry Goldwater in his run for the presidency against Johnson. Their extremism was manifested when Vernon made some crack about the "Birchers," and Mona wondered what was wrong with the right-wing John Birch Society.[161] He mentioned in a letter to Kay that he could honestly say he was not looking forward to an upcoming dinner with them: "I guess I no longer understand Alex; we seem to have so little in common! Still—outside of you, who is my *whole life*—they are closest to me—and it makes me sad to realize what poles apart we are; my brother and myself."[162] The dinner, however, went well, although he lost 70 cents at blackjack to Mona. But he held little hope that his brother would ever grow up.[163]

His hopes that Kay would succeed in Europe also were dashed. She wrote to him on December 10: "I can't say that most of the trip has been any joy at all! I really think I've done all I could under the circumstances to get auditions, but they just didn't pan out!"[164] Kay wired him from Munich that she would arrive in Los Angeles on December 22.[165]

If their career goals were not always achieved, their financial ones certainly were. In an interview in 1965, Vernon bragged that his finances were in such good shape that he could turn down many offers to compose film music, which takes four months or so to write. The pay was "somewhere between $10,000 and $17,500, but it was not enough for the amount of work."[166] He told Ogden Nash that even though he had had "no shows on the boards in 1964 (except for the short-lived revival of 'Cabin in the Sky'), it was the best year, so far, financially speaking. Those Golden Records of Standards certainly do help."[167]

How well *Frank Sinatra Sings Vernon Duke*, released the previous year, sold is not known. What Duke thought of the album also is unknown, but he may have been upset at being credited as the composer of only one of the four songs, "Autumn in New York." Lyricists of the other songs were identified as the composers. Nevertheless, he must have been pleased with the well-rendered and produced songs. "Autumn in New York" and "April in Paris" were arranged by Billy May, "I Can't Get Started" by Gordon Jenkins, and "Taking a Chance on Love" by Nelson Riddle.[168]

"Cabin in the Sky" was one of the songs Duke was asked to review in a blindfold test conducted in 1966 by Leonard Feather for *Down Beat* magazine. Presented with eight of his songs, he was asked to identify the performer and comment on the quality of each rendition. Ethel Waters's version of the song, first recorded in 1946, had "a nostalgic charm" but "not with any tangible improvements, especially in the piano playing; but it still has that same sure Ethel Waters touch." He was impressed with Sammy Davis Jr.'s interpretation of "April in Paris," although the "little bit of French music at the end was rather unfortunate—instead of giving it a poetic ending this made it more like a take-off." Pianist Bud Powell's version of "Autumn in New York" received a positive review, although "missing was the melancholy aspect of the song." Duke also liked singer Bobby Short's interpretation of "Island in the West Indies," pronouncing him "one of the best performers around." But Duke was rather critical of Ella Fitzgerald's rendition of "Taking a Chance on Love," preferring the first part at a slow tempo to her doubling the time later in the song. Three trumpet players got very good reviews: Harry Edison's "What Is There to Say," Al Hirt's "I Can't Get Started," and especially Dizzy Gillespie's medley of "I Can't Get Started" and "Round

Midnight." Regarding the latter, Duke noted, "The whole performance has a fresh, invigorating quality. From the composer's standpoint it is certainly one of the most imaginative things I have heard."[169]

The royalties from his "Golden Records" may have entered into a decision not to accept a position in the College of Fine Arts at the University of Utah. That he had little respect for the kind of composers that universities were producing may also have been a factor. But he was flattered and fascinated by the offer. In his response, he admitted lacking academic qualifications, noting that composition and orchestration were "the only fields in which I would consider myself qualified as a pedagogue." He was not qualified to teach "academic counterpoint, fugue, harmony and such."[170] Being married may have influenced his decision to decline the offer.

He was probably in the audience at Fiesta Hall on Santa Monica Boulevard on June 5, 1966, when Kay performed with tenor Arthur Ross-Jones, violinist Stanley Plummer, and pianist Howard Wells. The music and poetry were by Soviet and Russian émigré composers and writers.[171] And six days later Plummer and Wells also at Fiesta Hall performed Duke's music and that of Moralev, Botiarov, Shirinsky, and Alexei Haieff. Kay and Ross-Jones sang the works of Slonimsky, Hartmann, Horak, Nicolas Nabokov, Semenov, and Techerepnin.[172] Early the following year, Vernon and Kay presented the music of Scarlatti, Stradella, Strauss, Durey, Poulenc, Walton, and Duke in a concert at Hancock Auditorium on the campus of the University of Southern California.[173]

Always looking for a new project, Duke made plans to record an album of his vocal music and to include the songs from *Musical Zoo*, the book he and Ogden Nash had published in 1947. He wrote to Nash in mid-1968 about the project, noting that he found the music "surprisingly fresh and inventive; I think there is even a chance of it clicking at long last." He asked Nash to contact the publishers and have them send him copies of the book, which was long out of print.[174] Little, Brown did not respond, but a former employee sent him a copy.[175] In September he and Kay began rehearsing the songs.[176] And the next month he told Nash that Kay was "pretty familiar with the 'Zoo' and we looked forward to recording it."[177]

In November or December 1968, Duke agreed to review in manuscript form Alec Wilder's *American Popular Song: The Great Innovators,*

1900–1950. In his acknowledgments, Wilder noted that he "loved American music deeply and his affection was reflected in the astonishing scope and depth of his knowledge. Only weeks before his death he took the time to write a careful commentary on the concept and general scheme of the present project, suggesting certain correctives in early theater music. Then quite suddenly, this book lost an expert and sympathetic guide."[178]

On January 17, 1969, at St. John's Hospital in Santa Monica, Duke had died of lung cancer. The *Los Angeles Times* announced that the funeral service would be held on January 20 at St. Mathews Episcopal Church in Pacific Palisades and that Duke "leaves his wife, Kay and brother Alexis."[179] Although the priest conducting the service was a Russian, he was also an Episcopalian. Alex and the Russian community were offended. They wanted a Russian Orthodox funeral.[180]

The many letters of condolence Kay received indicate how well he was respected. Ira and Lee Gershwin telegraphed her: "We too are heart broken and send you our deepest sympathy."[181] Lyricist Howard Dietz wrote: "During the three shows I wrote with him I came to appreciate his individuality as well as his great talent. . . . Ballard, my wife, was also a friend and admirer of Vernon's. We both send you our deep regret."[182] Kay, of course, was devastated, but so was Nicolas Slonimsky:

> Dearest Kay—how can it be? Vernon, Vladimir, Dima—the most vital, the most imperishable, indestructible of my longtime friends, filling the world about him with wonderfully stimulating talk and action, marvelously gifted in so many different fields, full of intellectual and physical energy and inexhaustible vitality, establishing personal relationships in a vivid, lively, affectionate, assertive manner. . . . An enfilade of scenes passes before my mind. Fifty years! Kiev in 1919, Constantinople in 1920 and 1921, Paris, New York, Pacific Palisades. And Boston in between. I recall Vernon's sayings, his chuckles, his youthful triumphs in music, his amazing culture and eagerness for knowledge. There is no one like him in life, and I have a sense of loss that is a loss of a part of me that was related to Dima.[183]

Newspapers nationwide reported his death often with notices explaining who he was. The Boston paper, for example, apparently convinced that most of its readers had never heard of Duke, emphasized that he had composed dozens of classical works but was better known for such popular songs as "April in Paris" and "Autumn in New York." Those who appreciate classical music "knew him as Vladimir Dukelsky, the Russian-born composer of symphonies, concertos, and the Diaghilev-produced *Zepher and Flora*. . . . He used the name Duke for his popular songs, musical shows, and movie scores. 'Taking a Chance on Love' and 'I Can't Get Started with You' were among his longest lasting songs."[184] *The New York Times* noted the death with a much more extensive biography.[185]

A personal tribute came from friend and pianist Erno Balogh: "The general public does not know the name Vladimir Dukelsky and unfortunately even the musical world is scarcely acquainted with it. But Vernon Duke, Dukelsky's popular nom de plume is another matter." Balogh did not equate the music of Dukelsky with that of Stravinsky, but he predicted "that music history in the next generation will show that Dukelsky was underrated while Stravinsky has probably been overrated." Balogh noted that Dukelsky's output was "not negligible. It included one opera, six ballets, three symphonies, three concertos (for piano, violin, cello) as well as several songs and song cycles. Also pieces for woodwind, for piano, and chamber music work for different combinations. His composition 'Epitaph,' written for soprano, chorus, and orchestra upon the death of Diaghilev, is eloquent testimony to his gratitude."[186]

Critic Jack O'Brian, who admired Duke for many years before becoming his friend, also identified Duke's accomplishments. Duke "successfully created admirable serious music," and in the popular field he should be ranked "with Gershwin, Rodgers, Arlen, Kern, and their lilting ilk." But unlike other writers, O'Brian mentioned that Duke also wrote books, books that were "among the most literate, perceptive, urbane, and interesting we've ever encountered." O'Brian's concluding words could hardly be more fitting: "A charming, gifted man of music has gone to his Cabin in the Sky."[187]

CONCLUSION
DUKE AND DUKELSKY REDISCOVERED

The death of Vernon Duke in 1969 led to thirty years of relative obscurity, but he was not entirely neglected. Producers, musicians, and writers kept his name alive. In May 1969, for example, singers Bobby Short and Mabel Mercer devoted part of their Town Hall concert to songs by Duke. Subsequently released by Atlantic Records, the album includes "Round About," "Summer Is A-Comin' In," "Not a Care in the World," "I Like the Likes of You," and "I Can't Get Started."[1] Promoter Ben Bagley, who considered Duke the greatest composer of theater music, got several stage and screen personalities to participate in the project dedicated to the works of Duke. *Vernon Duke Revisited*, issued in 1970, includes many of Duke's lesser known songs, such as "Just Like a Man," "Low and Lazy," "If You Can't Get the Love You Want," and "Water under the Bridge." Movie actress Gloria DeHaven sings "Words without Music," and stage actors Tammy Grimes and Anthony Perkins interpret "Now," the song Duke recorded with Hildegarde in 1940. Because each song is rendered by a different person or persons, the album lacks continuity, but at least it gives the public a glimpse of Duke's genius. In his review John S. Wilson of the *New York Times* noted that "Bagley has gathered a collection of songs that go a long way toward supplying the elusive evidence that Duke deserves a high place in the musical theater to which one instinctively assigns him."[2] Jack O'Brian was particularly impressed with a song he had long forgotten, "Low and Lazy," mainly because it was presented in the "forgettable" *Sweet Bye and Bye*: "It is a sheer, moody delight, deeply romantic without cloying."[3]

VERNON DUKE: THE SERIOUS SONGS. Glendale Records, 1978.

Although his classical acclaim never equaled his popular fame, the composer also got some well-deserved attention. In 1978 Kay McCracken Duke and pianist David Berfield recorded *Vernon Duke: The Serious Songs.* The songs are based on the poems of Francis Carco, John V. A. Weaver, and five Victorian poets. Also included are the twenty songs Duke had composed for *Musical Zoo,* the book he and Ogden Nash published in 1947. Nicolas Slonimsky wrote in the liner notes that Dukelsky's zoo songs are "concise and humorous" and his "rhythmic treatment of the poet's assonant rhymes brings the music and the verse together in a fitting blend."[4] A critic for the *Los Angeles Times* suggested that Duke's art songs "should have gained at least a modicum of the acceptance granted his overtly popular tunes. Adventurous recitalists would do well to investigate these fragrant concoctions with their mildly tart vocal lines, perky accompaniments and deft, witty settings of some rather idiosyncratic texts."[5]

In 1980 Kay gave the Library of Congress Duke's library, papers, and music, which became the Vernon Duke Collection. And to celebrate the event, the Library presented a concert. The first half featured Duke's 1949 Sonata for Violin and Piano and a 1956 string quartet, neither of which impressed Octavio Roca of the *Washington Post*. Regarding Kay's recital, he claimed her voice had "too many hues," but her renditions of Duke's popular songs, including "I Can't Get Started" and "Ages Ago," which he called beautiful, turned the Coolidge Auditorium into "the nicest piano bar in town."[6]

English singer Sandra King, Scottish pianist Pat Smythe, and American bassist Tommy Cecil performed Duke's songs at the Corcoran Gallery of Art, also in Washington D.C., in April 1982. Tapes of the performance were converted into a CD a few years later. Along with Duke's standards, she included some of his relatively unknown pieces: "For Your Thoughts" and "Off Again, On Again" from *Walk a Little Faster*; "Love Turned the Lights Out" from *Cabin in the Sky*; and "You Took Me by Surprise" from *The Lady Comes Across*. "When a singer who is virtually unknown in this country records an album of songs by Vernon Duke, she is hitching her wagon to a star," wrote John Wilson. "It can be a helpful ride for her—certainly she will have good material. But it can also be dangerous because she invites comparison with established singers who have successfully drawn on Mr. Duke's catalogue of songs, and she can be overshadowed by the public perception of the high quality of those songs and by their familiarity." King easily met these challenges, Wilson being most impressed with her interpretation of "I Can't Get Started."[7]

From the late 1960s through the 1990s, historians and musicologists included Duke in their works about the golden age of American music. In *The World of Musical Comedy*, for example, Stanley Green placed him in a chapter with E. Y. Harburg, Harold Arlen, and Burton Lane and highly praised his work on *Cabin in the Sky*. Other than Arthur Schwartz, no other composer "contributed so many good songs to the reviews of the Thirties." The bad luck that plagued him during his later years "cannot obliterate the sound musicianship and superior quality that have distinguished his work for the musical stage. Graceful, elegant, imaginatively constructed, the songs of Vernon Duke have a durability and individuality that has made them part of the permanent literature of American popular songs."[8]

In *American Popular Song* (published in 1972), Alec Wilder included him in a chapter with Burton Lane and Hugh Martin and acknowledged Duke's contributions: "For although he was born in another culture, his absorption of American popular music writing was phenomenal. One never was aware in his songs of his not being rooted in this culture, as I was, for example, when I listened to the theatre songs of Kurt Weill." Why "Water under the Bridge" was overlooked by the public confounded Wilder, but he noted that "I Like the Likes of You" became a standard. It "is alive and undated (in terms of professional writing) as any great song should be." Wilder also praised "What Is There to Say?" He called it "one more great model of theater song writing. Again it's a case of every note counting and not one false move along the way." He was especially impressed with the four sets of quarter note triplets in the second phrase of the chorus.[9]

Wilder considered the verse to "Autumn in New York" possibly the most ambitious he had ever seen: "It begins simply enough, but halfway through it's almost as if the other musical half of the man couldn't be silent and the rest of the verse was finished by Dukelsky. It is extremely difficult and very lush." Duke, moreover, had come a long way as a lyric writer, a long way from "Spooning on a Crowded Bus." Wilder found the lyric of the verse of "Autumn in New York" compelling. It ends with

> I'll dispense with my rose-colored chattels
> And prepare for my share of adventures and battles
> Here on the twenty-seventh floor
> Looking down at the city I hate and adore.[10]

Three songs from *The Ziegfeld Follies of 1936* also got Wilder's attention. Although "I Can't Get Started" uses the conventional I-VI-II-V chord progression in the chorus, its bridge is "extremely ingenious in its insistent return to the whole note *a* each time supported by different harmony." "That Moment of Moments" is solid and "unbusy," and the bridge "contains an imitated phrase which is very ingenious." The song "managed to escape from the show and have a small standard life of its own." Wilder also praised "Words without Music," but was surprised it was included in the revue, since it was "so far out." What he meant is that the song is in the key of B-flat but begins on a high E natural. And except for the final cadence, the main strain of the song is in D minor and D major. "No matter what key it's in," wrote Wilder, "it's a good wailing song, perhaps more instrumental than vocal, but original and juicy."[11]

Wilder is critical of Duke for not breaking "out of the framework of popular music forms.... He has kept to the conventional forms and thirty-two measure lengths, and even when he does write a complex melody, such as 'Born Too Late,' he doesn't move out of the framework more than melodically." Wilder was puzzled "that a schooled composer who has written a body of complex concert music should have been the man least inclined to experiment in popular forms."[12] But as explained by Aaron Ziegel, "Given how Duke stretches the boundaries of popular songwriting with a classically hued harmonic and melodic style, the standard formal structure needed to remain intact in order to help preserve a popular song's generic identity."[13] To be added is that Duke, like all composers of musicals, did not have the freedom to experiment radically with structure but had to write songs for particular singers in distinct situations. He had to work within the thirty-two bar framework.

The same year Wilder published his book, Max Wilk was conducting interviews with some of the great lyricists and tunesmiths, resulting in *They're Playing Our Song*. In his chapter on Duke, he quotes several individuals who knew him. Duke was very talented, recalled Ira Gershwin: "He was very prolific, and he made the fastest piano copy I ever saw. He could do a whole verse and refrain, a good piano copy in twenty minutes—just put the whole thing down on paper." Bernard Herrmann remembered a very complicated man. Even though he had great success in both musical fields, he remained discontented because "he never really won the sweepstakes—the jackpot. Perhaps because he had very little taste in picking librettos to work on; he didn't know the difference between a good and a bad one—but he certainly worked with good lyricists." Cabaret performer Bobby Short met Duke while playing in Club Gala on Sunset Boulevard: "His sense of harmony was something that America hadn't ever heard before in popular music—it was a whole different approach!" Like Herrmann, Short acknowledged that Duke was "a little mean, because he never quite achieved the success he should have had, I guess. A little bitter because of that."[14]

Charles Hamm failed to mention Duke in *Yesterdays: Popular Songs in America*, published in 1979, but an anthology of songs collected by Steven Suskin and a bibliography of songwriters by David Ewen give Duke considerable credit for his popular works.[15] Suskin's *Opening Night on Broadway* saw print in 1990 and includes reviews of *Jackpot, The Littlest Revue, Sadie Thompson*, and *Two's Company*.[16] Although Duke's reputation, even his existence, is overlooked by William G. Hyland in *The Song Is Ended*, published in 1995, that year Allen Forte placed Duke in a chapter with Hoagy Carmichael, Arthur Schwartz, John Green, Burton Lane, and Jimmy Van Heusen in *The American Popular Ballad of the Golden Era, 1924–1950*. Forte has special praise for "April in Paris." He devoted a five-page in-depth analysis of it and considers it "one of the most resilient of standards, recorded by such diverse performers as Count Basie and his orchestra and jazz pianist-extraordinaire Bill Evans." Forte also mentions some of Duke's other songs, including "Suddenly" and "What Is There to Say?"[17]

In early March 1990, Kay McCracken Duke, accompanied by pianist Thomas Russell, sang some of his popular songs at the Westport Arts Center. Natalie Ryshna Maynard played five of Dukelsky's classical works for piano.[18] In a private home, friends and admirers reminisced, and local musicians performed some of Duke's works.[19] Westport, Connecticut, is the village where Duke wrote "Autumn in New York."

A few months later but far to the west, Duke's cousin, an actress/singer, opened an act called *Lisa Duke: Lost and Found* at the Gardenia in Hollywood.[20] Over the next few years, playing in several clubs, she refined her act into a seventy-minute bona fide theater piece that emphasized the Duke/Dukelsky dichotomy. In 1992 she mentioned to a critic that the most inspiring thing about Duke, "aside from the fact that he's a relative, is the way he integrated the two completely different sides of his creative life."[21] The following year she told another reporter, "I found those two different sides of him exciting and inspiring. . . . And so the theme of this show is how we embrace—and don't embrace—the different sides of our personalities, the masks we wear." She sang seven numbers by Duke, "spoke" to Vernon as herself, and played several characters gleaned from roles she had created over the years.[22]

Vernon's songs can be heard in the Ben Bagley 1991 album, *Harold Arlen and Vernon Duke Revisited, Vol. II*. Although he got some outstanding talent, such as Dolores Gray, Tammy Grimes, and Sandy Duncan, to perform, the album seems hastily put together, with no unifying theme, and the liner notes by Bagley contain glaring mistakes. Still, "Poor as a Church Mouse," "Let Her Not Be Beautiful," and "Sailing at Midnight" are well performed, as is the barely known "You Took Me by Surprise," sung up-tempo by Blossom

CONCLUSION

Dearie. Three years later, Bagley issued *Vernon Duke Revisited, Vol. III*. Nearly half of the twenty-five songs are from Duke's unproduced shows. "Once I Fall" came from the canceled *Casey Jones*. Bagley also included "I Used to Be above Love," one of several songs dropped from the *Ziegfeld Follies of 1936*. How well the albums sold is not known, but they probably did not significantly enhance Duke's reputation.

By the end of the 1990s, this began to change, as classical and popular performers were increasingly drawn to his music. In 1998 *Dawn Upshaw Sings Vernon Duke* was released. Upshaw, a well-known and highly respected soprano, included "April in Paris" and "Autumn in New York," but she wisely selected some of Duke's lesser known songs, such as "Words without Music," "Ages Ago," "Not a Care in the World," "Born Too Late," and "Round About." Of special interest is "Water under the Bridge," in which pianist Eric Stern and clarinetist John Manasse joined Dawn in an arrangement adapted from the 1934 recording by Duke, Bonnie Lake, and Ralph McLane. In the liner notes Steven Suskin predicted that Duke's "reputation seems poised for rehabilitation. And thanks to Dawn Upshaw—along with producer Tommy Krasker, music director Eric Stern, and a top-notch group of arrangers—I think it is safe to say that the music of Vernon Duke is hereby officially rediscovered and back in circulation."[23]

In an extended article in the *New York Times* entitled "A Neglected Master's Haunting Consolations," Barry Singer praised the Upshaw recording and had nothing but admiration for the man who wrote the songs. His article begins:

> There is something so improbably consoling about the sadness at the heart of the best Vernon Duke melodies. This redemptive afterglow could be a consequence of sheer melodic sophistication. Duke knew how to construct a song, elegantly, with surpassing craft and harmonic flair. Yet the earned wisdom behind the sadness in his music transcends flair and craft and goes beyond sophistication.
>
> It's not that the songs are even inherently unhappy. "Autumn in New York," "April in Paris," and "I Can't Get Started"—to name Duke's most identifiable trio—inhabit an emotional realm uncommon in the American popular song canon, that of dry-eyed ballads of unusual

poignancy. The melancholy induced by these songs, while hauntingly seductive, is never glum."

After briefly mentioning the highlights of Duke's life, Singer comments on Upshaw's renditions of the songs: "Ms. Upshaw may be Duke's ideal interpreter. The only opera diva on the scene today with a classic pop singer's gift for phrasing and a torch singer's emotional fearlessness, she possesses the craftsmanship and the soul to take on the full range of Duke's songwriting talent. His bittersweet chromaticism, unexpected key modulations, and dense harmonies are all sung with a crystalline simplicity that eloquently illuminates Duke's darker side." Singer was especially pleased that Upshaw included "The Love I Longed For," "Round About," and "Ages Ago."[24]

Were he at Joe's Pub in New York in mid-January 1999, when Upshaw sang most of the songs in the album, he would have been further pleased. Stephen Holden certainly was: "The relative formality of many of Duke's songs makes Ms. Upshaw an ideal interpreter of his work, since her careful balance of precision and breeziness matches the composer's in so many ways. Ms. Upshaw knows exactly how to confide a song without getting lost in its emotions. She is adept at sustaining an intimate conversational tone while keeping graceful musical reserve."[25]

From March 27 to 29, 1999, Encores presented the *Ziegfeld Follies of 1936* at New York's City Center without sets or costumes. Peter Marks of the *New York Times* reviewed the concert, which he called an "attenuated mishmash of a revue" that was not "uproariously funny, gloriously tuneful, or drenched in glamour." Still, he thought it "a swell idea" to bring back the *Follies* because it represented "a fascinating evening of time travel."[26] The revue included "I Can't Get Started," "Words without Music," "That Moment of Moments," and "5 A.M." Of the original score of the musical, only Don Walker's orchestration of "I Can't Get Started" was found intact. The search for the music had begun in 1976 when the Shubert Archive was created to preserve in one place the music, sketches, and librettos of all of the Shubert brothers' productions. In 2001 a Decca Broadway original cast album of the show was released on a CD.[27]

Although the late 1990s were very good to Duke, Dukelsky was not overlooked. In 1999 the Chandos label issued *Zéphyr et Flora*, the ballet that had launched Duke's career in 1925. It was presented by Residentie Orchestra of The Hague and conducted by Gennady Rozhdestvensky. On the same CD, the Netherlands Theater Choir with Russian soprano Ilma Achmadeeva presented *Epitaphe*. In the liner notes, Russian Natalya Savkina explained: "The clear and expressive melodies are nearly always simple and always unique, as a result of unexpected twists in the way the modal structure unfolds or a sudden harmonic colour, which allows the melodic line to achieve an unpredictable pirouette." Regarding *Epitaphe*, Dukelsky had "in mind not only the memory of Diaghilev but the disappearing Russia of his youth. The chorus and orchestra marvelously recreate the atmosphere of 'between two worlds' of ghostliness and cold."[28]

Scott Dunn knows the work well. With a bachelor of arts degree in music from University of Iowa, Scott moved to Los Angeles, where he studied piano at University of Southern California. Not sure about a career in music, he returned to Iowa, entered the medical school at the university, and after graduating moved back to USC for an internship. During this time, he did not neglect the piano, and taking the advice of film composer Leonard Rosenman, he began playing in public, winning piano competitions, and touring Europe and Russia on an artistic ambassadorship from the United States Information Service. Back in Los Angeles, Scott gave up his medical practice, returned to New York and entered the Manhattan School of Music, studying piano, conducting, and composition. He graduated in 1997 with a master's degree.[29]

Through Rosenman, Scott met Duke's widow (now Kay Duke Ingalls) and developed a special interest in Duke that would last to the present. In July 1998 he, soprano Marni Nixon, and violinist Masako Yanagita presented "Gershwin in Context" at one of the Mohawk Trail concerts. The program, which included works by Maurice Ravel, Alban Berg, Sigmund Romberg, W. C. Handy, and Scott Joplin, also featured seven songs from Ogden Nash and Duke's *Musical Zoo*, "Island in the West Indies" from the *Ziegfeld Follies of 1936*, and "April in Paris" from *Walk a Little Faster*.[30]

If there is a tipping point in the rediscovery of Vernon Duke, a case can be made that it came on January 10, 1999, at Carnegie Hall with the performance of his Concerto in C for Piano and Orchestra. This is the composition written in 1923 for Arthur Rubinstein that had so impressed Sergei Diaghilev in Paris the following year. A two-piano version was published

> **CARNEGIE HALL**
>
> **1998–99 SEASON**
>
> Sunday Afternoon, January 10, 1999, at 3:00
>
> CARNEGIE HALL Presents
>
> ## AMERICAN COMPOSERS ORCHESTRA
>
> Dennis Russell Davies, *Music Director*
> Paul Lustig Dunkel, *Resident Conductor*
> Robert Beaser, *Artistic Advisor*   Tania León, *Latin American Music Advisor*
>
> DENNIS RUSSELL DAVIES, *Conductor*
> LEON BATES, SCOTT DUNN, ALAN FEINBERG, URSULA OPPENS, *Piano*
>
> | | | |
> |---|---|---|
> | VERNON DUKE (a.k.a. Vladimir Dukelsky) *orch.* Scott Dunn | Concerto in C major for Piano and Orchestra (World Premiere) SCOTT DUNN, *piano* | |
> | OSCAR LEVANT | Concerto for Piano and Orchestra ALAN FEINBERG, *piano* | |
> | | *Intermission* | |
> | GEORGE GERSHWIN | Second Rhapsody for Piano and Orchestra LEON BATES, *piano* | |
> | MAURICE RAVEL | Piano Concerto for the Left Hand URSULA OPPENS, *piano* | |
>
> This Carnegie Hall presentation and the American Composers Orchestra's "20th Century Snapshots" series are generously sponsored by Fleet Bank.
>
> The Carnegie Hall Gershwin Centennial Project is made possible in part through the generous support of the Ira and Leonore Gershwin Trusts. Major additional support is provided by The Eleanor Naylor Dana Charitable Trust, The DuBose and Dorothy Heyward Memorial Fund, The Blanche and Irving Laurie Foundation, The Fan Fox and Leslie R. Samuels Foundation and The Alice Tully Foundation.

PROGRAM FOR A JANUARY 10, 1999, PERFORMANCE OF DUKELSKY'S CONCERTO IN C MAJOR AT CARNEGIE HALL. Author's Collection.

in 1926, but Dukelsky never orchestrated the work. In 1998 Scott Dunn, working from the two-piano version, orchestrated the concerto in time for its premiere with the American Composers Orchestra under Dennis Russell Davies and with Dunn at the piano. In the program Dunn wrote: "The influence of Dukelsky's hero and older colleague, Sergei Prokofiev, is easily heard in the music of this tuneful, 19-minute piece. Keeping that influence in mind, I've attempted, while orchestrating this one-movement concerto, to be faithful throughout to technical and stylistic practices which Dukelsky himself or Prokofiev might have utilized." As he later recalled, "I had to

> The New York Public Library for the Performing Arts
> Dorothy and Lewis B. Cullman Center
>
> # BRUNO WALTER
> ## AUDITORIUM
> 40 Lincoln Center Plaza
> New York, N.Y. 10023-7498
>
> ---
>
> ### Vernon Duke:
> A Centennial Celebration
>
> **Richard Rodney Bennett** and **Scott Dunn**, pianists
> Special guests
> **Angelina Réaux** and **Pinky Winters**, vocalists
> **Linc Milliman**, double bassist
> And
> **Kay Duke Ingalls**
>
> THURSDAY, OCTOBER 9, 2003
> 6:30 PM   ADMISSION FREE
>
> Baldwin piano courtesy of Deutsche Bank Foundation.
> Additional piano provided courtesy Baldwin/Gibson, Inc.
>
> Series Producer: Alan J. Pally
>
> Programs are subject to change and cancellation. Please telephone 212-642-0142 to confirm performance schedules. The use of cameras and recorders in the theater is not allowed.

ANNOUNCEMENT FOR "VERNON DUKE: A CENTENNIAL CELEBRATION," CONCERT IN BRUNO WALTER AUDITORIUM, NEW YORK CITY, 2003. Author's Collection.

intuit the orchestration (which I made for woodwinds and brass in pairs, four French horns, timpani, percussion, solo piano, and strings)."[31] A critic noted that Dunn's "love for the breezy little piece came through in his honest and rigorous performance."[32]

A few months later Dunn and pianist Richard Rodney Bennett were featured in a concert called *Crossover* in Weill Recital Hall at Carnegie Hall. They interpreted the works of composers influenced by jazz and popular genres—Lucas Foss, William Bolcom, Erwin Schulhoff, Scott Joplin, George Gershwin, and Vernon Duke. Dunn played Duke's *Romance* and *Ronde,* two piano pieces dedicated to Gershwin. A few years later, Dunn and Bennett joined vocalists Angelina Réaux and Pinky Winters and double bassist Linc Milliman in a series called *Vernon Duke: A Centennial Celebration*, beginning at the Bruno Walter Auditorium at the New York Performing Arts Library on October 9, 2003. Kay Ingalls and Bobby Short made a special appearance. This program included Duke's original two-piano version of his Concerto in C Major, Bennett's two-piano arrangements of "April in Paris" and "Taking a Chance on Love" (participated in by the entire ensemble), and select songs sung by Réaux and Winters and accompanied by Bonnett, Dunn, and Milliman. The celebration continued at various times in October, November, December, and January 2004, with themes such as *The Musical Diversity of Vernon Duke* and *Chamber Music of Vernon Duke*.[33]

Duke's songs continued to draw popular and jazz artists to them. Cabaret singer Klea Blackhurst put together a concert called *Autumn in New York: Vernon Duke's Broadway*, performed in October 2004 at the Opia in Manhattan. Backed up by the Pocket Change Trio, she, according to a critic, infused "Duke's songs with oxygen."[34] The following year, she recorded many of the songs in an album, including "Not a Care in the World," "Poor as a Church Mouse," and "Sailing at Midnight." In the liner notes, she wrote: "The irresistible texture of the music, not to mention the challenges of some uncharted vocal territory, won me over and presented some very green pastures for the talents of Michael Rice [arranger and conductor]. We embarked on this project with equal enthusiasm, hoping to give some of Duke's Broadway compositions a much deserved revival."[35]

Jazz at Lincoln Center presented a radio program of Duke's songs in late 2009. In a running commentary, Wendell Pierce informed the audience of Duke's early life and his transition from an exclusively classical composer to one who also wrote for musicals. Interspersed were songs by Duke performed by a band led by pianist Bill Charlap and featuring vocalist Ethel Ennis and tenor saxophonist Houston Person. The program featured Duke's most famous songs, but it also included "Round About," and "The Love I Long For," an indication of how stimulating Duke's melodies and harmonies are to jazz musicians.[36]

These songs were included in *Taking a Chance on Love: The Music of Vernon Duke*, a show put on by Lyrics and Lyricists, during three days in April

2013. David Loud created and directed the show and arranged the music. He noted in the program that shows that flop often "contain good songs, and in Duke's case, the wreckage proves astonishingly generous. Legendary disasters like *Sweet Bye and Bye, Two's Company, Sadie Thompson, Banjo Eyes, The Lady Comes Across,* and *Zenda* have left us with a delightful catalogue of urban treasures, largely unknown." From these shows, he chose "Born Too Late," "Good Little Girls," "A Nickel to My Name," "Where Have We Met Before?" "Just Like a Man," and several more.[37]

PS Classics issued a cast recording of *Sweet Bye and Bye* in 2014, featuring several Broadway and recording veterans. Aaron Ziegel reviewed the album, noting that the show is "no lost masterpiece, yet we are fortunate that its zany plot inspired such high-quality songwriting from Duke and Nash. Given that Duke's compositional language is primarily one that rewards a listener's close scrutiny rather than one of immediate appeal, a work like this is perhaps better served on record than on stage."[38]

Another music scholar found Duke's work worthy of investigation. Scott Holden discovered Duke while he was a graduate student playing popular music and jazz to earn some extra money. Dawn Upshaw's recording of Duke's songs made him curious about the man and his music, but none of his professors had "ever heard about the classical side—the Dukelsky side—of the Vernon Duke catalog. I realized I had discovered the topic of my dissertation."[39] Completed in 2002, he called it "Confrontations with Vladimir Dukelsky: A Study of the Composer and His Music." Holden pays particular attention to Dukelsky's classical piano pieces, noting that they "tend to be extremely angular and often cover a wide range of the instrument. They are deliberately deceptive, often with two melodic lines in the same hand." But much of his "solo piano music ends quietly, evading the big finish. Frequently there is a virtuosic climax towards the end, but then the tension resolves to a soft and simple conclusion." Holden considers the more than forty character pieces Dukelsky wrote for the piano to be his best work. And he sees parallels between them and Duke's popular tunes. Both mastered the short form. Duke often wrote in the AABA thirty-two-bar song form, Dukelsky in the ABA format.[40]

As he improved as a composer of the short form, continued Holden, "The serious Russian composer is reconciling his aesthetics with those of the

'Americanized' songwriters. Dukelsky successfully combines popular dance rhythms into his modern language." He became "a composer of genuine merit," and every "pianist curious about obscure and forgotten repertoire would enjoy exploring them. They would fit perfectly on a historical program containing works by Gershwin and Prokofiev, as Dukelsky shared so much personally and artistically with these composers." But much of his music can stand on its own, "regardless of the fact that the composer also happened to be [a] popular songwriter. Indeed, this dual aspect of Vladimir Dukelsky's career makes these same works even more fascinating. He was a pioneering 'cross-over' composer before this concept had a name."[41]

This cross-over aspect was implied in 2005 when Duke received equal time with George Balanchine and George Gershwin in a paper presented by Beth Genné and Christian Matjias at an international conference on music and dance held at Roehampton University in London. Especially insightful is their analysis of "Five A.M.," the song Duke and Ira Gershwin wrote and Balanchine choreographed for Josephine Baker in the *Ziegfeld Follies of 1936*. "Duke's score," they maintain, "combines classical compositional techniques with popular musical vernacular forms. Debussy, Stravinsky and others had done the same, but we would argue, as a kind of novelty add-on to a 'classical' foundation. Fully at home in both 'languages,' with love and respect for each. Duke synthesizes these elements to create something new. It is not a watered down version of his sources, but something his own."[42]

In 2004 Mark N. Grant published *The Rise and Fall of the Broadway Musical*, which included Duke in a discussion of "highbrow" composers such as Leonard Bernstein, Kurt Weill, and Marc Blitzstein, who also wrote for the theater. Duke, however, differed from them in one important way: "He did not always write 'to the book.' For all his literary and musical gifts, he somehow misunderstood the composer's function in the Broadway musical to write to character and situation." There may be some truth to this, but Duke clearly wrote "to the book" in *Cabin in the Sky*, which Grant considers his greatest work. He also acknowledged that "Duke's best songs are so good that he will never die. His rhapsodic ballads come closer to art songs than the songs of any other Broadway composer."[43]

In *Classic American Popular Song*, musicologists David Jenness and Don Velsey have much to say about those songwriters and lyricists who emerged in the 1930s and 1940s and continued to produce outstanding songs in the 1950s. They included nearly as much information on Duke as on Harold Arlen, Cole Porter, Richard Rodgers, Arthur Schwartz, Burton Lane, Johnny Mercer, Jimmy McHugh, and Jimmy Van Heusen. The section on Duke begins: "Another great melodist whose songs were well known before 1950 was Duke, whose lyrical gifts were first class and whose harmonic sophistication was unexcelled." Particular attention is paid to "The Love I Long For" ("a fine tune"), "Ages Ago" ("one of the most beautiful songs of Duke's career"), "Round About" ("perhaps his finest melody"), "Who's to Blame" ("a rapturously sad song, oddly unknown"), and "Madly in Love" ("a gem of a little song"). Each song is briefly analyzed. For example, they consider "Who's to Blame" as "harmonically and melodically elegant" as 'Autumn in New York." The chorus, "basically in C, opens over a ii chord, a distinctive Duke touch, and for half its length tries to go to D-flat and then D minor, all over a beguinelike rhythm." The authors conclude by stating, "There should be a Duke songbook."[44]

In 2010 two articles on Duke appeared in the same issue of the journal *American Music*. In "One Person, One Music: Reconsidering the Duke-Dukelsky Musical Style," Aaron Ziegel argues that Duke's classical and popular compositions are not as distinct as Duke claimed they were: "Wide leaps, disjunct contours, and chromatic meandering are the common features of Duke's melodies. While this is, of course, not uncharacteristic of art songs from the period, the frequent occurrence of these traits in his popular song melodies is noteworthy. Given a melody alone, the tonic can often be unidentifiable, since Duke generally avoids outlining the triad and prefers to begin his melodies on upward extension of the harmony. Only with the support of the bass and chords does a tonal center become apparent."[45]

Scott Holden discusses the often volatile relations Dukelsky had with composers, conductors, and music publishers in "The 'Adventure and Battles' of Vladimir Dukelsky (a.k.a. Vernon Duke)." He also acknowledges the important contributions Dukelsky made in the field of classical music. He worked with some of the greatest artists of his time, and his music was performed in places "ranging from Poland to Hawaii, including a number of coveted concerts at Carnegie Hall. These alone would be impressive credentials for any musician, yet they are even more astounding considering that this versatile man had a lifestyle that required him to be two separate composers."[46]

The Russians, too, rediscovered their native son. In 2011 Antonina S. Maximova published a paper in the Russian journal *Music Scholarship* called "Zefir and Flora: European Debut of Vladimir Dukelsky in the Ballets Russes of S. Dyagilev." Maximova analyses the stylistic components of the ballet, gives details of its formation and history, and argues that it should be considered part of the Russian national musical traditions.

Fulfilling the wishes of Jenness and Velsey for a Duke songbook, in 2012 Scott Dunn edited *The Vernon Duke Songbook*. It contains sixteen of Duke's songs arranged for piano and vocal. The choice of songs is significant, because five of them come from the largely forgotten musical *Sweet Bye and Bye*: "Born Too Late," "Just Like a Man," "Low and Lazy," "Round About," and "Sweet Bye and Bye." In the foreword, Steven Suskin points out that even though Duke's most popular songs remain the favorites of jazz musicians, the *Songbook* demonstrates that his other songs also contained "constantly modulating keys and shifting harmonies, beneath strong closely chromatic melodies."[47] Although "I Can't Get Started" was not included in the *Songbook*, it is the focus of my 2016 book, *The Tunesmith and the Lyricist: Vernon Duke, Ira Gershwin, and the Making of a Standard.*, which was the launching pad for this present work.

Duke's classical compositions continued to be performed and recorded. In 2012, ten years after completing his dissertation, Scott Holden accomplished what he advocated in that work: recognition of Dukelsky's piano compositions. *Beyond Vernon Duke* consists of a collection of piano pieces, organized as *"Parisian Suite," "Sonata: Souvenir de Venice," "Three Caprices," "Surrealist Suite," "Romance,"* and *Divertissements des Muses: Theme and Variations from Zephyr et Flora*. In the liner notes, Michael Hicks mentions that Duke believed music must instantly validate vitality or inevitability: "The pieces on this recording have vitality, yes, and instantly evoke a distinctive presence—a musical personality of superbly honed instincts. Whether or not the sets or single movements have enough 'inevitability' may be too soon to judge. This recording, though, is a start, enabling the hearers to glimpse the pieces through a dazzling prism of performance skill and sensitivity."[48]

CONCLUSION

In 2007 Scott Dunn performed Duke's *Homage to Boston Suite* for solo piano, and orchestrated and recorded Duke's Piano Concerto and *Home to Boston* suite with the Russian Philharmonic Orchestra conducted by Dimitry Yablonski for Naxos. Sam Magill performed the first recording of Duke's Cello Concerto on the same disk. In their liner notes, Scott and Kay Duke Ingalls briefly trace the histories of the compositions, noting that they "only partially represent the exceptional output of a great composing talent."[49] A part of that output was performed on September 16, 2010, at the New York Chamber Music Festival. Dunn and violinist Elmira Darvarova interpreted the works of John Adams, Georgy Catoire, Franco Alfano, as well as *Homage to Offenbach* and *Capriccio Méxicano* by Vernon Duke.[50]

The following year, the International Festival of the Arts presented *Diaghilev P.S.* in St. Petersburg, Russia. An important part of the festival was a concert featuring Duke's concert works connected to Diaghilev by numerous soloists. The Academic Symphony Orchestra of the St. Petersburg Philharmonic and the Choir of the St. Petersburg State Academic Capella performed, with Dunn conducting, *Epitaphe (On the Death of Diaghilev)* for orchestra, chorus, and mezzo, *Dédicaces* for orchestra solo piano and soprano obbligato, and the premiere of *The End of St. Petersburg* for soloists, chorus, and orchestra, which had never been performed in Russian: "Could there be a better way for Russia to welcome home an unjustly neglected composer—one who has nonetheless done so much to represent her musical culture to the world at large?"[51]

Early in 2012 Scott Dunn conducted the Symphony Orchestra of the University of Iowa in the first performance in seventy years of Duke's Concerto for Violin, with soloist Tricia Park.[52] Two years later he recorded *Violin Concerto: Complete Works for Violin,* with violinist Elmira Darvarova and others. In the all-Duke album, Dunn conducted the ORF Radio-Symphonieorchester Wien for the Violin Concerto and was the pianist on Sonata for Violin and Piano, *Homage to Offenbach,* and *Capriccio Méxicano.* The centerpiece of the recording is the Violin Concerto, originally written for Heifetz but introduced by Ruth Posselt in 1943 with the Boston Symphony Orchestra.[53]

Three years later, Dunn conducted the preproduction world premiere cast recording of *Misia: The Musical.* Some of the music is from Dukelsky's never-produced *Milord l'Arsouille*, but the other numbers are various incidental pieces and "trunk" songs that Dunn selected for the new show. Kay persuaded Barry Singer, as strong an admirer of Duke as anyone, to write a new libretto and create new lyrics. "Producer Tommy Krasker enlisted a cast of Broadway all-stars," recalled Singer, "(headed by the glorious Marin Mazzie) to fill the leading roles and if that wasn't enough, approached the legendary Jonathan Tunick about orchestrating. The two days of recording in March 2015 were as musically gratifying as anything I have ever experienced. What sounds! Scott conducted the orchestra. I just sat there, with Kay at my side, and Vernon very close by."[54]

In concluding this study of the exciting and turbulent life of Vernon Duke, I am tempted to speculate what he might have achieved absent his volatility and superego. But without these characteristics, his life would not have been as exciting and turbulent and therefore not nearly as fascinating as it turned out to be. Of course, it ended too soon, but the number and variety of his compositions, classical and popular, performed and recorded before and after his death, are impressive. Even more impressive is his complete repertoire. Three hundred of his works have been published, but many of them lie unexamined. Hundreds more have never been published. Locating, performing, recording, and evaluating them await the future efforts of researchers, musicians, producers, and critics.

NOTES

INTRODUCTION
1. Duke, *Passport*, 5–6.
2. Duke, *Passport*, 430.
3. Duke, *Passport*, 3.
4. Duke, *Passport*, 6.
5. *New York Times*, January 18, 1969.
6. Duke, "A Dichotomic Dialogue," Vernon Duke Collection, Music Division, box 108, file 8, Library of Congress. The article was published in *Down Beat* magazine, but a copy has not been found.
7. Early draft of *Passport*, Duke Collection.
8. Quoted in Kashner and Schoenberger, *A Talent for Genius*, 59.
9. Duke, *Passport*, 291–92.
10. Quoted in Duke, *Passport*, 362
11. Wilder, *American Popular Song*, 357.
12. Dolin, *Divertissement*, 106.
13. Quoted in Wilk, *They're Playing Our Song*, 196.
14. Quoted in Ben Bagley, liner notes, *Vernon Duke Revisited, Vol. III*, Painted Smiles Records PSCD-147.
15. Duke, *Passport*, 5.
16. Quoted in Holden, "Confrontations," 55n67.
17. Quoted in Holden, "Confrontations," 12. The January 1969 issue of *Variety* stated that the number was more than seven hundred.

CHAPTER 1: DUKELSKY EMERGES
1. Duke, *Passport*, 6–8. Duke gives his birthday as October 10 in his autobiography, but his birth is identified as September 27, 1903, in *The Twenty-Second Programme of the Boston Symphony Orchestra, Fifty-First Season, 1931–1932*, edited by Philip Hale (hereafter cited as *Programme*), 1320. Scott Holden has pointed out other discrepancies, noting that one source puts his birth as September 14, 1904, another the autumn of 1902. See Holden, "Confrontations," 11n6.
2. Duke, *Passport*, 8.
3. Duke, *Passport*, 8.
4. Duke, *Passport*, 8; Wikipedia's entry on Mykolaiv.
5. Duke, *Passport*, 8–9.
6. Duke, *Passport*, 9–10.
7. Holden, "The 'Adventures and Battles' of Vladimir Dukelsky (a.k.a.) Vernon Duke," 301.

8. Duke, *Passport*, 9–10
9. Wikipedia's entry on Kungur, 1–2.
10. Duke, *Passport*, 10–11.
11. Duke, *Passport*, 11.
12. Duke, *Passport*, 11.
13. Duke, *Passport*, 14.
14. Wikipedia's entry on Alupka.
15. Duke, *Passport*, 12.
16. Duke, *Passport*, 12–13.
17. Duke, *Passport*, 14–15.
18. Duke, *Passport*, 15–16.
19. Duke, *Passport*, 16–17.
20. Wikipedia's entry on "History of Kiev." Of the population, 56 percent spoke Russian, 23 percent Ukrainian, 12.5 percent Yiddish, 7 percent Polish, and 1 percent Belarusian.
21. Duke, *Passport*, 33.
22. Hamm, *Kiev*, 191.
23. Duke, *Passport*, 19.
24. Duke, *Passport*, 20–21.
25. Duke, *Passport*, 21–23.
26. Duke, *Passport*, 24–25. This event is recounted in Robinson, *Sergei Prokofiev: A Biography*, 122.
27. Wikipedia's entry on Reinhold Glière.
28. Duke, *Passport*, 30–31.
29. Duke, *Passport*, 31–32.
30. Duke, *Passport*, 35–37.
31. Duke, *Passport*, 36–37, 47.
32. Duke, *Passport*, 37–41.
33. Duke, *Passport*, 40.
34. Hamm, *Kiev*, 221–27.
35. Duke, *Passport*, 43.
36. Dukelsky to Boston Symphony Orchestra, *Programme*, 1324. In his letter, Dukelsky narrated a brief account of his life to 1932, details of which occasionally differ with what he wrote in *Passport*. Because the *Programme* was written twenty years before the autobiography, I consider it the more reliable of the two documents.
37. Duke, *Passport*, 46–47.
38. Duke, *Passport*, 47–48.
39. Duke, *Passport*, 48.
40. Duke, *Passport*, 49–52.
41. Duke, *Passport*, 53–54.
42. Duke, *Passport*, 53–54.
43. Duke, *Passport*, 54.
44. Duke, *Passport*, 54–59. Vladimir claimed that he persuaded his mother to depart the city. Written in dialogue and coming from a seventeen-year old, his claim seems manufactured. See *Passport*, 56–57.

45. Holden, "Confrontations," 112–16. The eighteen-page one movement piano piece is in the Duke Collection.
46. Quoted in Herlihy, *Odessa*, 262–65. A century after its founding it consisted of 9,786 buildings, including 661 stores, 3,600 shops, 413 restaurants, 127 bakeries, 55 tea shops, 371 spirit shops, and 745 artisan workshops.
47. Quoted in Herlihy, *Odessa*, 272.
48. Duke, *Passport*, 59–61.
49. Herlihy, *Odessa*, 273.
50. Duke, *Passport*, 61.
51. Duke, *Passport*, 61.
52. "The Odessa National A. V. Nezhdanova Academy of Music," http:/odma.edu.ua/eng/about.
53. Duke, *Passport*, 61–62.
54. Duke, *Passport*, 64–65.
55. Duke, *Passport*, 65.
56. Duke, *Passport*, 65.

CHAPTER 2. DUKE AWAKENS

1. MacMillan, *Paris, 1919*, 372.
2. Duke, *Passport*, 69–70.
3. Duke, *Passport*, 70–72.
4. Duke, *Passport*, 70.
5. Duke, *Passport*, 72–73.
6. Duke, *Passport*, 73–75.
7. Duke, *Passport*, 75. For an analysis of this work, see Holden, "Confrontations," 114–16.
8. Duke, *Passport*, 75–77.
9. Duke, *Passport*, 77–78.
10. Duke, *Passport*, 78.
11. Vladimir Dukelsky to Boston Symphony Orchestra, *Programme*, 1324.
12. Slonimsky, *Perfect Pitch*, 66.
13. Duke, *Passport*, 78.
14. Duke, *Passport*, 79.
15. Quote in *Boston Globe*, March 22, 1929.
16. Duke, *Passport*, 79–81.
17. Duke, *Passport*, 81–82.
18. Duke, *Passport*, 82.
19. Duke, *Passport*, 84.
20. Duke, *Passport*, 84.
21. Duke, *Passport*, 84–85.
22. Duke, *Passport*, 85–86.
23. Prokofiev, *Diaries*, June 15, 1929, 112. Because Prokofiev was in the United States between October 21, 1921, and February 25, 1923, Duke must have met him during this period.
24. Duke, *Passport*, 86–87. Emphasis added to song lyric.

25. Duke, *Passport*, 88.
26. Duke, *Passport*, 88.
27. Duke, *Passport*, 88–89.
28. *New York Tribune*, March 20, 1922.
29. Duke, *Passport*, 90. Scott Holden identified the composition created in Constantinople as the one performed for George Gershwin in New York. See Holden, "Confrontations," 116.
30. Duke, *Passport*, 91.
31. Duke, *Programme*, 1324.
32. Quoted in Duke, *Passport*, 91.
33. Quoted in *Programme*, 1322.
34. Duke, *Passport*, 91–92.
35. Duke, *Passport*, 92.
36. Duke, *Passport*, 93–94.
37. Duke, *Passport*, 95.
38. Duke, *Passport*, 95.
39. Duke, *Passport*, 95–96.
40. Duke, *Passport*, 96–97.
41. Duke, *Passport*, 98–100.
42. Duke, *Passport*, 100.
43. Duke, *Passport*, 101–2. Rubinstein kept a copy of the work, but he never performed it, at least in public.
44. Duke, *Passport*, 103–4.
45. Jablonski and Stewart, *Gershwin Years*, 92–94.
46. Duke to George Gershwin, May 25, 1924, Duke Collection.
47. Duke, *Passport*, 104.
48. Duke, *Passport*, 104–5.

CHAPTER 3. DUKELSKY TRIUMPHANT

1. McAuliffe, *When Paris Sizzled*, 2, 22–23.
2. McAuliffe, *When Paris Sizzled*, 69.
3. Duke, *Passport*, 107.
4. Duke, *Passport*, 110.
5. Duke, *Passport*, 108–11. See also Vladimir Dukelsky, "Friendship's Tribute, Dukelsky to Nabokov," *Boston Evening Transcript*, 1931.
6. Wikipedia's entry on Sergei Diaghilev.
7. Duke, *Passport*, 113.
8. Duke, *Passport*, 115.
9. Duke, *Passport*, 115–17.
10. Duke, *Passport*, 118.
11. Duke, *Passport*, 119–20.
12. Duke, *Passport*, 120–21. Duke mistakenly gave the date of the performance as June 17, 1924.
13. Prokofiev, *Diaries*, June 18, 1924, 73.

14. This part of Prokofiev's life is detailed in Robinson, *Sergei Prokofiev*, 7–138. See also Robinson, *Selected Letters of Sergei Prokofiev*, 62.
15. Duke, *Passport*, 121–23.
16. Duke to George Gershwin, Paris, August 4, 1924, Duke Collection (also quoted in Duke, *Passport*, 123–24).
17. Duke to George Gershwin, Monte Carlo, August 14, 1924, Duke Collection.
18. Quoted in Lifar, *Serge Diaghilev*, 241.
19. Braude, *Making Monte Carlo*, 1, 144–52.
20. Quoted in Braude, *Making Monte Carlo*, 171.
21. Duke, *Passport*, 127–28.
22. Prokofiev, *Diaries*, March 24, 1925, 148.
23. Prokofiev, *Diaries*, March 25, 1925, 150.
24. Grigoriev, *Diaghilev Ballet*, 206.
25. Beaumont, *Diaghilev Ballet in London*, 252.
26. Grigor'ev, *Diaghilev Ballet*, 205–6.
27. Duke, *Passport*, 128–30.
28. Braude, *Making Monte Carlo*, 154, 157.
29. Duke, *Passport*, 130–32. In an earlier draft of his relationship with Khaki, Vladimir claimed that later she had a change of heart and wrote him several letters about resuming their relationship. Her father told him she had some kind of illness and entreated him to make up with his daughter. By this time, however, Vladimir had returned full time to his music. See Duke Collection.
30. Duke Collection. In this earlier draft of this episode, she is known as Polly. In *Passport*, Duke makes no mention of Sally infecting him. Evidently such frankness did not suit the editors of the book.
31. Taper, *Balanchine*, 3–84; Duke, *Passport*, 141.
32. Duke, *Passport*, 141.
33. Quoted in Duke, *Passport*, 141–42.
34. Dolin, *Divertissement*, 106.
35. Duke, *Passport*, 144.
36. Lifar, *Serge Diaghilev*, 191.
37. Philip Hale, notes in *Programme*, 1330.
38. Grigoriev, *Diaghilev Ballet*, 207.
39. Duke, *Passport*, 145.
40. Prokofiev, *Diaries*, May 12, 1925, 162.
41. Prokofiev, *Diaries*, May 17, 1925, 163. Apparently it was this meeting that Duke describes in some detail, giving himself and Prokofiev dialogue and claiming that Sergei was so impressed with the work that he kissed him on the mouth. See *Passport*, 148–49.
42. Prokofiev, *Diaries*, May 22, 1925, 165.
43. Prokofiev, *Diaries*, June 15, 1925, 177.
44. Prokofiev, *Diaries*, June 16, 1925, 178.
45. Quoted in Duke, *Passport*, 152–53.
46. Quoted in Garafola, *Diaghilev's Ballets Russes*, 113.
47. Sergei Prokofiev to Nikolai Miaskousky, Bourron-Marlotte, Seine et Marne, August 4, 1925, in Robinson, *Selected Letters*, 259.

48. Quoted in Duke, *Passport,* 153–55.
49. Duke, *Passport,* 153–54
50. Prokofiev, *Diaries,* July 1, 1925, 192.
51. Prokofiev, *Diaries,* July 3, 1925, 195.
52. Duke, *Passport,* 161.
53. *Stage,* October 22, 1925.
54. Duke, *Passport,* 166.
55. *Era,* November 18, 1925.
56. *Stage,* November 19, 1925.
57. Beaumont, *Diaghilev Ballet in London,* 252–53.
58. Duke, *Passport,* 166.
59. Quoted in Duke, *Passport,* 168–69. The ballet was performed for the fourth time in Berlin in December 1925.
60. Duke, *Passport,* 199.
61. Duke, *Passport,* 199–200
62. Dukelsky, "Friendship's Tribute, Dukelsky to Nabokov," *Boston Evening Transcript,* 1931.
63. Duke, *Passport,* 199–200.
64. Duke, *Passport,* 147.
65. Vladimir Dukelsky to Boston Symphony Orchestra, *Programme,* 1326.

CHAPTER 4. DUKE TAKES CHARGE

1. Duke, *Passport,* 158.
2. Duke, *Passport,* 158–59.
3. Balfour, *Society Racket,* 59–60.
4. Balfour, *Society Racket,* 64.
5. Duke, *Passport,* 163.
6. Duke, *Passport,* 167–68.
7. Duke, *Passport,* 174.
8. Duke, *Passport,* 169.
9. Quoted in Holden, "The 'Adventures and Battles' of Vladimir Dukelsky," 300–301.
10. Duke *Passport,* 175.
11. Duke, *Passport,* 176–77.
12. Suskin, *Show Tunes,* 273.
13. Duke, *Passport,* 177.
14. Prokofiev, *Diaries,* March 22, 1926, 278.
15. Duke, *Passport,* 178–79.
16. Quoted in Duke, *Passport,* 182–84.
17. Beaumont, *Diaghilev Ballet in London,* 256.
18. Duke, *Passport,* 185.
19. *Sphere,* July 3, 1926.
20. Prokofiev, *Diaries,* June 5, 1926, 332.
21. Prokofiev, *Diaries,* June 5, 1926, 332.
22. Duke, *Passport,* 184.
23. *Britannia and Eve,* June 16, 1926.

NOTES TO CHAPTER 4   217

24. *Illustrated London News*, July 14, 1926.
25. Prokofiev, *Diaries*, August 10, 11, 1926, 357–58.
26. Prokofiev, *Diaries* , August 21, 22, 1926, 361. This translates as "The Russian gents have drunk too much!"
27. Duke, *Passport,* 187.
28. *Programme*, 1328.
29. Duke, *Passport,* 189.
30. Duke, *Passport,* 190–93.
31. Suskin, *Show Tunes*, 274–75
32. Duke to George Gershwin, May 24, 1927, Duke Collection.
33. Quoted in Duke, *Passport,* 4.
34. Scheijen, *Diaghilev: A Life*, 415–16.
35. Duke, *Passport,* 196. The ballet was extensively reviewed by J. Turner, "The World of Music," *Illustrated London News*, July 23, 1927.
36. Duke, *Passport,* 196–97. In *Diaghilev: A Life*, Scheijen offers a shorter and slightly different account of the episode.
37. Quoted in Prokofiev, *Diaries*, 596n4.
38. Duke, *Passport,* 199.
39. Prokofiev, *Diaries*, February 21, 1928, 691.
40. Duke, *Passport,* 201.
41. Duke, *Passport,* 201–2.
42. Suskin, *Show Tunes*, 274–75.
43. Duke, *Passport,* 202.
44. *Era*, November 23, 1927.
45. Duke, *Passport,* 206.
46. *Stage*, February, 16, 1928, 18.
47. *Diss Express*, April 20, 1928.
48. *Tattler*, February 22, 1928. Steven Suskin finds some Gershwin in "Blowing the Blues Away" but with more complex harmonies. See Suskin, *Show Tunes*, 272.
49. *Diss Express*, February 24, 1928.
50. *Programme*, 1328; Duke, *Passport,* 203.
51. Prokofiev, *Diaries*, December 6, 1927, 670–71.
52. Prokofiev to Natalia Konstantinovna, Paris, January 31, 1928, in Robinson, *Selected Letters*, 197.
53. Sergei Prokofiev to Nikolai Yakovlevich, Paris, January 25, 1928, in Robinson, *Selected Letters*, 271.
54. Prokofiev, *Dairies*, December 7, 1927, 671.
55. Prokofiev, *Dairies*, December 9, 1927, 671.
56. Duke, *Passport,* 204–5.
57. Gershwin, *Lyrics on Several Occasions*, 246–47.
58. Prokofiev, *Diaries*, May 31, 1928, 704.
59. Duke, *Passport,* 209.
60. Duke, *Passport,* 210. Prokofiev's account of the concert can be found in Robinson, *Sergei Prokofiev*, 219.

61. Prokofiev, *Diaries*, June 14, 1928, 712–13.
62. Prokofiev to Nikolai Yakovlevich, Paris, July 9, 1928, in Robinson, *Selected Letters*, 275.
63. Duke, *Passport*, 210.
64. Duke, *Passport*, 169–70.
65. Duke, *Passport*, 210.
66. Duke, *Passport*, 210–11.
67. Duke, *Passport*, 213–15.
68. Prokofiev, *Diaries*, November 25, 1928, 740.
69. Prokofiev, *Diaries*, November 27, 1928, 741.
70. Prokofiev, *Diaries*, November 28, 1928, 741–42.
71. Duke, *Passport*, 214–15. The Bogdanovich songs were composed in 1925. See notes in *Programme*, 1330.
72. Duke, *Passport*, 215.
73. Nicholas Slonimsky, "Bouncing into Fortune's Lap and Out Again," in *Nicholas Slonimsky: Writings on Music*, ed. Electra Slonimsky Yourke, 51–54.
74. Duke, *Passport*, 216.
75. *Boston Globe*, March 22, 1929.
76. *Boston Herald*, March 16, 1929.
77. Quoted in McAuliffe, *When Paris Sizzled*, 253.
78. Duke, *Passport*, 217–18.
79. Prokofiev, *Diaries*, March 21, 1929, 800.
80. Prokofiev, *Diaries*, March 22, 1929. 800.
81. Duke, *Passport*, 216–17.
82. Suskin, *Show Tunes*, 276.
83. *Era*, August 28, 1929.
84. *Era*, September 10, 1930.
85. Duke, *Passport*, 228.
86. Duke, *Passport*, 169.
87. Duke, *Passport*, 218.

CHAPTER 5. DUKE AND DUKELSKY CELEBRATED

1. Mordden, *Sing for Your Supper*, 1–3; Young and Young, *Music of the Great Depression*, 68; Laufe, *Broadway's Greatest Musicals*, 31–36; Odets, *Six Plays of Clifford Odets*, 1–31.
2. Duke, *Passport*, 220.
3. Duke, *Passport*, 221–22.
4. Prokofiev, *Diaries*, January 14, 1930, 904.
5. Prokofiev, *Diaries*, January 18, 1930, 907.
6. Prokofiev, *Diaries*, January 29 to February 1, 1930, 913–14; February 3, 1930, 915.
7. Vladimir Dukelsky, "With Justice, in Admiration, in Friendship," *Boston Evening Transcript*, February 21, 1930.
8. Vladimir Dukelsky, "Friendship's Tribute, Dukelsky to Nabokov," *Boston Evening Transcript*, October 31, 1931.
9. Duke to George Gershwin, n.d. (late 1929), Duke Collection.
10. Duke to George Gershwin, n.d. (different letter, late 1929), Duke Collection.

NOTES TO CHAPTER 5   219

11. Duke to George Gershwin, n.p, January 1, 1930, Duke Collection.
12. Duke to George Gershwin, New York, n.d. (c. 1930), Duke Collection.
13. Duke, *Passport,* 229–30.
14. *New York Times*, October 12, 1930.
15. Duke, *Passport,* 238.
16. Duke, *Passport,* 240–41.
17. *New York Times*, June 11, 1931.
18. Duke, *Passport,* 242.
19. *New York Times*, April 30, 1931.
20. This short film can be seen YouTube. Duke barely mentioned the film in his autobiography. See, p 230.
21. *Morning Star,* August 17, 1930.
22. Duke, *Passport,* 239–40.
23. IMDb's entry on *Honor among Lovers*.
24. Duke, *Passport,* 241. In his review of the film, Jose Arroyo notes that the soundtrack "is by the great Vernon Duke that features jazz and classical, placing both on an equal footing." See "First Impressions: Notes on Film and Culture." Sections of the film can be seen on *You Tube,*
25. Duke, *Passport,* 242.
26. *New York Times*, June 22, 1930.
27. *New York Times*, October 6, 1930; Duke, *Passport,* 243–44.
28. Phillips, *Tunesmith and the Lyricist,* 33.
29. Prokofiev to Dima [Vladimir Dukelsky], Paris, November 9, 1930, in Robinson, *Selected Letters,* 145–47.
30. Duke to George Gershwin, April 23, 1930, Duke Collection.
31. Duke, *Passport,* 237.
32. Notes in *Programme,* 1330.
33. Prokofiev to Nikolai Yakovlevich, Paris, May 22, 1931, in Robinson, *Selected Letters,* 292.
34. Holden, "Confrontations," 110.
35. Duke, *Passport,* 255.
36. Suskin, *Show Tunes,* 277.
37. *New York Times*, July 20, 1931.
38. Dukelsky to Philip Hale, in *Programme,* 1316–18.
39. Dukelsky to Philip Hale, in *Programme,* 1316–18.
40. *Springfield Republican*, May 1, 1932.
41. Prokofiev to Dima, Paris, June 3, 1932, in Robinson, *Selected Letters,* 147–48.
42. Duke, *Passport,* 258–61.
43. Duke, *Passport,* 261–62.
44. Duke, *Passport,* 262–63.
45. Duke, *Passport,* 263.
46. Duke, *Passport,* 264–67.
47. Duke, *Passport,* 267–68.
48. Wilk, *They're Playing Our Song,* 232n.
49. Wilk, *They're Playing Our Song,* 233.

50. Quoted in Duke, *Passport*, 274.
51. Duke, *Passport*, 276.
52. Duke, *Passport*, 276.
53. Duke, *Passport*, 277.
54. Samuel Steatton, *Dallas Morning News*, February 3, 1935.
55. Quoted in Duke, *Passport*, 276–77.
56. Quoted in Duke, *Passport*, 277.
57. For an analysis of Winchell's influence on popular culture, see Gabler, *Winchell: Gossip, Power, and the Culture of Celebrity*.
58. *Richmond Times Dispatch*, October 19, 1932.
59. Duke, *Passport*, 278.
60. *Evansville Courier*, September 9, 1933.
61. Duke, *Passport*, 269–70.
62. Duke, *Passport*, 282.
63. *Brooklyn Daily Eagle*, April 5, 1933.
64. Duke, *Passport*, 284.
65. Duke, *Passport*, 280. See also *New York Times*, May 31, 1933.
66. *Springfield Republican*, July 6, 1933.
67. Duke, *Passport*, 284–85.
68. Duke, *Passport*, 292.
69. Kendrick, *Musical Theater*, 210.
70. *Stage*, January 1934.
71. *New York Times*, January 5, 1934.
72. David Cunard, liner notes, *NineteenThirty-Fourth Edition of the Ziegfeld Follies*.
73. Meyerson and Harburg, *Who Put the Rainbow*, 39.
74. Duke, *Passport*, 292.
75. *New York Times*, March 29, 1934.
76. *Boston Herald*, April 22, 1934.
77. *Boston Herald*, April 22, 1934.
78. Duke, *Passport*, 302–3.
79. Gioia, *Jazz Standards*, 23. In his review in the *Daily News* of December 28, Burns Mantle mentioned that "Words without Music" was included in the show, but did not identify the writer or lyricist. If it was the song Duke and Ira Gershwin composed, it would soon have a second life.
80. *Boston Herald*, February 22, 1934.
81. Quoted in Duke, *Passport*, 305.
82. Duke, *Passport*, 295.
83. Duke, *Passport*, 305–6.
84. Duke, *Passport*, 303.
85. Duke, *Passport*, 306.
86. *New York Times*, March 22, 1935.
87. *Greensboro Daily News*, September 27, 1935.
88. Duke, *Passport*, 308.

CHAPTER 6. DUKE AT HIS VERY BEST

1. *Stage*, September 1935, 13–15.
2. In his autobiography Duke fails to recognize the importance of the *Follies* in his career, devoting only two and a half pages to it and thus relegating it to a small place in his musical life and in the history of Broadway shows.
3. Duke, *Passport*, 308.
4. *Greensboro Daily News*, October 20, 1935.
5. Duke, *Passport*, 309.
6. Duke, *Passport*, 315–16.
7. Duke, *Passport*, 312.
8. Green, *Encyclopedia of the Musical Theatre*, 8, 21, 179.
9. *New York Times*, May 10, 1936.
10. See Kirstein, *Choreography by George Balanchine*, 66–127.
11. Duke, *Passport*, 311.
12. Green, *Encyclopedia of the Musical Theatre*, 15, 195.
13. Duke, *Passport*, 311–12.
14. *Boston Herald*, December 25, 1935.
15. Duke, *Passport*, 311.
16. The history of *Shuffle Along* is discussed in detail by John Jeremiah Sullivan in "American" in *New York Times Magazine*, March 17, 2016. Included is a photograph of Baker in the chorus line.
17. *Boston Herald*, January 5, 1936.
18. Kimball, *Complete Lyrics of Ira Gershwin*, 259.
19. Duke, *Passport*, 316.
20. Gershwin, *Lyrics on Several Occasions*, 194–95.
21. Kimball, *Complete Lyrics of Ira Gershwin*, 258–62.
22. *Boston Herald*, December 31, 1935.
23. Duke, *Passport*, 316.
24. Kimball, *Complete Lyrics of Ira Gershwin*, 244–45.
25. Gershwin, *Lyrics on Several Occasions*, 53.
26. *Greensboro Daily News*, February 1, 1936.
27. *New York Times*, January 31, 1936.
28. Duke, *Passport*, 315–16.
29. Genné, *Dance Me a Song*, 77.
30. Kimball, *Complete Lyrics of Ira Gershwin*, 246.
31. Gershwin, *Lyrics on Several Occasions*, 248.
32. Genné, *Dance Me a Song*, 77.
33. *Stage*, March 1936.
34. Quoted in Genné, *Dance Me a Song*, 31.
35. Genné and Matijas, "Collaborating in the Melting Pot," 58–60. See also Mordden, *Sing for Your Supper*, 195–96, and Kimball, *Complete Lyrics of Ira Gershwin*, 254.
36. Genné and Matijas, "Collaborating in the Melting Pot," 58–60
37. Genné, *Dance Me a Song*, 82.

38. *New York Times*, February 10, 1936.
39. *New York Times*, January 31, 1936.
40. *Springfield Republican*, February 9, 1936.
41. Gershwin, *Lyrics on Several Occasions*, 246.
42. Mordden, *Sing for Your Supper*, 139.
43. *San Francisco Chronicle*, April 4, 1936.
44. *Evening Star*, May 11, 1936.
45. Duke to Ira Gershwin, October 21, 1936, Duke Collection.
46. *New York Times*, September 15, 1936.
47. Ira Gershwin to Vernon Duke, Beverly Hills, October 6, 1936, Gershwin Collection.
48. Duke to Ira Gershwin, New York, October 21, 1936, Duke Collection.
49. Duke to Ira Gershwin, October 21, 1936, Duke Collection.
50. *Evening Star*, May 11, 1937.
51. *Greensboro Record*, November 19, 1937.
52. Ewen, *American Songwriters*, 136.
53. Quoted in Rosenberg, *Fascinating Rhythm*, 323.
54. Vernon and Ira's relationship is discussed in chapters 7 and 8 of Phillips, *Tunesmith and the Lyricist*.
55. Phillips, *Tunesmith*, 88–89.
56. Phillips, *Tunesmith*, See chapter 6 for analyses of those interpreting the song.
57. *Scotsman*, July 24, 1935.
58. *Yorkshire Post*, July 24, 1935.
59. *Illustrated Sporting and Dramatic News*, August 2, 1935.
60. *Sphere*, August 3, 1935.
61. Duke, *Passport*, 319.
62. Duke, *Passport*, 319–23.
63. Duke, *Passport*, 326.
64. Duke, "John Field," unpublished essay in Duke Collection.
65. *Scotsman*, June 30, 1936.
66. *Illustrated Sporting and Dramatic News*, July 10, 1936.
67. *Sphere*, July 11, 1936.
68. Duke, *Passport*, 331–33.
69. *Boston Herald*, July 21, 1936.
70. *Boston Herald*, September 24, 1936.
71. *Boston Herald*, November 12, 1936.
72. Duke, *Passport*, 337.
73. *Daily News*, January 20, 1937.
74. Duke, deleted chapter from *Passport*, 14–15, Duke Collection.
75. Gershwin to Vernon Duke, Beverly Hills, May 5, 1937, Gershwin Collection.
76. On the illness and death of Gershwin, see Jablonski and Stewart, *Gershwin Years*, 289–96.
77. Duke intimated that his salary was between $30,000 and $50,000. See Duke, *Passport*, 358.

78. Taper, *Balanchine*, 303–5.
79. *New York Times*, November 14, 1937. Duke also worked on "I Love to Rhyme" and "Just Another Rhumba," the latter, although the longest and most ambitious, was not included.
80. *Trenton Evening Times*, September 21, 1937.
81. Genné, *Dance Me a Song*, 98.
82. Duke, *Passport*, 358.
83. Genné, *Dance Me a Song*, 105.
84. Duke, *Passport*, 358.
85. Duke, *Passport*, 359.
86. *New York Times*, January 9, 1938.
87. *New York Times*, January 13, 1938.
88. Oscar Thompson, quoted in eliminated chapter of *Passport*, Duke Collection.
89. Samuel Chotzinoff, quoted in eliminated chapter of *Passport*, Duke Collection.
90. Quoted in Duke, *Passport*, 362.
91. Duke, *Passport*, 362.
92. Sergei Prokofiev to Dima [Vladimir Dukelsky], Paris, January 14, 1938, in Robinson, *Selected Letters*, 157.
93. Duke, *Passport*, 367.
94. Duke, *Passport*, 248–49, 359.
95. Duke to Ira Gershwin, New York, June 21, 1938, Duke Collection.
96. Duke to Ira Gershwin, New York, December 3, 1938, Duke Collection.
97. Quoted in Duke, *Passport*, 372. The war scare was probably the outbreak of the Spanish Civil War in 1936.
98. *New York Times*, January 8, 1939.
99. *Edinburg Daily Courier*, March 15, 1939.
100. Duke, *Passport*, 372.
101. Suskin, *Show Tunes*, 281.
102. *New York Times*, February 22, 1940.
103. Duke, *Passport*, 373–87.
104. Prokofiev to Mon cher Ami [Vernon Duke], Moscow, April 5, 1940, in Robinson, *Selected Letters*, 158.
105. Duke, *Passport*, 379–82.
106. Duke, *Passport*, 349–50.
107. *Springfield Republican*, October 25, 1940.
108. *Richmond Times Dispatch*, November 5, 1940.
109. Duke, *Passport*, 388.
110. Duke, *Passport*, 382–83.
111. Duke to Ira Gershwin, New York, February 16, 1940, Duke Collection.
112. Duke, *Passport*, 383.
113. Quoted in Meyerson and Harburg, *Who Put the Rainbow*, 176.
114. *Boston Herald*, February 8, 1942.
115. Duke, *Passport*, 389; Pollack, *Ballad of John Latouche*, 117.

116. The songs are listed on the back of the 1940 sheet music of "Taking a Chance on Love."
117. Aschenbrenner, *Katherine Dunham*, 19–140.
118. Mason, ed., *I Remember Balanchine*, 190.
119. Kirstein, *Choreography by Balanchine*, 146. John Martin assessed the dancing of Dunham and her troupe in a long article in the *New York Times*, November 10, 1940.
120. Genné, *Dance Me a Song*, 112–17.
121. Pollack, *Ballad of John Latouche*, 126.
122. Duke, *Passport*, 388–39.
123. Pollack, *Ballad of John Latouche*, 123.
124. Mason, *I Remember Balanchine*, 193.
125. Duke, *Passport*, 391.
126. *Pittsburgh Press*, October 22, 1940.
127. Duke, *Passport*, 392.
128. *New York Times*, October 26, 1940.
129. *San Francisco Chronicle*, July 27. 1941.
130. Pollack, *Ballad of John Latouche*, 127–28.
131. Duke, *Passport*, 393.

CHAPTER 7. DUKE SERVES HIS COUNTRY

1. Strangely, Duke only occasionally mentioned the war in his autobiography.
2. Kirstein, *Choreography of George Balanchine*, 145.
3. Duke, *Passport*, 395–96.
4. Pollack, *Ballad of John Latouche*, 109.
5. *Brooklyn Daily Eagle*, September 28, 1941.
6. *Pittsburgh Press*, September 18, 1941.
7. Duke, *Passport*, 396.
8. Pollack, *Ballad of John Latouche*, 142. Pollack devoted an entire chapter to the show.
9. Duke, *Passport*, 400–401.
10. Duke, *Passport*, 401.
11. Pollack, *Ballad of John Latouche*, 144–45.
12. *New York Times*, December 26, 1941.
13. Duke, *Passport*, 404.
14. Pollack, *Ballad of John Latouche*, 150–51.
15. *Daily News*, November 24, 1941.
16. Pollack, *Ballad of John Latouche*, 157. Pollack also spent an entire chapter on this show.
17. Duke, *Passport*, 400.
18. Matthews, *Over My Shoulder*, 173. The difficulties Matthews claimed she experienced after leaving the show indicate a woman psychologically disturbed or someone with a very creative imagination.
19. Pollack, *Ballad of John Latouche*, 157.
20. *New York Times*, January 10, 1942.
21. Duke, *Passport*, 403.

22. Duke, *Passport*, 404.
23. *New York Times*, April 16, 1942.
24. *Brooklyn Daily Eagle*, January 5, 1942.
25. *Brooklyn Daily Eagle*, February 11, 1942.
26. *Oakland Tribune*, March 8, 1942.
27. Duke, *Passport*, 405-6.
28. *Brooklyn Daily Eagle*, January 28, 1942.
29. Duke, *Passport*, 406.
30. Duke, *Passport*, 407-8.
31. Duke, *Passport*, 426.
32. I thank Scott Dunn for providing me with a recording of this work.
33. Duke, *Passport*, 409-10.
34. Duke, *Passport*, 410.
35. Duke, *Passport*, 414-17.
36. Pollock, *Ballad of John Latouche*, 130.
37. *New York Times*, May 28, 1943.
38. Quoted in Pollack, *Ballad of John Latouche*, 131.
39. Diana Burgin, quoted in Scott Dunn, liner notes, *Vernon Duke Violin Concertos*, Naxos, 8.559286, 2007. See also *Boston Herald*, March 17, 18, 1943. On January 5 and 7, 1944, it was badly conducted at Carnegie Hall by Artur Rodzinski who at the last minute had replaced Leonard Bernstein who had rehearsed the work.
40. *Boston Globe*, March 20, 1943.
41. Duke, *Passport*, 410-11.
42. Duke, *Passport*, 412.
43. Caesar, *Caesar's Hours*, 46-48.
44. Duke, *Passport*, 418-19; *New York Times*, December 29, 1943.
45. Duke, *Passport*, 419-20.
46. Meyerson and Harburg, *Who Put the Rainbow*, 176-77.
47. *Evening Star*, January 4, 1944.
48. *Daily Illinois State Journal*, March 20, 1944.
49. Duke, *Passport*, 422-23.
50. Quoted in Suskin, *Opening Night*, 342.
51. *New York Times*, January 14, 1944.
52. Duke, *Listen Here!* 242.
53. Duke, *Passport*, 421-22.
54. Caesar, *Caesar's Hour*, 52-53.
55. Duke, *Passport*, 424.
56. Duke, *Passport*, 424-25.
57. *Miami News*, April 5, 1944; *Boston Herald*, June 4, 1944.
58. *New York Times*, November 16, 1944.
59. *San Diego Union*, September 23, 1944.
60. Duke, *Passport*, 426-27.
61. *New York Times*, September 30, October 2, 1944.

62. Dietz, *Dancing in the Dark*, 270–73.
63. Duke, *Passport*, 427.
64. Duke, *Passport*, 428.
65. Quoted in Suskin, *Opening Night*, 579.
66. *New York Times*, November 17, 1944.
67. *Plain Dealer*, November 19, 1944.
68. *Augusta Chronicle*, November 10, 1944.
69. Quoted in Suskin, *Opening Night*, 581.
70. Duke, *Passport*, 428.
71. Duke, *Passport*, 429.
72. Duke, *Passport*, 426–29. Evidently Duke was discharged in September 1945.

CHAPTER 8. DUKELSKY REEMERGES
1. Dukelsky, "The Composer's Lot in America," 6–7, 44–45.
2. Duke, *Passport*, 428–29.
3. *New York Times*, December 4, 1944.
4. *New York Times*, December 11, 1944.
5. *New York Times*, December 3, 1944.
6. *New York Times*, May 1, 1945.
7. *Boston Globe*, January 5, 1946.
8. *New York Times*, January 10, 1946.
9. *New York Times*, June 4, 1946.
10. *Omaha World Herald*, July 14, 1946.
11. Quoted in Grant, *Rise and Fall of the Broadway Musical*, 105.
12. Duke, *Passport*, 436–37.
13. Parker, *Ogden Nash*, 134.
14. Duke, *Passport*, 436–37.
15. Parker, *Ogden Nash*, 134.
16. Duke, *Passport*, 431–34.
17. Duke, *Passport*, 408, 438.
18. Duke, *Passport*, 438–39.
19. *Springfield Republican*, August 22, 1946.
20. Duke, *Passport*, 435–36.
21. Duke, *Passport*, 441.
22. Duke, *Listen Here*, 201.
23. Quoted in Duke, *Passport*, 440.
24. *Tattler and Bystander*, January 8, 1947.
25. Duke, *Passport*, 455.
26. *Stage*, June 12, 1947.
27. *Richmond Times Dispatch*, September 14, 1947.
28. Nash and Duke, *Musical Zoo*, flyleaf.
29. *New York Times*, January 11, 1948.
30. Duke, *Passport*, 444, 448.
31. Duke, *Passport*, 449–50.

32. Duke, "The Society for Forgotten Music," *Down Beat*, August 20, 1959, 29, 80.
33. Duke, *Passport*, 455.
34. Duke, untitled article, Duke Collection.
35. Duke to Ira Gershwin, Paris, July 9, 1947, Duke Collection. An émigré journal, *Novosselye* was published in New York in Russian from 1942 to 1950. Duke's article, "The Crossroads of Modern Music," was included in the 1947 winter edition. The January edition of *Musical Quarterly* included Duke's "Gershwin, Schillinger, and Dukelsky: Some Reminiscences." It briefly recounts how Gershwin benefited from working with music theoretical practitioner Joseph Schillinger.
36. Ira Gershwin to Duke, Beverly Hills, October 6, 1947, Gershwin Collection.
37. Duke, *Passport*, 453–55.
38. Zimmers, *Lyrical Satirical Harold Rome*, 55.
39. Duke, *Passport*, 455.
40. *New York Times*, June 2, 1948.
41. Duke, *Passport*, 456.
42. Program, Second Regular Concert, December 12, 1948, Society for Forgotten Music, New York State Library.
43. Program, Fourth Regular Concert, March 6, 1949, Society for Forgotten Music, New York State Library.
44. *New York Times*, October 29, 1949.
45. Wikipedia's entry on Walter Benton.
46. Benton, *This Is My Beloved*, 15.
47. *Dallas Morning News*, September 11, 1949.
48. *New York Times*, June 5, 1949.
49. Duke, *Passport*, 464.
50. *San Diego Union*, March 8, 1949.
51. Quoted in Greenfield, *Last Sultan*, 53–54.
52. Duke, *Passport*, 463–65.
53. Duke, *Passport*, 464–65.
54. Quoted in Holden, "Confrontations," 92–94. Holden identified Estelle as Marie-Adele Bishop, an Irish woman. But Duke's claim that she was part Irish sounds about right, because she lived with her mother and sister in New York.
55. Duke, *Passport*, 469–70.
56. Duke, *Passport*, 470.
57. *New York Times*, September 25, 1949.
58. *Daily News*, September 24, 1949; *Springfield Union*, October 2, 1949.
59. Duke, *Passport*, 470.
60. *New York Times*, October 15, 1949.
61. Holden, "Confrontations," 173.
62. Quoted in Holden, "The Adventures and Battles of Vernon Duke," 303–4.
63. Quoted in Holden, "Adventures," 309–10.
64. Cahn to Duke, Los Angeles, September 25, 1950, Duke Collection.
65. Cahn, *I Should Care*, 193.
66. Duke, *Passport*, 476.

CHAPTER 9. DUKE AND DUKELSKY BECOME ONE

1. Bowman, *Los Angeles: Epic of a City*, 1–73.
2. Robert M. Fogelson entitled his history of Los Angeles *The Fragmented Metropolis*.
3. Bowman, *Los Angeles: Epic of a City*, 289–91, 201–11, 313–14, 387.
4. Day, *Russians in Hollywood*, 3–5.
5. See Robinson, *Russians in Hollywood*, *Hollywood's Russians*, especially 59–145.
6. Duke, *Passport*, 353.
7. Duke, "A Rosy Posy to Hollywood," unpublished article, Duke Collection.
8. Duke, *Passport*, 476.
9. *Los Angeles Times*, June 29, 1952.
10. Duke, *Passport*, 476.
11. Duke, "Canyon Anyone?" *Canyon Cryer*, November 13, 1958.
12. Duke, *Listen Here!* 309–10.
13. *Los Angeles Times*, January 2, 1952.
14. Quoted in Holden, "The 'Adventures and Battles' of Vladimir Dukelsky," 308.
15. Quoted in Holden, "Adventures," 309.
16. Quoted in Holden, "Adventures," 307–8.
17. Duke, *Passport*, 478–79.
18. Parker, *Ogden Nash*, 137.
19. Duke, *Listen Here!* 305–6.
20. Quoted in Holden, "Adventures," 319.
21. *Repository*, July 23, 1952.
22. *Omaha World-Herald*, July 3, 1952.
23. Cahn, *I Should Care*, 193–94.
24. *Boston Daily Record*, January 1. 1953.
25. *San Diego Union*, January 1, 1953.
26. Spada discusses the play in *More than a Woman: An Intimate Biography of Bette Davis*, 305–5.
27. Duke to Nash, May 30, 1952, Duke Collection.
28. *New York Times*, October 19, 1952.
29. *Boston Herald*, November 2, 1952.
30. *New York Times*, August 28, 1952.
31. *New York Times*, October 20, 1952.
32. *New York Times*, October 23, 1952.
33. *New York Times*, November 30, 1952.
34. *Boston Globe*, November 23, 1952.
35. *New York Times*, November 29, 1952.
36. *New York Times*, December 4, 1952.
37. *Oregonian*, December 16, 1952.
38. *New York Times*, December 16, 1952.
39. Duke, *Passport*, 480.
40. Quoted in Parker, *Ogden Nash*, 139.
41. *Los Angeles Times*, January 27, 1953.

42. Duke, *Passport*, 482–84.
43. Pollack, *Ballad of John Latouche*, 131.
44. George Frazier, liner notes, *Vernon Duke Plays Vernon Duke*, Atlantic Records, ALS 407, 1953.
45. Liner notes, *Autumn in New York: Dick Hyman Plays the Music of Vernon Duke*, Proscenium Inc. CE 4002-A, n.d.
46. *Los Angeles Times*, September 22, 1953.
47. Quoted in Pollack, *Ballad of John Latouche*, 168.
48. Duke to Latouche, New York, November 23, 1953, Duke Collection.
49. *Los Angeles Times*, January 28, 1954, February 3, 1954.
50. *Los Angeles Times*, July 13, 1954.
51. *Times* (San Mateo), March 20, 1954.
52. *Los Angeles Times*, May 20, 1954.
53. *Los Angeles Times*, September 1, 1954.
54. *San Diego Union*, May 6, 1955.
55. *San Diego Union*, May 16, 1955.
56. *Long Beach Independent*, May 31, 1955.
57. *Quad-City Times*, May 26, 1956.
58. *Richmond Times Dispatch*, May 26, 1955.
59. Duke, *Passport*, 484.
60. *Lake Review*, June 30, 1960.
61. *New York Times*, March 27, 1955.
62. *Chicago Sunday Times*, April 17, 1955.
63. *Sacramento Bee*, June 4, 1955.
64. Nicolas Slonimsky to Dima, Boston, April 29, 1955, Duke Collection. Document courtesy of Scott Holden.
65. Howard Dietz to Duke, New York, May 2, 1955, Duke Collection.
66. Duke to Ogden Nash, May 6, 1955, Duke Collection.
67. Dietz, "Schizo on the Musical Staff," 26. Duke reviewed the review in a letter to Dietz. He was very appreciative but pointed out that Dietz made a mistake regarding the origin of a particular song and questioned the inference that he had not written anything successful except *Cabin in the Sky*. In his response to the response, Dietz apologized for his "cavalierness with the details" and mentioned that he had received many letters and comments on his review. See Dietz to Duke, New York, July 6, 1955, Duke Collection.
68. Duke, *Listen Here!* 204–5; *Daily Republican*, August 4, 1955.
69. Pollack, *Ballad of John Latouche*, 420.
70. Parker, *Ogden Nash*, 140.
71. Ben Bagley, "List of Songs," *Littlest Revue*, Epic LN 3257, n.d. See also Suskin, *Show Tunes*, 288–89.
72. *Augustus Chronicle*, May 11, 1956.
73. *New York Times*, May 22, 1956.
74. *Boston American*, May 17, 1956.
75. *Dallas Morning News*, May 23, 1956.

76. Quoted in Suskin, *Opening Night*, 394.
77. *Dallas Morning News*, June 24, 1956.
78. Parker, *Ogden Nash*, 139–41.
79. Nash, liner notes, *Littlest Revue*, Epic LN 3257, n.d.
80. Pollack, *Ballad of John Latouche*, 463.
81. Duke, *Theater Arts*, March 1957, 24–26, 96.
82. Duke to Effie Latouche, March 20, 1957, Duke Collection.
83. *Los Angeles Times*, April 19, 1957.
84. Duke, *Passport*, 171.
85. Kay McCracken Duke, "Vernon Duke," January 1990, Duke Collection. Document courtesy of Scott Holden.
86. McCracken to Duke, September 14, 1956, Duke Collection.
87. Duke to McCracken, New York, November 6, 1956, Duke Collection. Why Duke was in New York is not known.
88. Liner notes, *Time Remembered.*, Mercury Records, MG 20380.
89. *Stage*, August 1, 1957.
90. *Los Angeles Times*, July 17 and August 30, 1957.
91. Duke to McCracken, n.p., September 25, 1957, Duke Collection.
92. Duke to Kay McCracken, n.p., September 29, 1957, Duke Collection.
93. Duke to Kay McCracken, n.p., September 30, 1957, Duke Collection. This is a different letter written on the same day.
94. Duke to McCracken, New Haven, September or early October, 1957, Duke Collection.
95. *New York Times*, November 24, 1957.
96. *Time Remembered* reproduces act 2, which is divided into ten sections in which can be heard "The Tango," "Waltz Codetta," "The Polka," "Ages Ago," and "Time Remembered."
97. *Los Angeles Times*, October 24, 1957.
98. Duke to McCracken, New Haven, September 1957, Duke Collection.
99. *Los Angeles Times*, November 1, 1957.
100. *Montana Standard,* December 8, 1957.
101. *Lincoln Star,* November 3, 1957.
102. *Oakland Tribune*, November 9, 1957.
103. *Van Nuys News*, August 14, 1958.
104. *El Gaucho*, December 12, 1958.
105. *Van Nuys News*, March 15, 1959.
106. Duke, "The Society for Forgotten Music," *Down Beat*, August 20, 1959, 80.
107. Duke, liner notes, *Sonata in D, Etude for Violin Bassoon, Souvenir de Venise & Parisian Suite*, Contemporary Composers Series, S 8007, 1960.
108. Nicolas Slonimsky, liner notes, *Vernon Duke String Quartet in C, Three Caprices for Piano, Variations on an Old Russian Chant for Oboe and Strings, and Surrealist Suite*, Stereo Records in association with Contemporary Records, S7024, 1958.
109. Duke, liner notes, *Sonata in D.*

110. Kay McCracken Duke, "Vernon Duke," January 1990, Duke Collection. Document courtesy of Scott Holden.
111. Duke, liner notes, *Andre Previn Plays the Songs of Vernon Duke*, Proscenium Inc., n.d.
112. Duke, liner notes, *Barney Kessel Plays Carmen*, Contemporary Records 513172K, 1958.
113. Duke, "Manors and Manners," *Variety*, January 8, 1958.
114. Duke, "Agents on the Agenda," *Variety*, January 9, 1959.
115. *Down Beat*, August 20, 1959, 29, 80.
116. Duke, "Plight of the Perishable Composer," 49–54.
117. Duke to Ira Gershwin, October 2, 1959, Duke Collection.
118. Gershwin, *Lyrics on Several Occasions*, 246.
119. Duke to Ira Gershwin, n.p., October 2, 1959, Duke Collection.
120. Duke, "Le Cas Ginger," Duke Collection.
121. *San Diego Union*, October 11, 1959.
122. *Sacramento Bee*, October 21, 1959.
123. *Los Angeles Times*, October 16, 1959.
124. *Los Angeles Times*, November 4, 1959.
125. Duke to McCracken, n.p., November 12, 1959, Duke Collection.
126. Duke to McCracken, Detroit, November 17, 1959, Duke Collection.
127. Duke to McCracken, Detroit, n.d., Duke Collection.
128. *New York Times*, December 8, 1959.
129. *Boston Herald*, December 6, 1959.
130. *Los Angeles Times*, February 20, 1960.
131. Duke, liner notes, *Lekeu: Piano Quartet, Cello Sonata (3rd movement), Poemes*, Society for Forgotten Music, Contemporary Records, R60-1092, 1958.
132. Quoted in Holden, "Adventures," 306–7.
133. *New York Times*, February 21, 1961.
134. *San Bernardino County Sun*, December 4, 1961.
135. *Los Angeles Times*, February 19, 1962.
136. *Los Angeles Times*, April 23, 1962.
137. Quoted in Holden, "Adventures," 317–18. Two years later, Dukelsky would sing in Russian two of his songs that were beamed over Radio Liberty to Moscow. See *Boston Herald*, June 14, 1964.
138. Duke, "About Myself," April 2, 1962, Duke Collection. Document courtesy of Scott Holden.
139. Duke to McCracken, Pacific Palisades, April 7, 1963, and April 11, 1963, Duke Collection.
140. *San Diego Union*, June 30, 1963.
141. *Democrat and Chronicle*, June 23, 1963.
142. *Independent Star-News*, August 4, 1963.
143. *Independent Star-News*, August 4, 1963.
144. *Los Angeles Times*, September 26, 1963.
145. *Los Angeles Times*, October 18, 20, 1963.

146. *Journal News*, January 6, 1964.
147. Slonimsky to Dima, Boston, January 10, 1964, Duke Collection. Document courtesy of Scott Holden.
148. Duke, *Listen Here!* 272.
149. *Los Angeles Times*, February 16, 1964.
150. *Omaha Herald*, July 5, 1964.
151. Igor Stravinsky, "Stravinsky Proposes a Cure for V.D.," *Listen: A Music Monthly*, September/October 1964, 1–2.
152. Holden, "Confrontations," 67.
153. Duke, "Dichotomic Dialogue." Unable to locate a published copy of this strangely titled article, I had to rely on the unpublished version in the Duke Collection.
154. *San Bernardino County Sun*, December 27, 1963.
155. *Los Angeles Times*, February 23, 1964.
156. *San Diego Union*, August 2, 1964.
157. Between November 8 and December 7, 1964, Vernon and Kay exchanged forty-one letters and postcards, twenty-seven written by Duke.
158. Duke to McCracken, Pacific Palisades, November 11, 1964, Duke Collection.
159. Duke to McCracken, November 14, 1964, Duke Collection.
160. Duke to McCracken, November 13, 1964, Duke Collection.
161. Duke to McCracken, November 14, 1964, Duke Collection.
162. Duke to McCracken, November 22, 1964, Duke Collection.
163. Duke to McCracken, November 29, 1964, Duke Collection.
164. McCracken to Duke, Munich, December 10, 1964, Duke Collection.
165. McCracken to Duke, telegram, Munich, December 10, 1964, Duke Collection.
166. *Poughkeepsie Journal*, January 31, 1965.
167. Duke to Nash, Pacific Palisades, March 9, 1965, Duke Collection.
168. *Frank Sinatra Sings Vernon Duke*, Capitol EAP-1 20423.
169. *Down Beat*, February 10, 1966, 34–35.
170. Duke to Forrest D. Stoll, Pacific Palisades, May 22, 1966, Duke Collection. Document courtesy of Scott Holden.
171. *Los Angeles Times*, June 5, 1966.
172. *Los Angeles Times*, May 29, 1966.
173. *Los Angeles Times*, February 19, 1967.
174. Duke to Nash, n.p., August 23, 1968, Duke Collection.
175. Duke to Nash, n.p., October 1, 1968, Duke Collection.
176. Duke to Nash, n.p., September 5, 1968, Duke Collection.
177. Duke to Nash, North Hampton, N.H., October 1, 1968, Duke Collection.
178. Wilder, "Acknowledgments," *American Popular Song*, xxvi.
179. *Los Angeles Times*, January 18, 1969.
180. Kay Duke Ingalls, pers. comm., December 17, 2018.
181. Ira and Lee Gershwin to McCracken, Western Union telegram, January 20, 1969, box 4, folder 21, Gershwin Collection.
182. Howard Dietz to McCracken Duke, Duke, n.p., January 21, 1968, Duke Collection.

183. Nicolas Slonimsky to Kay McCracken Duke, New York, January 18, 1969, Duke Collection. Document courtesy of Scott Holden. Inexplicably, Slonimsky barely mentions Duke in his autobiography, *Perfect Pitch*.
184. *Boston Record American*, January 19, 1969.
185. *New York Times*, January 18, 1969.
186. *Evening Star*, February 23, 1969.
187. *Journal News*, January 22, 1969.

CONCLUSION
1. *New York Times*, April 26, 1970.
2. *New York Times*, April 16, 1970.
3. *Boston Record American*, June 2, 1970.
4. Slonimsky, liner notes, *Vernon Duke: The Serious Songs*.
5. *Los Angeles Times*, June 20, 1980.
6. *Washington Post*, October 15, 1980.
7. *Sandra King Accompanied by Pat Smythe in a Concert of Vernon Duke*. Audiophile Records, ACD-197, 1985; *New York Times*, May 19, 1985.
8. Green, *The World of Musical Comedy*, 221–26.
9. Wilder, *American Popular Song*, 360.
10. Wilder, *American Popular Song*, 360.
11. Wilder, *American Popular Song*, 363–64.
12. Wilder, *American Popular Song*, 368.
13. Ziegel, "One Person, One Music," 332.
14. Wilk, *They're Playing Our Song*, 195–98.
15. Suskin, *Show Tunes 1905–1985*, 273–90; Ewen, *American Songwriters*, 133–37.
16. Suskin, *Opening Night on Broadway*, 341–42, 394–95, 579–82, 681–84.
17. Forte, *The American Popular Ballad of the Golden Era*, 29–96.
18. *New York Times*, March 4, 1990.
19. *Westport News*, March 2, 1990.
20. *Los Angeles Times*, July 1, 1990.
21. *Los Angeles Times*, March 7, 1992.
22. *Los Angeles Times*, August 6, 1993.
23. Suskin, liner notes, *Dawn Upshaw Sings Vernon Duke*.
24. *New York Times*, January 24, 1999.
25. *New York Times*, January 15, 1999.
26. *New York Times*, March 27, 1999.
27. Goldberg, liner notes, *Ziegfeld Follies of 1936*.
28. Savkina, liner notes, *Dukelsky, Zéphyr et Flora, Epitaphe,*
29. Scott Dunn, pers. comm., April 28, 2018.
30. Program, *Mohawk Trail Concerts*, 29th season, 1998, 36.
31. Scott Dunn and Kay Duke Ingalls, liner notes, *Vernon Duke, Piano Concertos*, Naxos 8.559289, 2007.
32. *New York Times*, January 12, 1999.

33. Program, *Vernon Duke: A Centennial Celebration*, October 9, 2003.
34. *New York Times*, October 27, 2004.
35. Blackhurst, liner notes, *Autumn in New York: Vernon Duke's Broadway*.
36. "Jazz at Lincoln Center Radio: Duke of the Songbook," season 17, program 8, airdate November 4, 2009.
37. Lyrics and Lyricists, *Taking a Chance on Love: The Music of Vernon Duke*, program, April 6–8, 2013.
38. Ziegel, "An Historical Flop Flips Back into Existence." *American Music Review* 41, no. 1 (Fall 2011).
39. Scott Holden to Ron Simpson, liner notes, *Beyond Vernon Duke*.
40. Holden, "Confrontations with Vladimir Dukelsky," 106–9.
41. Holden, "Confrontations with Vladimir Dukelsky," 205–7.
42. Genné and Matjias, "Collaborating in the Melting Pot," 59–60. In 2018 Genné published *Dance Me a Song*, which also discusses Duke's music for the show. See 74–84.
43. Grant, *The Rise and Fall of the Broadway Musical*, 106.
44. Jenness and Velsey, *Classic American Popular Song*, 87–90
45. Ziegel, "One Person, One Music," 321–45.
46. Holden, "The 'Adventures and Battles' of Vladimir Dukelsky," 316.
47. Suskine, *The Vernon Duke Songbook*, ii.
48. Hicks, liner notes, *Beyond Vernon Duke*.
49. Dunn and Ingalls, liner notes, *Vernon Duke Concertos*, Naxos, 8.559286, 2007.
50. New York Chamber Music Festival, program, September 10–16, 2010.
51. *Diaghilev P.S.*, program, October 23, 2011.
52. "Orchestrating a Rare Performance," *Iowa Now*, March, 2012.
53. Dunn and Ingalls, liner notes, *Violin Concerto: Complete Works for Violin,* Unrich, UATV-5990, 2014.
54. Singer, liner notes, *Misa*.

BIBLIOGRAPHY

UNPUBLISHED MATERIALS

George and Ira Gershwin Collection, Music Division, Library of Congress.

Holden, Scott. "Confrontations with Vladimir Dukelsky: A Study of the Composer and His Music." PhD diss., Manhattan School of Music, 2002.

Vernon Duke Collection, Music Division, Library of Congress.

PUBLISHED MATERIALS

Aschenbrenner, Joyce. *Katherine Dunham: Dancing a Life*. Urbana: University of Illinois Press, 2002.

Austin, William W. *Music in the 20th Century*. New York: W. W. Norton, 1966.

Ben Bagley. Liner notes. *Harold Arlen and Vernon Duke Revisited, Vol. II*. Painted Smiles Records PSCD-127, 1991.

———. Liner notes. *Vernon Duke Revisited, Vol III*. Painted Smiles Records, PSCD-147, 1994.

———. List of songs. *Littlest Revue*. Epic LN 3257, n.d.

Balfour, Patrick. *Society Racket: A Critical Survey of Modern Social Life*. London: John Long, 1932.

Beaumont, Cyril W. *The Diaghilev Ballet in London: A Personal Record*. London: Adam and Charles Black, 1951.

Benton, Walter. *This Is My Beloved*. New York: Alfred A. Knopf, 1951.

Blackhurst, Klea. Liner notes, *Autumn in New York: Vernon Duke's Broadway*. Lunch Money, 7915583302–2, 2005.

Braude, Mark. *Making Monte Carlo: A History of Speculation and Spectacle*. New York: Simon & Schuster, 2016.

Caesar, Sid, with Eddy Friedfeld. *Caesar's Hours: My Life in Comedy with Love and Laughter*. New York: Public Affairs, 2003.

Cahn, Sammy. *I Should Care: The Sammy Cahn Story*. New York: Arbor House, 1974.

Cunard, David. Liner notes to *The Nineteen Thirty-Four Edition of the Ziegfeld Follies*. AEI-CD-039, 1997.

Day, George Martin. *The Russians in Hollywood: A Study in Culture Conflict*. Los Angeles: University of Southern California Press, 1934.

Dietz, Howard. *Dancing in the Dark*. New York: Quadrangle/New York Times Book, 1974.

———. "Schizo on the — Musical Staff." *Atlantic Review*, 1955.

Dolin, Anton. *Divertissement*. London: Simpson Low, Marston, 1931.

Duke, Vernon. "Agents on the Agenda." *Variety*, January 7, 1959.

———. "Gershwin, Schillinger, and Dukelsky: Some Reminiscences." *Musical Quarterly* 33 (January 1947): 102–15. Reprinted in *The George Gershwin Reader*, ed. Robert Wyatt and John Andrew Johnson, 289–93. New York: Oxford University Press, 2004.
———. *Listen Here! A Critical Essay on Music Depreciation*. New York: Ivan Obolensky, 1963.
———. "Manors and Manners." *Variety*, January 8, 1958.
———. "Musical Antics and Antiques: The Modern Composer Is Sacrificed on the Alter of Ancestor Worship." *Stage*, March 1937, 46–47.
———. *Passport to Paris*. Boston: Little, Brown, 1955.
———. "The Composer's Lot in America." *Music Publishers Journal*, September–October 1944, 6–7, 44–45.
———. "The History of an Effort: The Society for Forgotten Music." *Down Beat Magazine* (August 20, 1959), 29, 80.
———. "The Plight of the Perishable Composer. *HiFi Review*, October 1959, 49–54, 74.
———. "Tribute to a Poet." *Theatre Arts* 41, no. 3 (March 1957): 24–26, 96.
Dunn, Scott, ed. *The Vernon Duke Songbook, Vol. 1*. Milwaukee: Boosey & Hawkes, 2012.
Ewen, David. *American Songwriters: An H. W. Wilson Biographical Dictionary*. New York: H. W. Wilson, 1987.
Fitzgerald, F. Scott. *This Side of Paradise*. Introduction by Aaron John Loeb. New York: Barnes & Noble, 1966.
Forte, Allen. *The American Popular Ballad of the Golden Era, 1924–1950*. Princeton: Princeton University Press, 1995.
Furia, Philip. *Ira Gershwin: The Art of the Lyricist*. New York: Oxford University Press, 1996.
Gabler, Neil. *Winchell: Gossip, Power, and the Culture of Celebrity*. New York: Vintage, 1994.
Garafola, Lynn. *Diaghilev's Ballets Russes*. New York: Oxford University Press, 1989.
Genné, Beth. *Dance Me a Song: Astaire, Balanchine, Kelly, and the America Musical*. New York: Oxford University Press, 2018.
Genné, Beth, and Christian Matjias. "Collaborating in the Melting Pot: Balanchine, Duke, and Gershwin." In *Proceedings, Sound Moves Conference*, sponsored by Princeton University and University of Surrey, published online, 2006.
Gershwin, Ira. Lyrics on Several Occasions. New York: Knopf, 1959.
Gioia, Ted. *The Jazz Standards: A Guide to the Repertoire*. New York: University of Oxford Press, 1012.
Goldberg, Mark Trent. Liner notes, *Ziegfeld Follies of 1936: Encore's Great American Musicals in Concerts*. Decca 440 016 056-2 BK02, 2001.
Grant, Mark N. *The Rise and Fall of the Broadway Musical*. Boston: Northeastern University Press, 2004.
Green, Stanley. *Encyclopedia* of the *Musical Theatre: An Updated Reference Guide to Over 2,000 Performers, Writers, Directors, Productions, and Songs of the Musical Stage, Both in New York and London*. New York: Da Capo, 1980.

———. *The World of Musical Comedy: The Story of the American Musical Stage as Told through the Careers of Its Foremost Composers and Lyricists*. Rev. ed. South Brunswick, NJ: A. S. Barnes, 1968.

Grigoriev, S. L. *Diaghilev Ballet, 1909–1929*. Translated and edited by Vera Bowen. London: Constable, 1953.

Hamm, Charles. *Yesterdays: Popular Song in America*. New York: W. W. Norton, 1979.

Hamm, Michael F. *Kiev: A Portrait, 1800–1997*. Princeton: Princeton University Press, 1993.

Herlihy, Patricia. *Odessa: A History, 1794–1914*. Cambridge: Distributed by Harvard University Press for the Ukrainian Research Institute, 1986.

Hicks, Michael. Liner notes, *Beyond Vernon Duke: Piano Works by Vladimir Dukelsky*. Tantara Records, TCD-0212BVD, 2012.

Holden, Scott. "The 'Adventures and Battles' of Vladimir Dukelsky (a.k.a. Vernon Duke)." *American Music*, Fall 2010, 297–319.

———. Liner notes, *Beyond Vernon Duke: Piano Works of Vladimir Dukelsky*. Tantara Records, TCD0212 BVD, 2014.

Jablonski, Edward, and Lawrence D. Stewart. *The Gershwin Years*. 2nd ed. Garden City, NY: Doubleday, 1973.

Jenness, David, and Don Vesey. *Classic American Popular Song: The Second Half-Century, 1950–2000*. New York: Routledge, 2006.

Joseph, Charles M. *Stravinsky and Balanchine: A Journey of Invention*. New Haven: Yale University Press, 2002.

Kashner, Sam, and Nancy Schoenberger. *A Talent for Genius: The Life and Times of Oscar Levant*. Los Angeles: Silman-James Press, 1994.

Kendrick, John. *Musical Theater: A History*. New York: Continuum International, 2008.

Kimball, Robert, ed. *The Complete Lyrics of Ira Gershwin*. New York: Knopf, 1993.

Kirstein, Lincoln, ed. *Choreography by George Balanchine: A Catalogue of Works*. New York: Viking, 1984.

Lambert, Constant. *Music Ho! A Study of Music in Decline*. London: Faber and Faber, 1941.

Laufe, Abe. *Broadway's Greatest Musicals*. Rev. ed. New York: Funk & Wagnalls, 1977.

Lifar, Serge. *Serge Diaghilev: His Life, His Work, His Legend: An Intimate Biography*. New York: G. P. Putnam's Sons, 1940.

MacMillan, Margaret. *Paris, 1919: Six Months That Changed the World*. New York: Random House, 2001.

Mason, Francis, ed. *I Remember Balanchine: Recollections of the Ballet Master by Those Who Knew Him*. New York: Doubleday, 1991.

Matthews, Jessie. *Over My Shoulder: An Autobiography as Told to Muriel Burgess*. New Rochelle, NY: Arlington House, 1974.

Maximova, Antonia S. "Zefir and Flora: European Debut of Vladimir Dukelsky in the Ballets Russes of S. Dyagilev." *Ballet Stock Library* 9, no. 2 (2011).

McAuliffe, Mary. *When Paris Sizzled: The 1920s Paris of Hemingway, Chanel, Cocteau, Cole Porter, Josephine Baker, and Their Friends*. New York: Rowman & Littlefield, 2006.

Meyerson, Harold, and Arthur Harburg. *Who Put the Rainbow in* The Wizard of Oz? *Yip Harburg Lyricist*. Ann Arbor: University of Michigan Press, 1993.

Mordden, Ethan. *Sing for Your Supper: The Broadway Musical in the 1930s*. New York: Palgrave Macmillan, 2005.

Nash, Ogden. "Tunes by Vernon Duke and Illustrations by Frank Owen." *Musical Zoo*. Boston: Little, Brown, 1947

Nice, David. *Prokofiev: From Russia to the West, 1891–1935*. New Haven: Yale University Press, 2003.

Norton, Leslie. *Léonide Massine and the 20th Century Ballet*. Jefferson, NC: McFarland, 2004.

Parker, Douglas M. *Ogden Nash: The Life and Work of America's Laureate of Light Verse*. Chicago: Ivan R. Dee, 2005.

Phillips, George Harwood. *The Tunesmith and the Lyricist: Vernon Duke, Ira Gershwin, and the Making of a Standard*. Camano Island, WA: Coyote Hill Press, 2016.

Pollack, Howard. *The Ballad of John Latouche: An America Lyricist's Life and Work*. New York: Oxford University Press, 2017.

Prokofiev, Sergey. *Diaries, 1915–1923: Behind the Mask*. Translated by Anthony Phillips. London: Faber and Faber, 2008.

———. *Diaries, 1924–1933: Prodigal Son*. Translated by Anthony Phillips. London: Faber and Faber, 2012.

Reis, Claire R. *Composers in America: Biographical Sketches of Contemporary Composers with a Record of Their Works*. Rev. ed. New York: Da Capo Press, 1977.

Robinson, Harlow, trans. and ed. *Selected Letters of Sergei Prokofiev*. Boston: Northeastern University Press, 1998.

———. *Sergei Prokofiev: A Biography*. New York: Viking Penguin, 1987.

———. *Russians in Hollywood, Hollywood's Russians: Biography of an Image*. Lebanon, NH: University Press of New England, 2007.

Rosenberg, Deena. *Fascinating Rhythm: The Collaboration of George and Ira Gershwin*. New York: Dutton, 1991.

Sanjek, Russell. *American Popular Music and Its Business: The First Four Hundred Years*. Vol. 3, *From 1900 to 1984*. New York: Oxford University Press, 1988.

Savkina, Natalya. Liner notes, *Dukelsky, Zephyr et Flore, Epitaphe*. Chandos, 9766, 1999.

Scheijen, Sjeng. *Diaghilev: A Life*. Trans. Jane Hedly-Prole and S. J. Leinbach. Oxford: Oxford University Press, 2009.

Sheed. Wilfrid. *The House That George Built: With a Little Help from Irving, Cole, and a Crew of About Fifty*. New York: Random House, 2007.

Singer, Barry. Liner notes, *Misa*. PS Classics, PS-1526, 2015.

Slonimsky, Nicolas. Liner notes, *Vernon Duke: The Serious Songs*. Glendale Records, GLS 6016, 1978.

———. *Perfect Pitch: A Life Story*. New York: Oxford University Press, 1988.

Spada, James. *More than a Woman: An Intimate Biography of Bette Davis*. New York: Bantam Books, 1993.

Stravinsky, Igor. "A Cure for V.D." *Listen: A Music Monthly*, September–October 1964, 1–2.
Struble, John Warthen. *The History of American Classical Music*. New York: Facts on File, 1995.
Sullivan, John Jeremiah. "American Shuffle." *New York Times Magazine*, March 27, 2016, 32–41, 53–55.
Suskin, Steven. Liner notes, *Dawn Upshaw Sings Vernon Duke*, Nonesuch Records, 79531-2, 1999.
———. *Opening Night on Broadway*. New York: Schirmer Books, 1990.
———. *Show Tunes, 1905–1985*. New York: Dodd, Mead, 1986.
Taper, Bernard. *Balanchine*. New York: Harper & Row, 1963.
The Twenty-Second Programme of the Boston Symphony Orchestra, Fifty-First Season, 1931–1932. Historical and descriptive notes by Philip Hale. Boston: Boston Symphony Orchestra, 1932.
Wilder, Alec. *American Popular Song: The Great Innovators, 1900–1950*. Edited by James T. Maher. New York: Oxford University Press, 1972.
Wilk, Max. *They're Playing Our Song: The Truth behind the Words and Music of Three Generations*. Mount Kisco, NY: Moyer Bell, 1991.
Yagoda, Ben. *The B Side: The Death of Tin Pan Alley and the Rebirth of the Great American Song*. New York: Riverhead Books, 2015.
Young, William H., and Nancy K. Young. *Music of the Great Depression*. Westport, CT: Greenwood Press, 2005.
Yourke, Electra Slonimsky, ed. *Nicholas Slonimsky: Writings on Music*. Vol. 1, *Early Articles for the Boston Evening Transcript*. New York: Routledge, 2004.
Ziegel, Aaron. "An Historical Flop Flips Back into Existence: Vernon Duke's *Sweet Bye and Bye*." *American Music Review* 41, no. 1 (Fall 2011).
———. "One Person, One Music: Reconsidering the Duke-Dukelsky Musical Style." *American Music* (Fall 2010): 321–45.
Zimmers, Tighe E. *Lyrical Satirical Harold Rome: A Biography of the Broadway Composer and Lyricist*. Jefferson, NC: McFarland, 2014.

INDEX

African American music and culture, 54, 121
African American performers, 104–5, 124, 125–26
agents, 177–78, 187
Alberts, Adelle, 85
albums. *See* recordings of Vernon Duke's music
All Star Dance Gala for British War Relief, 127–28
Alton, Robert, 99, 133
Alupka, Russia, 12–13
American Composers Orchestra, 202, *202*
American expatriates, 41, 74
American in Paris, An (Goldwyn film), 113
American popular music, 35; dances, 17, 24, 29; financial benefits of, 28, 58, 61–63, 73, 154; musical films, 160; musical theater, 73, 77, 108, 185, 206. *See also* Broadway; Duke-Dukelsky musical dichotomy; Duke, Vernon, popular music; jazz
Amor, Carolina, 86
Anderson, John Murray, 38, 92, 94, 99–100, 103, 104, 119, 162
Apollinaire, Guillaume, 117
April in Paris (film), 161, 223n78
"April in Paris" (song), 87–89, 96, 115, 117, 120, 132, 147, 164, 179, 184, 188, 191, 198, 199, 201, 204
April in Paris Fantasy (1942 radio broadcast), 131–32
Arden, Eve, 91, 99, 106
Arlen, Harold, 133, 191, 195, 198, 207
Aronson, Boris, 121–22, 125, 143–44

Atkinson, Brooks, 92, 103, 105, 125, 129, 130, 162–63, 169, 173. *See also* reviews and commentary, popular music
Auric, George, 49, 54, 65
"Autumn in New York," 94, 164, 171, 179, 188, 191, 196, 198, 199, 207
Autumn in New York (Hyman), 164–65

Bagley, Ben, 5, 169–70, 193, 198–99
Baird, Sir David and Lady, 68–69
Baker, Israel, 175
Baker, Josephine, 41, 100–105, 106, 206
Balanchine, George, 50, 63, 99, 113, 118, 130; *Cabin in the Sky*, 121–25; *Goldwyn Follies*, 113–14; *The Lady Comes Across*, 130; other collaborations with Vernon Duke, 119, 129–30; *Three Seasons*, 63, 66; *Ziegfeld Follies of 1936*, 99–100, 103–4, 106, 206; World War II relief efforts, 127–28
Ballets Russes, 43, 46, 47, 50, 64, 95, 208
Ballets Russes de Monte Carlo, 47, 95, 110
Balogh, Erno, 191
Banjo Eyes, 128–29, 205
Bankhead, Tallulah, 38, 81, 138
Barber, Samuel, 141, 145
Barney Kessel Plays "Carmen," 177
Baron, Aaron, 32
Barzin, Léon, 90, 142
Basil, Wassili de, 95, 110
Bennett, Richard Rodney, 203–4
Benton, Walter, 150
Berfield, David, 194
Berigan, Bunny, 109, 112
Berlin, Germany, 72

241

Berlin, Irving, 29
Bernhardt, Isolde von, 32
Bernstein, Leonard, 4, 141, 145, 178, 181, 206, 225n39
Blackhurst, Klea, 204
Black Sea, 12
Bogdanovitch, Ippolit Fyodorovich, 73
Bolger, Ray, 119, 129, 161
Bolsheviks. *See* Russian Revolution (1917–21)
Boston Symphony Orchestra, 55, 67, 74, 79, 83–84, 88, 114, 117, 134, 142–43, 174, 209. *See also* Koussevitsky, Serge
Boston theater, 88, 92, 100–101, 112, 128, 129–30, 133, 162, 180
Bowman, Patricia, 91–92
Brahms, Johannes, 65, 84, 143
Braque, Georges, 48, 52, 53, 54, 143
Bren, Milton, 140
Brice, Fanny, 91–92, 97–98, 99, 102–3, 106, 108
British War Relief, 127–28
Broadway, 31, 38, 70, 73, 84, 92, 108, 136, 139, 141. *See also* American popular music; New York City
Bruno Walter Auditorium (N.Y.), *203*, 204
Burgin, Richard, 134

Cabin in the Sky (film), 133–34
Cabin in the Sky (musical), 120–26, *122*, *124*, 170, 195, 206
Cabin in the Sky (revivals), 164, 184, 188
"Cabin in the Sky" (song), 121, *124*, 165, 176
Caesar, Sid, 135–36, 137–38
Cahn, Sammy, 140, 154, 161, 169
cantatas, 18, 110, 114, 147–49
Cantor, Eddie, 128, 133, 143
Carnegie Hall (N.Y.), 4, 34, 90, 117, 142, 143, 153, 201–3, 207, 225n39
Carroll, Nancy, 81, 82
Carter, Desmond, 69
Carter, Elliott, 5, 115

CBS Symphony Orchestra, 106, 146, 153
Champion, Gower, 130, 137, 138
Chanel, Coco, 44, 47
Chaplin, Charlie, 161
Charig, Phil, 35, 108
Charlie Barnet Orchestra, 119, 186
Chautauqua, N.Y., 169
Chavez, Carlos, 86
Chevreuse Valley, France, 46
Chicago, Ill., 95
Clark, Bobby, 106, 108
Claude, Francis, 151
Coast Guard, 132, 134–40. *See also* World War II
Cochran, Charles B., 61–62, 76
Cocteau, Jean, 44, 49, 67–68, 168
Communist Party (Soviet Union), 20–21
Composers' Protective Society, 91, 141
Connolly, Bobby, 91–92
Constantinople (Istanbul, Turkey), 26
Contemporary Records, 174
Copland, Aaron, 141, 153
Coward, Noel, 38, 57, 87
Crimea, 12
critics and criticism. *See* reviews and commentary, classical compositions; reviews and commentary, popular music
Cukor, George, 81

Dall, John, 150–51
Dassin, Jules, 162
David, Lee, 33
Davis, Bette, 161–63
Davis, Sammy, Jr., 188
Day, Doris, 161
Debussy, Claude, 23, 43, 99, 104, 175, 181, 206
Denenholz, Barbara, 153
Detroit, Mich., 180
Diaghilev, Serge Pavlovitch: death, 84, 85; relationship with Vernon Duke, 43–45, 47, 48, 51–52, 55, 57, 61–62, 68,

71, 75, 76, 84, 147, 201, 209; and Sergei
Prokofiev, 43, 45, 46, 48, 67; and Igor
Stravinsky, 58; *Three Seasons*, 63, 64,
66; *Zephyr and Flora*, 46, 48–49, 50,
53–57, 64, 67, 110, 115, 191
Dietz, Howard, 84, 133, 136–37, 138–39,
168, 190, 229n67
Dirman, Rose, 141–42, 149
Dixon, Dean, 152, 187
Doble, Francis, 60–61
Dolin, Anton, 5, 49, 51, 52, 53, 127
Dombrovsky, Marian, 16
Drake, Alfred, 140, 183
Dreyfus, Max, 35, 39, 42, 80, 90
Duke, Kay McCracken, 210; marriage to
Vernon Duke, 171–73, 176, 186–87;
performing and recording Duke's
music, 189, 194–95, 198, 204; singing
career, 181, 182, 186–87, 189
Duke, Lisa (cousin), 198
Duke, Vernon (Dukelsky, Vladimir), *36,
61, 163*; American citizenship, 86, 118,
149; appearance, 9, 37, 57, 64, 67, 68,
94, 121, 128, 154; autobiography, 3–4,
6, 7, 166–68, 182–83, 211n1; Ballets
Russes, 44–46; Broadway, 31, 38, 84,
128, 185; childhood and family, 9–14;
childhood musical development, 12,
15–17, 24, 29; commercial success,
84, 93, 96, 126, 195, 198, 207; on composing, 31, 34, 93, 142, 174, 175–76,
178–79, 185, 189; Constantinople,
young man in, 26–31; death, 190–91;
and Serge Diaghilev, 43–45, 47, 48,
51–52, 55, 57, 61–62, 68, 71, 75, 76, 79,
84, 147, 201, 209; early career playing
for money, 28–29, 31–35; education,
13, 15–16, 17; film work, 80–81, 113;
financial compensation as classical
composer, 34, 55, 58, 80, 154; financial
compensation from popular music,
34, 39, 58, 61–63, 73, 80, 93, 107, 114,
117, 154, 188; on forgotten composers
and music, 111, 141, 148, 149, 158, 174,
178, 181–82; and George Gershwin,
34, 35, 38–39, 46, 51, 62, 69, 74–75,
79–80, 83, 110, 113, 116, 148, 179, 204;
and Ira Gershwin, 5, 35, 67, 71, 82, 96,
97–98, 112–13, *113*, 114, 116–17, 120,
125, 140, 148, 179; health, 21, 26–27,
50, 61, 85–86, 118, 136, 183; jazz, 29,
50, 54, 58, 69, 82, 88, 93, 109, 111, 114,
150, 168, 177, 186; Kiev Conservatory,
16–18, 20–21; and Serge Koussevitzky,
55, 67, 68, 72, 74, 76, 83, 85, 146, 153,
174, 178; and John Latouche, 121,
123, *124*, 125, 127–29, 165–66, 169,
170; lyrics, 33, 67; marriage to Kay
McCracken, 171–73, 176, 186–87;
Monte Carlo, 46–53, *51*; mother's
death, 131, 132; musicals, 5, 58, 61–62;
name change, 8, 62, 118, 166–67; as
pianist, 13, 17, 28–29, 32, 33, 37, 38,
64, 73, 82, 149–50, 153, 164, 175, 176,
181; pen names, 29, 33; personality
and temperament, 3, 5–6, 10, 17, 66,
71, 159, 184; poetry, 15, 27, 127, 182;
political views, 20–21, 70, 126, 187,
131; professional musical connections,
25, 28, 32, 38, 42–43, 116, 125; professional theater and film connections,
81–82, 140; and Sergei Prokofiev,
32, 45–46, 48, 53–56, 63–68, 70–73,
75, 78, 79, 82–85, 115–16, 119, 202,
213n23; publications, 68, 79, 141,
148, 170, 177–79, 182, 184; radio and
television broadcasts, 93, 166, 182,
184, 186, 204, 231n137; romantic relationships, 36, 49–50, 60–61, 70, 80, 97,
98, 118, 112, 120, 151–52, 171, 215n29,
215n30; Russian Revolution (1917–21),
18–22, 24–25; sexuality, 13, 30, 32, 37,
45, 49–50, 53–54, 65; social life, 37, 39,
49, 60, 70, 73, 78, 89–90, 111, 112, 125,
130, 133, 140, 147–48, 159–60, 166;
and Igor Stravinsky, 34, 43–45, 51,

Duke, Vernon (Dukelsky, Vladimir) (*continued*)
54, 68, 115, 185–86, 191, 206; World War II Coast Guard service, 132–33, 134–36, 138, 140, 145, 226n72; World War II relief efforts, 127–28

Duke, Vernon, classical compositions: albums, 175; arrangements, 111; cantatas, 18, 110, 114, 147–49; in Constantinople, 28–29, 34; early New York songs, 33, 35, 38; early performances, 19, 22; Kiev Conservatory, 17, 19, 20–21, 22; other pieces, 67, 73, 152–53, 175, 195, 208; performances and recordings by other musicians, 176–77, 194, *194*, 200–205, 208–9

Duke, Vernon, classical compositions—selections and shows: Concerto in C for Piano and Orchestra (1923), 38, 201–2, *202*, 204; Concerto for Cello and Orchestra (1946), 142–43, 146; Concerto for Violin (1941), 131, 134, 209; First Symphony, 68–69, 70, 72, 73–74, 90; G Minor Piano Sonata, 28, 34; Quartet in C Major, 170–71; Second Symphony, 80, 83, 84, 142; Third Symphony, 145–46, 148–49, 153, 159, 168–69, 178, 181; Violin Sonata in D Major, 153; "Loveliest of Trees," 181; "New York Nocturne," 119; "Tragedian," 112; *April in Paris Fantasy* (1942 radio broadcast), 131–32; *Le Bal des Blanchisseuses*, 146, 149; *Dédicaces*, 117, 209; *Emperor Norton*, 174–74; *The End of St. Petersburg (Leningrad)*, 114–15, 209; *Epitaphe*, 84–85, 200–201, 209; *Gondla*, 34; *Jardin Public*, 93, 94–95, 109–11; *Mistress into Maid*, 73, 174; *Ode to the Milky Way*, 145, 153; *Paris Aller et Retour*, 147, 148–49; *Song of Songs*, 37; *Surrealist Suite*, 175, 208; *Three Caprices*, 153, 175, 208; *Three Seasons*, 63, 66; *Zephyr and Flora*, 46–50, 52–57, 64–65, 72, 208

Duke, Vernon, popular music: albums, 164, 189; arrangements, 39, 62, 80, 113; introduction to, 17, 24, 29; for movie scenes, 80–81, 82; other songs, 63–64, 67, 112, 118, 129, 147, 161, 163, 176, 179, 184, 195, 198–99, 208; performances and recordings by other musicians, 90, 108–9, 130, 134, 140, 176–77, 188–89, 193, 195, 198–200, 204–5; success and musical influence, 125, 164, 190–91, 195–99, 205–7; World War II music, 135–38

Duke, Vernon, popular music—musicals and shows: *The Angry God*, 149; *April in Paris* (film), 161; *Banjo Eyes*, 128–29, 164, 205; *The Bow-Wows*, 69; *Cabin in the Sky* (film), 133–34; *Cabin in the Sky* (musical), 120–26, *122*, *124*, 170, 195, 206; *Cabin in the Sky* (revival), 164; *Casey Jones*, 154, 199; *Dancing in the Streets*, 133; *Dilly*, 165–66; *Goldwyn Follies*, 113–14; *Honor among Lovers*, 82; *It Happened on Ice*, 120; *Jackpot*, 136–37; *Katja the Dancer* (operetta), 62–66; *The Lady Comes Across*, 129–30, 164, 170, 195, 205; *Laughter*, 82, 219n24; *The Littlest Revue*, 169; *Milord l'Arsouille*, 151, 209–10; *Misia*, 209–10; *Musical Zoo*, 146–47, 189, 194, 201; *Open Your Eyes*, 75–76, 82; *The Pink Jungle*, 179–80; *Raffles*, 119; *Romeo and Juliet*, 114; *Sadie Thompson*, 138–40; *The Sap from Syracuse*, 81; *Serena Blandish*, 116; *She's Working Her Way through College*, 160–61; *Sweet Bye and Bye*, 143–45, 205, 208; *Tars and Spars* (musical), 137–38; *Tars and Spars* (film), 140; *This Is My Beloved*, 150–51; *Time Remembered*, 172, 173, 230n96; *Two Little Girls in Blue*, 67;

Two's Company, 161–64, 197, 205; *Vernon Duke Plays Vernon Duke,* 164, 165; *Yellow Mask,* 69, 72, 76; *Yvonne,* 63–64; *Walk a Little Faster,* 87–89, 132, 195; *Water Nymph,* 114; *Zenda,* 183–84; *Ziegfeld Follies of 1934,* 91–93; *Ziegfeld Follies of 1936,* 97–101, 103–4, 106, 107–8, 201

Duke, Vernon, popular music—songs: "Ages Ago," 173, 176, 195, 199, 200, 207; "A Little Privacy," 82; "April in Paris," 87–89, 96, 115, 117, 120, 132, 147, 164, 179, 184, 188, 191, 198, 199, 201, 204; "Autumn in New York," 94, 164, 171, 179, 188, 191, 196, 198, 199, 207; "Back to My Heart," 62; "The Ballad of Baby Face McGinty," 100–101; "Blowing the Blues Away," 69; "Cabin in the Sky," 121, *124,* 165, 176; "Day Dreams," 64; "Deep Sea," 69; "Don't Blow That Horn, Gabriel," 120; "Do What You Wanna Do," 121, *124*; "Five A.M.," 103, 104, 206; "Fog," 127–28; "For Goodness' Sake," 69; "Half a Kiss," 69; "He Hasn't a Thing except Me," 102; "Honey in the Honeycomb," 121, *124*; "I Am Only Human after All," 82, *83*; "I Can't Get Started," *105,* 106, 108–9, *109,* 112, 120, 179, 188, 191, 193, 195, 196, 199, 200, 208; "I Cling to You," 120; "I Like the Likes of You," 93, 196; "I'm Grover," 82; "I'm Mad about a Man about Town," 93; "Island in the West Indies," 108, 201; "I Was Doing All Right," 113; "Just Like a Man," 144, 163, 193, 205, 208; "Let Her Not Be Beautiful," 184, 198; "Long Ago," 120; "The Love I Long For," 140, 165, 176, 204, 207; "Love Is Still for Free," 161; "Love Turned the Light Out," 121, *124,* 195; "Love Walked In," 113; "Magic of the Moon," 63–64; "Mary," 69; "The Mouse," 146–47; "Mu-Cha-Cha," 84; "My Old Virginia Home," 121; "A Nickel to My Name," 129, 130, 205; "Night Flight," 103, 104; "Not a Care in the World," 164, 193, 199, 204; "Now," 112, 120, 165; "Old Devil Sea," 81; "Our Love Is Here to Stay," 113–14; "Pas De Deux—Blues," 127; "Round About," 144, 163, 176, 193, 199, 200, 204, 207, 208; "Sailing at Midnight," 140, 198, 204; "Shavian Shivers," 82; "Somebody's Sunday," 67; "So Nonchalant," 88; "Speaking of Love," 88; "The Stuff That Dreams Are Made Of," 161; "Suddenly," 93, 120; "Summer Is A-Comin' In," 130, 164, 193; "Sway Britannia," 112; "Taking a Chance on Love," 123, *123, 124,* 125, 134, 188, 191, 204; "Talkative Toes," 84; "That Moment of Moments," 108, 196; "This Is Romance," 90; "Try a Little Kiss," 62; "Unaccustomed as I Am," 82; "Water under the Bridge," 92, 93, 196; "What Has He Got?" 112; "What Is There to Say," 92, 93, 120, 165, 176, 196; "Where Do You Go," 179; "Where Have We Met Before?" 88; "Who's to Blame," 164, 207; "Words without Music," 103, 108, 179, 196, 199

Duke-Dukelsky musical dichotomy, 4–5, 58, *135,* 166–67; contemporaries' perspectives on, 5, 33, 34–35, 51–52, 62, 175, 190–91, 198; critics' commentary on, 88–89, 95–96, 111–12, 115, 117–18, 143, 206, 207; Duke's commentary on, 4–5, 29, 33, 69–70, 89; name change, 62, 166–67; Prokofiev's criticism of, 45, 65–66, 82–83; public recognition of, 69–70, 118, 132. *See also* American popular music

Dukelsky, Alexander Vladimirovitch (father), 9–13

Dukelsky, Alexis (brother), 74, 88, 173, 187; childhood, 10–13, 15; Russian Revolution, 18–19, 20, 22–23; Constantinople, 26–27; education in the United States, 31, 32, 72; Paris, 72; New York, 78, 80, 90; California, 140, 154, 157, 172; Duke's death, 190

Dukelsky, Anna Alexeevna (mother), *20*, 118; Duke's childhood, 9–15; Duke's musical education, 16–17; Constantinople, 26–27, 30–31; World War I, 18; Russian Revolution (1917–21), 21–22; New York, 31–33, 78, 80, 85–86, 90; and Duke's music, 72, 74; death, 131, 132

Dukelsky, Col. Ilya Vladimirovitch (uncle), 23, 24, 26, 27, 111

Dukelsky, Vladimir Alexandrovich. *See* Duke, Vernon (Dukelsky, Vladimir)

Dunham, Katherine, 121, 123, 124

Dunn, Scott, 201, 202–4, 208, 209–10

Duquette, Tony, 159, 166, 173

Dyrenforth, James, 69

Eben, Gala, 165, 166

Ebsen, Buddy and Vilma, 91–92

Edison, Harry, 188

Edwards, Leo, 33

Eliscu, Edward, 84

Epitaphe, 84–85, 200–201, 209

Ertegun, Ahmet, 150–51

Fetter, Ted, 106, 112, 123

Field, John, 111

Fire Island, N.Y., 97–98

Fitzgerald, Ella, 188

Florence, Italy, 66

Fokine, Michel, 43

forgotten composers and music, 111, 141, 142, 148, 149, 158, 174, 178, 181, 183

Forte, Alan, 198

Foss, Lukas, 141, 203

Freed, Arthur, 133, 166

Freedley, Vinton, 137, 138

Freedman, David, 99, 103

French music, 71, 147, 151

French people, 41–42, 147

Garrick Gaieties, The, 82, *83*, 84

Gauthier, Éva, 33

Gay Divorce, The, 84, 87

German music, 72

Gershwin, Frances, 71

Gershwin, George, 4, 73, 89, 97, 227n35; *An American in Paris*, 71, 104; and Vernon Duke, 34, 35, 38–39, 46, 62, 69, 71, 79–80, 83, 110, 113–14, 179, 204; on popular music, 34; *Porgy and Bess*, working on, 4, 96, 97, 99; and Sergei Prokofiev, 71–72; *Rhapsody in Blue*, 39, 104; "Swanee," 29; other songs and musicals, 38, 67, 74–75, 78; death, 113; legacy, 148

Gershwin, Ira, 5, 108, 113, 179; and Broadway, 108, 116–17; and Vernon Duke, 5, 35, 67, 71, 82, 96, 97–99, 101, 103, 106–7, 108, 112–13, *113*, 114, 116–17, 120, 125, 148, 190, 197; *Goldwyn Follies*, 113–14; parties, 159–60, 166; *Ziegfeld Follies*, 96, 97–101, 103, 104, 107, 206

Gershwin, Leonore, 71, 97, 98, 99, 159, 160, 166

Gesualdo, Don Carlos, 158

Geva, Tamara, 50, 84

Gide, André, 94

Gillespie, Dizzy, 109, 188–89

Gilson, Paul, 147, 151

Glebov, Igor, 74–75

Glière, Reinhold, 16, 17, 20, 22, 45

Goldberg, Issac, 88–89

Goldwyn, Samuel, 113

Goodman, Benny, 130, 165

Gorney, Jay, 84

Goulding, Edmund, 81

Grant, Mark N., 206

Great Britain, 127–28. *See also* London, England
Great Depression, 77, 108, 155
Greek Orthodox, 13, 40
Green, Johnny, 81–82, 84, 91
Green, Stanley, 195
Grigoriev, Serge Leonidovich (S. L.), 49, 52–53

Haifetz, Jascha, 39, 160, 209
Harburg, E. Y. (Edgar Yipsel, "Yip"), 5, 80, 81, 82, 84, 87–88, 91–93, 120, 133, 195
Harms, Inc., 35, 39, 82, *83*, 90
Hart, Lorenz, 82, 112, 128, 145
Hart, Moss, 97, 99, 101
Havoc, June, 139
Helburn, Theresa, 82
Hemingway, Ernest, 41, 74
Hendl, Walter, 168–69
Herrmann, Bernard, 5, 90, 91, 141, 153, 159, 197
Heyman, Edward, 90
Hildegarde, *119*, 120, 193
Hirschfeld, Al, 143–44
Hirt, Al, 188
Hoctor, Harriet, 99, 103, 104
Hoey, Evelyn, 88
Holden, Scott, 200, 205, 207–8
Hollywood, Calif., 108, 112, 115, 140, 155–58
Holm, John Cecil, 128, 133
Hope, Bob, 99, 106
Hopper, Hedda, 173
Horowitz, Vladimir, 18, 156
Hyman, Dick, 164–65

"I Can't Get Started," *105*, 106, 108–9, *109*, 112, 120, 179, 188, 191, 193, 195, 196, 199, 200, 208
Ingalls, Kay Duke. *See* Duke, Kay McCracken
Irwin, Will, 107
Istanbul. *See* Constantinople (Istanbul, Turkey)

Ives, Charles, 141, 146
Ivin, Ivan. *See under* Duke, Vernon (Dukelsky, Vladimir)

James, Edna, 37
Jardin Public, 93, 94–95, 109–11
jazz, 29, 31–33, 71, 104, 109; and Vernon Duke, 50, 54, 58, 69, 82, 88, 93, 109, 111, 114, 150, 168, 177, 186; interpretations and recordings of Duke's music, 109, 119, 164–65, 203–4, 208. *See also* American popular music
Jazz Age, 31
Jazz Babies, 32, 33
Jenness, David, 206–7, 208

Kahn, Leo, *119*, 120
Kaufman, Harry, 99, 106, 107
Keep off the Grass, 119
Kemp, Hal, 90, 108
Kern, Jerome, 63–64, 88, 89, 90, 113, 191
Kessel, Barney, 177
Kiev, Russia, 14–16, 18, 20
Kiev Conservatory of Music, 16–17, 18, 19, 20
King, Sandra, 195
Knox, Collie, 75
Kochanski, Paul and Zosia, 32
Kochno, Boris, 28, 44, 46, 47, 52, 56, 59, *61*, 65, 111, 146
Koenig, Lester, 174
Koshetz, Nina, 32, 33, 35, 156
Koussevitzky, Serge, 16, 45, 78, 146; and Leonard Bernstein, 145; meeting Vernon Duke, 55; and Vernon Duke's compositions, 67, 68, 72, 74, 76, 83, 85, 145–46, 153, 178. *See also* Boston Symphony Orchestra
Koussevitzky Music Foundation, 145–46
Kungur, Russia, 11–12

Lady Comes Across, The, 129–30, 164, 195, 205

Lake, Bonnie, 93, 199
Lane, Alan. *See under* Duke, Vernon (Dukelsky, Vladimir)
Lannin, Paul, 67
Latouche, John, 121–23, *124*, 125–26, 127–29, 134, 164, 165–66, 169, 170
Lawrence, Gertrude, 38, 128, 138
Lawrence, Jerry, 165
League of Composers, 146, 153
Lee, Gypsy Rose, 106, 139
Lee, Robert, 165, 166
Lehár, Franz, 67
Lekeu, Guillaume, 181–82
Leskevitch, Josephine, 15
Levant, Oscar, 4, 35, 159–60
Library of Congress, 194–95
Lifar, Serge, 46, 49, 52–53, 57, 111
Listen Here! A Critical Essay on Music Depreciation, 184–86
Ljubljana, Yugoslavia, 164
London, England, 56, 59–60, 73, 127
Los Angeles, Calif., 155–58, 170. *See also* Hollywood, Calif.
Lvov, Col. Alexis Fedorovitch, 22, 26–27, 31, 78

Malishevsky, Vitold, 23–24
Mamoulian, Rouben, 138–39
March, Fredric, 81, 82
Marshall, Everett, 91–92
Martin, Mary, 133
Massine, Léonide, 43, 52, 53, 56, 62, 68, 95, 110
Matthews, Jessie, 129–30, 224n18
Mature, Victor, 137–38
Maugham, W. Somerset, 38, 138–39
McCracken, Kay. *See* Duke, Kay McCracken
McLane, Ralph, 93, 131, 199
Medtner, Nikolai, 28, 141
Mejigorye Convent, 13, 19
Mercer, Johnny, 5, 120, 207
Merman, Ethel, 81, 138–39

Messel, Oliver, 48
Meth, Max, 122, 125
Mexico, 86–87
Meyer, Baron Adolph de, 39, 44
Minnelli, Vincente, 99, 100, 103, 112, 116, 133–34, 159
Misia, 151, 209–10
Mitropoulos, Dimitri, 158–59
Monte Carlo, Monaco, 47, 49
Moorehead, Agnes, 180
Morris, Harold, 91, 141
Mundy, Meg, 118
Murray, John Creighton, 153
musical theater, 62, 73, 77, 108, 185, 206. *See also* American popular music; Broadway

Nabokov, Nicolas, 43, 58, 79, 189
Nash, Ogden, 160, 168, 188; *The Littlest Revue*, 169–70; *Musical Zoo*, 146–47, 189, 194, 201; *Sweet Bye and Bye*, 143–45, 205; *Two's Company*, 161–63
National Orchestral Association, 90
Navaho (ship), 24–26
New England, 78
New Haven, Conn., theater, 92, 128, 129, 144, 172–73
New York City, 31, 33, 77–78, 82, 94, 203, 204. *See also* Broadway, Carnegie Hall
New York City Symphony, 34
Nicholas Brothers, 99, 106
Niesen, Gertrude, 99–100, 101, 103, 106
Nikitina, Alice, 49, 53, 57
Nikolaiev, Russia, 10, 11
Nouvel, Valitchka, 43–44, 46, 56, 59
nudism, 13, 19

O'Connell, Hugh, 99, 106
Odessa, Russian Empire (now Ukraine), 22–25
Odessa Conservatory, 24
operettas, 17, 62–63, 65–66, 70, 72, 75, 79, 183

Palm Beach, Fla., 130, 137–38
Paramount Publix Corporation, 80
Paris, France, 41, 74, 147, 151, 164
Parker, Charlie, 109
Parker, Dorothy, 38, 87
Passport to Paris, 3–4, 6, 7, 166–68
Perelman, S. J. (Sidney Joseph), 116, 143–45
Philadelphia theater, 128, 139, 144–45
Piatigorsky, Gregor, 142–43
Pickens, Jane, 106–7
Piston, Walter, 141, 146, 149
poetry, 28, 150
popular music. *See* American popular music
Porter, Cole, 41, 87, 89, 116, 133, 207
Posselt, Ruth, 131, 134, 209
Poulenc, Francis, 43, 50–51, 65, 189
Powell, Bud, 188
Previn, André, 176–77, 182
Prokofiev, Lina (Ptashka), 48, 53, 56, 66, 75, 78
Prokofiev, Sergei, 16, 164, 202; compositions, 66, 67, 70, 72, 75, 79; and Serge Diaghilev, 43, 45, 46, 48, 67; on Vernon Duke's music, 48, 53–55, 63–66, 70, 73, 75, 79, 82–84, 85, 115, 119; and George Gershwin, 71–72; relationship with Vernon Duke, 32, 45–46, 54, 56, 63, 65–68, 71, 78, 115–16, 213n23; return to the Soviet Union, 115–16; *Zephyr and Flora*, 48, 54–55, 70
Proti, Turkey, 26–27, 78
publishers, 5, 35, 39, 42, 58, 73, 141, 207
Pushkin, Alexander, 49, 63, 73, 151

ragtime, 17, 38, 146
Rascoe, Burton, 38, 140
Ravel, Maurice, 43, 99, 104, 175, 201
Réaux, Angelina, 203, 204
recording industry, 174, 175, 178
recordings of Vernon Duke's music: classical compositions, 176–77, 194, *194*, 200–205, 208–9; popular music, 90, 108–9, 130, 134, 140, 176–77, 188–89, 193, 195, 198–200, 204–5
Red Cross, 24
reviews and commentary, classical compositions, 205–6; *Dédicaces*, 117; *End of St. Petersburg*, 114–15; *Epitaphe*, 84–85; First Symphony, 70, 74, 90–91; *Jardin Public*, 95, 109–10, 111; *Paris Aller et Retour*, 148–49; Quartet in C Major, 170–71; Second Symphony, 91; Third Symphony, 148–49, 181; *Zephyr and Flora*, 50–57, 64–65; other orchestral music, 28, 33–34, 67, 142–43, 146, 152–53, 175, 181, 184, 202
reviews and commentary, popular music: "April in Paris," 88–89; *Cabin in the Sky*, 125–26, 164; *Musical Zoo*, 146–47, 194; *Open Your Eyes*, 75–76; *Sadie Thompson*, 139–40; *Sweet Bye and Bye*, 144–45, 205; "Taking a Chance on Love," 125, 134; *Tars and Spars*, 136–37; *This Is My Beloved*, 150–51; *Two's Company*, 162–63; *Yvonne*, 63–64; *Walk a Little Faster*, 87–89; *Ziegfeld Follies of 1934*, 92; *Ziegfeld Follies of 1936*, 101, 102–3, 108; other musicals and popular songs, 35, 73, 69, 80, 82, 120, 129–30, 133, 160–61, 169, 173, 184, 199–200
Revueltas, Silvestre, 86
Rieger, Wallingford, 141, 149
Rieti, Vittorio, 56, *61*, 71
Rimsky-Korsakov, Nicolai, 24, 43, 54, 168, 181
Robbins, Jerome, 162
Rodgers, Richard, 83, 89, 112, 128, 191
Rogers, Ginger, 81–82, 112, 116, 179–80
Roosevelt, Franklin Delano, 130
Root, Lynn, 120, 125
Rose, Billy, 87, 97
"Round About," 144, 163, 176, 193, 199, 200, 204, 207, 208

Rubinstein, Arthur, 38, 201, 214n43
Russian immigrants, 155–56
Russian Revolution (1917–21), 18–22, 24–25, 155–56. *See also* Soviet Union (Russia), politics
Russky Myak (Constantinople), 27–29

Sadie Thompson, 138–40
Salabert, Francis, 39, 42
Saminsky, Lazare, 32, 35
San Francisco theater, 180, 183–84
Satie, Eric, 43, 99, 137, 175
Schaefer, George, 183
Schillinger, Joseph, 110, 227n35
Schmitz, E. Robert, 71
Schuller, Gunther, 186
Schumann, Clara, 150, 175
Schwartz, Arthur, 84, 195, 198, 207
Scriabin, Alexander, 71, 104
Shaw, Artie, 90, 109
Sherman, Hal, 64
Shoot the Works, 84
Short, Bobby, 188, 193, 197, 204
Show Is On, The, 112
Shubert, Lee, 91–92, 96, 103, 200
Shubert Theater (Boston), 112, 133
Shubert Theater (New Haven), 128, 129
Singer, Barry, 210
Slonimsky, Nicolas, 18, 156; compositions, 29–30, 189; and Vernon Duke, 55, 73–74, 153–54, 159, 160, 168, 175, 184, 190, 194
Society for Forgotten Music, 142, 148, 149, 158, 178, 181, 183
Sokolova, Lydia, 47, 53
Souvtchinsky, Pierre, 28, 53, 73
Soviet Union (Russia), politics, 18–22, 67, 74–75, 127, 131
Stember, Nicholas, 28, 32, 38
Stereo Records, 175
Stevens, Leslie, 180
Stillman, Al, 120
Stokowski, Leopold, 35, 39

Stravinsky, Igor, 3, 84, 156; comparisons to Duke as Dukelsky, 34, 51, 54, 115, 191, 206; criticism of Serge Diaghilev, 58; Vernon Duke's criticism of, 68, 185–86; *Les Noces*, 43, 44, 64; in Paris with Vernon Duke, 43–45
Suskin, Steven, 197, 199, 208
Sweet Bye and Bye, 143–45, 205, 208
Szymanowski, Karol, 32, 39, 150

"Taking a Chance on Love," 123, *123*, *124*, 125, 134, 188, 191, 204
Tanner, Alan, 43
Tansman, Alexandre, 71
Tars and Spars (film), 140
Tars and Spars (musical), 137–38
Tchelitchev, Pavlik, 29, 42–43
Tcherepnin, Nikolai, 43
Tcheresky, Luba, 171, 173
theaters (N.Y.). *See* Broadway
Theatre Guild (N.Y.), 82
Three's a Crowd, 84
Three Seasons, 63, 66
Thumbs Up! 94
Tin Pan Alley, 33, 89, 95, 128
Tiomkin, Dimitri, 71
Tresmand, Ivy, 64
Trotsky, Leon, 20
Two's Company, 161–64, 197, 205

University of California at Los Angeles (UCLA), 157, 170, 181
Upshaw, Dawn, 199–200
Ural Mountains, Russia, 11–12

Vajeersla, Vera, 79
Vajevska, Vera, 73
Velsey, Don, 206–7, 208
Vernon Duke Plays Vernon Duke, 164, *165*
Vries, John de, 109

Walk a Little Faster, 87–89, 132, 195
Walton, Sir William, 71, 189

Washington, D.C., 108, 118, 136, 194–95
Wasserman, Herman, 76
Waters, Ethel, 116, 122–26, 134, 188
Webster, Ben, 109
Weill, Kurt, 4, 141, 196, 203, 206
Westport, Conn., 94, 198
White, George, 31, 39
White, James, 62, 63
Whiteman, Paul, 39
Whitney, Robert, 159
Wilder, Alec, 5, 189–90, 195–97
Wilk, Max, 197
Wilson, Teddy, 109, 165
Winchell, Walter, 88, 89–90, 120, 169
Winter Garden, 92, 108, 126
Winters, Pinky, 203, 204

World War I, 18, 26, 41. *See also* Russian Revolution (1917–21)
World War II, 127, 129, 130–31, 140, 145. *See also* Coast Guard

Yaddo Festival of American Music, 152
Youmans, Vincent, 35, 67, 108, 139
Young, Lester, 109

Zephyr and Flora, 46, 48–49, 50, 52–57, 64–65, 67, 110, 115, 191
Ziegfeld Follies of 1934, 91–93
Ziegfeld Follies of 1936, 97–108, 201
Ziegfeld Follies of 1936 (1999 concert), 200
Zorina, Vera, 114, 118, 125, 127–28

www.ingramcontent.com/pod-product-compliance
Lightning Source LLC
Chambersburg PA
CBHW031433160426
43195CB00010BB/715